Routledge Revivals

Early Economic Thought in Spain

The growth of serious interest during the last fifty years in the scholastic contribution to the development of economic thought has been very marked, and no-where more so than in the history of economic thought in Spain. First published in 1978, this book begins in the Middle Ages and traces the effect on business practice and on thought of the presence of the Christian, Islamic and Jewish communities who lived side by side in the Peninsula. It shows how the economics of Plato and Aristotle were transmitted by way of Toledo to the Latin West.

In the second half of the book the author considers 'Salamancan' ideas and the views of the political economists and 'projectors' who preceded the Enlightenment. At the same time she surveys the present state of the subject and offers bibliographical guidance for the reader.

Early Economic Thought in Spain

1177 – 1740

Marjorie Grice-Hutchinson

Routledge
Taylor & Francis Group

First published in 1978
by George Allen & Unwin Ltd

This edition first published in 2012 by Routledge
2 Park Square, Milton Park, Abingdon, Oxon, OX14 4RN

Simultaneously published in the USA and Canada
by Routledge
711 Third Avenue, New York, NY 10017

Routledge is an imprint of the Taylor & Francis Group, an informa business

Publisher's Note
The publisher has gone to great lengths to ensure the quality of this reprint but
points out that some imperfections in the original copies may be apparent.

Disclaimer
The publisher has made every effort to trace copyright holders and welcomes
correspondence from those they have been unable to contact.

A Library of Congress record exists under ISBN: 78317485

ISBN 13: 978-0-415-68255-8 (hbk)
ISBN 13: 978-0-415-63104-4 (pbk)

Early Economic Thought in Spain 1177-1740

by

Marjorie Grice-Hutchinson

London
GEORGE ALLEN & UNWIN
Boston   Sydney

First published in 1978

© George Allen & Unwin (Publishers) Ltd, 1978

ISBN 0 04 946011 0

Printed in Great Britain
in 10 on 11 point Plantin
at the Alden Press, Oxford

Foreword

In the course of the last twenty years there has been a certain quickening of interest in the history of economic thought in Spain. Not only have the old economists been consulted as witnesses to the economic facts of their time, but their doctrines have been examined and found to be of interest for their own sake. A considerable number of long-forgotten texts have been brought to light, and some judged worthy of re-publication. I hope that this collection of essays may help to draw attention to the work done in this field, and perhaps suggest some lines of approach that invite further exploration.

My first two chapters are concerned with the medieval period. In them I have tried to see how far, if at all, Professor Américo Castro's main theme, the interpenetration of the Christian, Hebrew, and Islamic cultures in the Iberian Peninsula and their joint contribution to the making of modern Spain, may be applicable to our subject. The chapter on usury doctrine and business practice (the two things must be considered together) offers conclusions that I put forward tentatively, in the hope that others may be led to support or disprove them. With my second chapter we come on to firmer ground. The economic doctrines of Plato and Aristotle were first transmitted to western Europe by way of Spain, and I have tried to show in some detail the part played by scholars of the three religions in this achievement.

The second half of this book deals with the so-called age of mercantilism, which, in the field of economic thought, lasted in Spain from about the middle of the sixteenth century until well into the eighteenth. Coming into this period we find ourselves caught up in current controversy. Like the people of Spain in the age of mercantilism, we live in a time of inflation. Our economists, like theirs, are concerned with its causes and consequences, and some of them look back to the Spanish price revolution in search of a solution to our own problems. The monetarists among them point to the work of Professor Earl J. Hamilton, and ascribe the rise in the Spanish price level to the influx of gold and silver that reached Spain from the New World. The anti-monetarists adduce more recent researches in the field of Spanish economic history which have sought to modify Hamilton's conclusions.[1]

Before we form our own opinion we should do well to listen to the old Spanish economists, who were often shrewd observers and who felt the effects of the inflation at first hand. Broadly speaking, we shall find that the scholastic writers based their teaching on the quantity theory of money, and that the political economists, though they mostly attributed the increase in prices to monetary expansion of one kind or another, also brought forward other reasons for the inflation and subsequent economic decay of Spain. My third chapter will deal with the monetary theory of the Spanish late-scholastics (that being, I think, the most interesting feature of their work), and my fourth with the views of the political economists and 'projectors'.

I have to thank Mr Marrack I. Goulding for his advice on the transliteration of Arabic words.

NOTE

1 *Inflation: Causes, Consequences, Cures*, a debate between Lord Robbins, Samuel Brittan, A. W. Coats, Milton Friedman, Peter Jay and David Laidler, with Addenda by F. A. Hayek and Peter Jay (Institute of Economic Affairs, London, 1974), pp. 14, 15 and 22.

Contents

PART ONE

The Middle Ages

I

In Concealment of Usury

INTRODUCTION

To be told that Africa begins at the Pyrenees is apt to irritate Spaniards. Yet if by Africa we mean Islamic Africa there is some truth in the cliché. For over seven hundred years, from 711 to 1492, a gradually shrinking portion of the Iberian Peninsula was under Moslem rule. And, as Ibn Khaldun says, referring to the glorious Andalusian civilisation of his forebears, when once the dye is well taken the cloth keeps its colour for ever. Even the least observant of modern travellers, when he comes into Spain, is forced to consider, perhaps for the first time, the civilisation of Spanish Islam.

This civilisation was of eastern origin. Hence, by an accident of history, North Africa and Spain, the most westerly regions in their respective continents, shared throughout most of the Middle Ages an oriental culture. They formed a single bloc, the Maghreb or Moslem West, which balanced the other two blocs, of eastern and western Christianity, that made up the civilised world familiar to the medieval European. The theme-song of Spanish history during this period is that of the winning of Spain from the Maghreb and its return to the Christian West.

The oriental element in the life of medieval Spain was intensified by the presence of the Jews who lived under both Moslem and Christian protection. There were times when the Jews, here too, were persecuted. But, in the main, it was a golden age for Jewry. Some Jews were rich and powerful, moving between the Islamic and Christian princes whom they served as physicians, translators, diplomats, financial advisers and tax-gatherers. Others led humble lives as shopkeepers and artisans. They were a pious, clever, frugal, hard-working people, clinging to the traditions that held them together, and devoting to the study of their sacred books the hours that were not spent in business.

As the Reconquest progressed and political power passed more and more into Christian hands, the cultural and commercial life of the newly acquired territories was still dependent on an urban middle class that included many families of Moslem and Jewish origin. The Spanish Christians had mostly been forced to adopt other ideals – those of

13

soldiers and colonisers. In a famous book of laws Alphonso X of Castile lays down the duties of his subjects. Apart from fulfilling their obligations towards God and their king they must 'understand the land . . . and cultivate it well, not despising it and finding fault, because land that is useless for one crop will always serve for another', and, if need arises, they must 'break rocks, cut down forests, level the ground, and rid the country of wild beasts'.[1] Though Alphonso himself was a lover of learning and Christian Spain had never lacked for scholars, yet, in those pioneering days, the labours he prescribes must often have interrupted the work of the library.

Speculation about economic matters had reached a more advanced stage among Jews and Moslems than among Christians. In all three peoples a great part of such studies had centred round the problem of usury. The subject held an extraordinary fascination for countless thinkers over a period of some two thousand years. The vast body of teaching on usury that has come down to us reflects the religious spirit of the Semitic peoples and those who followed in their faith. We may contrast this spirit with the rationalistic standpoint of the Greeks, whose contribution to economic thought I shall consider in my second chapter. Our immediate task will be to find out what Moslems, Jews and Christians thought about usury in medieval Spain and how they reconciled, or failed to reconcile, accepted doctrine with their personal convictions and interests.

The tenet, common to the three religions of Spain, that usury is one of the gravest of sins has its source in the Old Testament. We need not labour the point in the case of Judaism and Christianity. But it is sometimes forgotten that Muhammad, who saw himself as the successor of the Hebrew prophets and of Christ, and as the renewer and purifier of a common faith in the One God, took over a hatred of usury from the Mosaic law.

Our three religions went through the stages that are common to many bodies of doctrine. In all three, the original and revolutionary teaching of their founders came to pass through a period of so-called 'tradition', in which it was handed down from generation to generation, undergoing some development but not entirely losing its early freshness and glow. And, in all three, there came a time when the first inspiration had faded, when prophets and saints gave way to scholars, when the broad lines of doctrine had been laid down, and when debate became a matter for professionals who used a language and method of their own: in short, a time of scholasticism.

The three religions thus followed parallel paths, but at long intervals from each other. Hence we find discussed among Christians, as late as the seventeenth century, typically scholastic problems that had been

14

thrashed out among Jews and Moslems long before. That of usury (by which I shall mean in this chapter any interest, however small, that is charged on a loan) provides an instructive example. In order to examine it we shall have to go far back into the past, and consider writings that at first sight may seem to bear little relation to the Spain of comparatively recent times.

USURY AMONG THE JEWS

The Bible and Talmud

The chief biblical sources of Jewish teaching on usury are the following:

(1) Psalms XV: 5. He that putteth not out his money to usury [shall abide in the tabernacle of the Lord].
(2) Exodus XXII: 25. If thou lend money to any of my people that is poor by thee, thou shalt not be to him as an usurer, neither shalt thou lay upon him usury.
(3) Leviticus XXV: 35-7. And if thy brother be waxen poor, and fallen into decay with thee, then thou shalt relieve him; yea, though he be a stranger, or a sojourner, that he may live with thee. Take thou no usury of him, or increase; but fear thy God, that thy brother may live with thee. Thou shalt not give him thy money upon usury, nor lend him thy victuals for increase.
(4) Deuteronomy XXIII: 19-20. Thou shalt not lend upon usury to thy brother; usury of money, usury of victuals, usury of anything that is lent upon usury. Unto a stranger thou mayest lend upon usury: but unto thy brother thou shalt not lend upon usury.
(5) Ezekiel XVIII: 8-9. He that hath not given forth upon usury, neither hath taken any increase . . . he is just, he shall surely live, saith the Lord God.
(6) Ezekiel XXII: 12. Thou hast taken usury and increase, and thou hast greedily gained of thy neighbours by extortion, and hast forgotten me, saith the Lord God.

It will be noticed that (2) and (3) seek to protect only the Jew who has fallen on hard times, whereas (4) forbids altogether the practice of usury between Israelites.

These texts formed part of the scriptures that were studied by generation after generation of pious Jews, and with especial care by the rabbis, who applied their conclusions in their legal decisions. There came into being, side by side with the Pentateuch, an oral law, which was probably set down in writing about the year AD 200. This compilation is known as the *Mishna* ('instruction' or commentary on the Tora

or revealed law), which in turn became the subject of fresh interpretation. The resulting new commentary, the *Gemara*, together with
the *Mishna*, make up the Talmud, which was completed about the year
500.

The word *mishna*, besides meaning the traditional doctrine of the
Jews, denotes among other things a single tenet. Each section of the
Talmud is made up of an introductory *mishna*, followed by a *gemara*
or commentary, in which are set forth the often conflicting opinions of
the leading rabbis on the subject dealt with in the *mishna*. The method
is essentially the same as that which was later to be adopted by the
Christian scholastics.

The rabbinical or Jewish doctrine of usury may conveniently be
studied in that tractate of the Talmud which is known as the *Baba
Mezi'a* or *Middle Gate*. The relevant passages are based on the biblical
injunctions against usury. They are of considerable interest in so far
as they reflect the efforts of the early rabbis to reconcile the needs of
commerce with the Mosaic law.

A *mishna* posited on Leviticus XXV: 36, 'Take thou no usury of him,
nor increase', seeks to distinguish between legitimate and usurious
profit.[2] In the *gemara* that follows are summarised the commentaries
of the leading rabbis or 'sages'. Some interpreted the *mishna* as approving
dealings in futures, but only where the future price was not known in
advance. A man might therefore contract to buy or sell goods for future
delivery at whatever price might be current when payment fell due.
This ruling was not universally accepted, but it was generally agreed
that lending money or goods for a stipulated bigger return is biblically
forbidden, whereas buying ahead, if forbidden at all, is only forbidden
by the rabbis. The distinction was of great practical significance, since
'Pentateuchal' or 'direct' usury was held to be reclaimable through the
Jewish courts, whereas merely 'rabbinical' or 'indirect' usury, the result
of luck or good judgement in business affairs, could not be so reclaimed.

Among the various ways in which a lender may try to charge usury,
the same *gemara* describes a device that was to be used throughout
Europe until quite recent times. This was the double contract of sale,
otherwise known as the *mohatra* or *barata* contract:

Some things are [essentially] permitted, yet forbidden as [con-
stituting] an evasion of usury. How so? If A. requested B. 'Lend
me a *maneh*', to which he replied, 'I have no *maneh*, but wheat to the
value thereof, which I will give you,' and thereupon he gave him a
maneh's worth of wheat [calculated on the current price] and repurchased it for 24 *selas*; now, this is essentially permitted, yet may
not be done on account of evasion of usury.

A *maneh* was equal to 100 *zuz* and a *sela* to 4 *zuz*; hence, 24 *selas* equalled 96 *zuz*. Thus, in the above case, B, the creditor, sells or pretends to sell wheat on credit to A, the debtor, who contracts to repay, in cash or in kind, 100 *zuz* in return for 96.

In order to make the matter quite clear, our *gemara* provides a second example of the same evasionary device:

A. said to B., 'Lend me 30 *denarii*', to which he replied, 'I have not 30 *denarii*, but wheat for the same, which I can give you.' He then gave him 30 *denarii's* worth of wheat [calculated at the current price] and repurchased it for a golden dinar.

A gold *dinar* was worth 25 *denarii*. The debtor thus receives 25 *denarii* in cash immediately and owes 30 repayable at some future date.

I would now ask the reader to compare the two last-quoted texts with the following passage taken from a sermon preached at Bury St Edmunds about the year 1595 by the Rev. Miles Mosse or Moses, a Protestant divine who was minister at Norwich and pastor of Combes in Suffolk:

I come to a man, and desire him to lend me an hundred pound upon usury. He answereth, he hath not so much ready money by him, but to do me a pleasure he will lend me an hundred pounds worth of plate to sell, and so to make money: the plate perhaps being hardly worth the money. I am no sooner gone out of the door, but the usurer provideth a broker to meet me, and to buy his plate of me again. Now for ready money perhaps I sell the plate for four score pound. The broker carrieth back the plate to the owner, and from him bringeth four score pound in ready money to the borrower. The borrower must pay the lender an hundred pound for his plate at the day appointed, and ten pound for the usury in the mean season. So in fine, the poor man payeth loan after thirty pound in the hundred, and yet must think himself befriended of the merchant. Thus and a thousand ways more is usury committed under pretence and colour of buying and selling.[3]

It is clear that the fictitious sale as described in the Talmud and by Mosse is one and the same device. As late as 1656, the intellectual world was reminded of the then moribund *mohatra* contract by Pascal, who, in the wittiest of his *Provincial Letters*, used it as a stick to beat the Jesuits with.[4] The *mohatra* seems to have flourished with especial vigour in Spain. We shall see later something of its history there.

Returning to our *gemara* on usury, we note that attention is paid to the subject of money-changing. A case is cited which suggests that money-changing was already being used among the Jews as a cover for money-lending. This popular way of evading the usury laws continued to occupy Jewish, Moslem and Christian writers on usury until the end of the seventeenth century.

Various other evasionary devices are mentioned in the Talmud. One is the enjoyment by the money-lender of the fruits of property given as a pledge or sold conditionally as cover for a loan. 'If a man lends to his neighbour,' runs a *mishna*, 'he must not live rent-free in his court, nor at a low rent, because that constitutes usury.'[5] What we should regard as interest on a mortgage was, however, permissible, because in Jewish law a mortgage was regarded as a temporary sale, and a man may naturally enjoy the fruits of his own property.

The Talmud forbids an Israelite to accept from another an 'iron flock' (i.e. sheep that cannot come to harm, or an investment that carries no risk for the investor), because that is nothing but a loan at usury. Such an investment may be accepted from Gentiles. It was also generally agreed that a Jew might borrow from and lend to Gentiles at usury. An Israelite may lend a Gentile's money at usury to another Israelite with the knowledge of the Gentile but not of the Jewish borrower.[6]

Another class of transactions that sometimes served as a cover for usury involved the transfer of money from place to place. In talmudic times (and, indeed, for long afterwards) money was transported in sealed purses containing gold or silver coins whose weight and number were indicated on the outside. This dangerous and cumbersome procedure was supplemented by various forms of transfer of debt, and more especially by the Jewish *diokne* or Moslem *suftaja*, defined by Moslem lawyers as 'a loan of money made in order to avoid the risk of transport'.[7]

The talmudic sages generally resisted the transfer of money by means of such instruments of credit. There were several reasons for this. Firstly, the banker's charge for issuing the document might be construed as usurious gain on a loan. Secondly, according to biblical law one could not acquire title to a non-existent thing; and a debt was non-existent, since in theory a loan was freely expendable. Finally, the transfer of money from place to place often entailed an exchange of currency, and we have seen that money-changing was in itself suspect.

The Responsa

In the early Middle Ages the great centres of Jewish learning were still in the east, at Sura and Pimbedith in Mesopotamia. The ever-increasing number of Jews who lived outside these centres continued to appeal to the heads of the eastern academies for the interpretation of obscure passages in the Talmud, in order to reconcile talmudic principles with the conditions of life that prevailed in the different countries where they had settled. Queries on doubtful points of Jewish law were sent by the scattered Jewish communities to the eastern academies, and in due course, sometimes after a delay of several years, the answers came back in the form of the so-called 'responsa'. Thanks to recent work based on this and other material, we now have a wonderfully complete and vivid picture of Jewish life in the Islamic countries of the Mediterranean, including Spain and Italy, as it existed between the tenth and the thirteenth centuries.[8]

From the tenth century onward the eastern centres of Jewish learning declined, and important rabbinical schools arose in Europe and North Africa. The first Spanish school was founded at Cordova in 948. As time went on the Spanish rabbis came to play an increasingly important part in guiding the conscience of Jewry, at first from Moslem and later from Christian Spain. The first noteworthy collections of *responsa* that relate wholly or largely to Spain are those of Isaac ben Jacob, of Fez, better known as Alfasi, who came to Spain in 1104 and directed the academy at Lucena; of his disciple and successor, Joseph ben Migash and of the Cordovan philosopher and rabbi, Moses ben Maimon, known as Maimonides (1135–1204).

To a later period belong the *responsa* of the celebrated talmudic scholar, Asher ben Yehiel of Cologne (1250–1327), who came to Spain in 1303 and settled in Toledo; of his son, Jacob ben Asher (*d.* 1340), whose *Turim* remained the standard code of Jewish law up to the sixteenth century; and of Solomon ben Abraham ben Adret (*d.* 1310), head of the academy at Gerona. The difficulties of the Jewish communities of Spain, who had to adapt themselves to a way of life for which the Talmud made no provision, are reflected in the copious volumes of the *responsa* (Adret's contain over three thousand cases and Asher's about one thousand). The flow of *responsa* continued up to the eve of the expulsion of the Jews from Spain in 1492.

Except for a short-lived attempt at the beginning of the twelfth century to put the clock back by rejecting casuistry and returning to a biblical simplicity of doctrine, the authority of the Talmud stood unchallenged in Spain. Commentaries and abridgements were poured out by learned rabbis as long as the Jews dwelled in the Peninsula; and after their expulsion talmudic law, together with the doctrines of the Spanish rabbis, were summarised by R. José Caro of Toledo (1481–1575), whose *Shulhan' Aruk* replaced Asher's *Turim* and still constitutes a standard textbook of Jewish law.

The Medieval Rabbis and Credit

When the medieval rabbis came to consider the ethics of business life the problem of usury was often in their minds. To exact usury in defiance of the biblical precepts was, as the Talmud taught, tantamount to a rejection of God and the highest degree of wickedness. Yet usury flourished on every side. To control the writhings of the monster was a matter of spiritual life and death, and the rabbis did not shrink from the struggle. Their chief weapons were the traditional taboos, to which they clung tenaciously. But here and there they were forced to give ground. They never openly relaxed the principles of the prohibition; but in course of time they tended to sanction contracts that had formerly been suspect, and to look leniently on those that had become customary in business life.

This tendency is illustrated by the attitude of the Maghrebian rabbis towards credit instruments, which, as we have seen, the talmudic sages had disapproved of. By the eleventh century the use of this form of paper money had become so common that the rabbis were forced to reconsider their position. In a query addressed to the head of the academy at Baghdad, a Kairuwan rabbi of the early eleventh century remarked that: 'It has been the custom among the inhabitants of Kairuwan from the days of their forefathers until today to issue letters of authorisation permitting the recipient to receive money in countries across the sea.' Another *responsum* of the same period confirms that in this matter doctrine followed established custom. We read that 'there exists nothing in the fundamentals of our law to permit the dispatch of a *suftaja* . . . but since we have seen people making use of it, we have begun accepting it as a basis for our judgements, lest the commercial transactions of the people be nullified'. Isaac Alfasi, whose *responsa* reflect Spanish conditions at the beginning of the twelfth century, likewise approves this 'contemporary practice among merchants' in the Maghreb.[9]

By the thirteenth and fourteenth centuries the use of negotiable instruments had become commonplace. Asher (1250–1327) sanctions them without question: 'If A. sends money to B. and C., and notes in his bill "payable to bearer by B. and C.", payment must be made accordingly.' So also Joseph Caro: 'If in any bill no name is mentioned but the direction is to "pay bearer", then whoever presents the bill receives payment.'[10]

Maimonides on Usury

The greatest of the medieval rabbis, and the only one whose name is familiar to the Christian West, is the Spanish Jew, Maimonides. Born at Cordova in 1135, he came of a family distinguished by its learning.

The conquest of Cordova in 1148 by the puritanical Moslem sect of the Almohades, followed by the persecution of the Jewish and Christian inhabitants of the conquered territories, forced the family of Maimonides to leave their home and wander through Andalusia until at last, in 1160, they left Spain for Fez. Here again they met persecution, and fled into Egypt, where they were finally able to settle. Maimonides, now a man of 30, was at last able to make full use of his gifts. He became court physician to the sultan, founded a school of philosophy at Fustat, and was appointed chief judge of the Jewish communities in Egypt, where he died in 1204.

Maimonides' vast literary production covers a wide range of topics that extend from the most elevated metaphysical problems to the proper treatment for haemorrhoids. Our wonder at his versatility is deepened when we remember the busy life he led as a physician. Yet Maimonides' writings bear no mark of haste. They are all order and serenity, all clarity and good sense. Most of his books were written in Arabic and translated immediately into Hebrew by members of the Tibbonides family of Andalusian Jews who had established themselves at Lunel. His code of Jewish law, however, was written in Hebrew for the benefit of his fellow Israelites. It was chiefly through this work, which was completed about 1180, that the medieval Catholic Church derived its knowledge of the Synagogue.

The *Code* is based on a large number of sources, including the Bible, the Mishna, the Talmud, the geonic literature and the opinions of the Spanish rabbis whom Maimonides regarded as his teachers. While most of the laws formulated in the *Code* are drawn from the Mishna and its main auxiliary, the Babylonian Gemara, Maimonides follows his own judgement in the choice of the treatises that make up each of the fourteen books of the *Code*, and also in the arrangement of the topics within a given treatise. He thus clarifies and systematises whole collections of laws that in the Talmud were submerged and scattered.

The subject of usury is discussed in the thirteenth book of the *Code*, the *Book of the Civil Laws*, and also touched upon in the twelfth, the *Book of Acquisition*. Maimonides keeps broadly to the principles laid down by Jewish tradition, but in certain cases permits some relaxation of traditional doctrine. His teaching may be summarised as follows.

To lend or borrow money at usury is forbidden between Israelites. In doing so the lender transgresses no less than six negative commandments, and the borrower two. Nevertheless, even though they are breaking all these commandments, the parties are not subject to punishment by flogging, because usury is restorable. Direct usury, which is forbidden by the Pentateuch, may be recovered by the debtor through the court. Indirect or quasi-usury, which is forbidden only by rabbinical law, may not legally be reclaimed by the creditor, but neither is it recoverable by the borrower if he has paid it already.[11]

It is obligatory for a Jew to make a gratuitous loan to a poor fellow-Jew. Repayment of the principal may not be exacted from a poor Jewish debtor, but it can and must be reclaimed from a Gentile. It is permissible for a Jew to borrow at usury from a Gentile or an alien resident, and to lend to him at usury. The Sages forbade Israelites to lend to Gentiles at directly stipulated interest, except in so far as this may be necessary for the Israelite in order to earn a livelihood, because they feared that the Jewish lender might be corrupted by the misdeeds of the Gentile borrower if he were to consort with him frequently. This consideration does not apply in the case of an Israelite who borrows from a Gentile, because he is more likely to avoid his creditor than to consort with him. A scholar, who is unlikely to be corrupted by association with a Gentile, may lend to him at usury merely in order to make a profit.[12]

Maimonides classes so many kinds of transactions as only quasi-usurious, permissible though reprehensible, that the ancient Jewish prohibition of usury is considerably whittled away. Forbidden indeed, but only quasi-usury, is the letting of money at hire, 'the letting of dinar being unlike the letting of a utensil since in the latter case the same utensil is returned, while in the former the dinars are spent and others returned in their place'.[13] Mere quasi-usury, too, is involved in the evasionary device by which A (the lender) is given a field as a pledge by B (the borrower), and lets it back to him, the rent being concealed interest on the loan;[14] and in the investment of money in a business on condition that the investor shares in the profit but not in any possible loss – the 'iron flock' of Jewish tradition.[15] As for the double contract of sale half-condemned by the sages, this 'is not even quasi-usury', and the full amount lent is recoverable at law.[16]

The later Spanish rabbis adhered to the doctrine of the Talmud and of Maimonides. They still taught that usury between Jews was to be condemned, and between a Jew and a Gentile condoned if not actively encouraged. But there was always an unpleasant stigma attached to the nation of direct, 'biting' usury as well as the risk that the borrower might try by legal means to cancel the debt. It fell to the parties concerned in a loan transaction to arrange matters in such a way that if inquiry were made they could at worst be found guilty only of indirect or quasi-usury.

By this time, the later Middle Ages, there were many well-recognised ways of doing so. For instance, if a Jew wanted to lend to another Jew he could employ a Gentile as intermediary, so that usury did not pass directly between his co-religionist and himself.[17] He could make a contract in which the usury would appear in the form of a penalty for (prearranged) failure to return the loan by a certain date.[18] He could resort to one of the numerous subterfuges connected with the use of houses and land as pledges.[19] He could enter into a fictitious contract of sale, of which there were by this time several forms to choose from.[20] He could fall back on the false *commenda* contract, in appearance a partnership agreement but one in which the lender's risk was minimised and his profit fixed in advance. By writing in the clause 'on the basis of the permissibility of the *commenda*' it seems that 'many a pious Jew, even in the 20th century, salved his conscience while charging or paying whatever rate of interest had been stipulated'.[21] Finally, he could defer payment for an object sold, the price being fixed above its market value. This practice was forbidden by Maimonides, who however held that 'if a man purchases something from his fellow at its market value on condition that he may pay therefor at the end of a year, the seller may say, "Pay me now, and I will take less"'.[22]

Altogether, with such an array of evasionary devices to choose from, it is unlikely that any Jew who was seeking a profitable investment would be unduly troubled by the fact that usury (between Israelites at least) was in principle forbidden by the law of his people.

The Maghrebian Rabbis and Money-changing

One of the many difficulties that hampered commercial life in the Middle Ages was the confusing labyrinth of currencies that were in use in the various trading areas that made up the business world. To gain a working knowledge of the more important systems required years of experience, and the trade of a money-changer was highly skilled.

In general, the value of a coin was judged by its weight, by the purity of its metal content, by its condition and by whether it was legal tender in a given district.[23] Coins called by the same name might be current in different areas, and yet, because (for example) in one place they had been debased, or because the metal they were made of had come to be more highly prized in one district than in another, and the coins more sought after in consequence, be valued very differently by the money-changer. Thus, for example, in Aragon, Catalonia, Valencia and Navarre, the *sueldo* or shilling was at one time worth 12 pennies, and in Leon and Gallicia only 8. The ratio might also vary from time to time within a single district. It was not difficult to make a profit by buying coins where and when they were cheap, and selling them where and when they were dear.

Monetary conditions were chaotic in medieval Spain. The rabbis were constantly plagued by inquiries from creditors and debtors as to the form of currency in which debts should be paid. Naturally, the debtors always wanted to pay in debased coins, while the creditors demanded currency that had been revalued. The doctrinal problems were intensified by the fact that a loan at usury could easily be disguised as an exchange of currency, the creditor obtaining a more favourable rate than that which prevailed on the market.[24]

To sum up the foregoing remarks, we note among the Maghrebian rabbis a tenacious clinging to the fundamental principles of the ancient prohibition of usury, accompanied by a gradual, reluctant approval of a series of legal fictions or evasionary devices that tended to weaken the taboo. We shall notice that Christian doctrine followed a similar course. But Spain was a predominantly Moslem country for much of the Middle Ages, and before turning to Christian teaching we must touch upon the Islamic attitude toward usury.

USURY IN ISLAM

The Koran and Tradition

In the Islamic community, teaching on usury followed a similar course to that which we have traced in the Jewish. At the time of Muhammad's birth in 570, the period of Jewish scholasticism had already come to maturity. For the Jews of Arabia it was a time not of reforming zeal but of compromise and adaptation. 'And ... they take usury while it was forbidden them, and devour uselessly the substance of the people' is a reproach levelled in the Koran against the Jews. The fact that the principal passages forbidding usury belong to the Medina period of Muhammad's life suggests that he was shocked by the backsliding of the three small tribes of that town who practised the Jewish faith. The men of these tribes were artisans, and they are said also to have been goldsmiths and money-lenders. They had schools and rabbis (it was, indeed, their skill in casuistry, which they used in order to mock the Prophet and his followers, that eventually goaded the Moslems into making a clean sweep of them all). It is probable that they paid lip-service to the biblical prohibition of usury while evading it by some of the methods I have described.

The Messenger of God would have none of this. The Koran renews the Mosaic prohibition in vehement language:

O ye who believe, devour not usury, doubling it again and again! But fear God, that ye may prosper![25]

And bestow not favours that thou mayest receive again with increase . . .[26]

They who swallow down usury shall arise in the resurrection only as he ariseth whom Satan hath infected by his touch. This, for that they say, 'Selling is only the like of usury', and yet God hath allowed selling and forbidden usury.[27]

And so on.

The Koranic condemnation of usury was upheld during the period of Islamic tradition, and emerged in the early legal textbooks as a rigid prohibition: according to a leading authority, 'the structure of the greater part of the Moslem law of contract is explained by the endeavour to enforce prohibition of *riba* (usury) and *maisir* (gambling) to the last detail of the law'.[28]

Riba, in Islamic law, is an excess, according to a legal standard of measurement (of capacity, not length) or weight, in one of two counter-values opposed to each other in a contract of exchange, in which such excess is stipulated as an obligation falling on one of the parties, without any compensatory advantage being received by that party. A few examples will make the matter clearer. Thus, the exchange of 2 measures of barley for 1 of wheat is not usurious, because, though both grains may be measured by capacity, they are not homogeneous. Again, the exchange of 10 yards of Granadine silk for 5 of Sevillian is not usurious, because silk is measured by length, not capacity or weight. A further principal of *riba* is that the two articles must be exchanged simultaneously. Any stipulation that one of the parties may delay performance renders the contract usurious, and therefore defective and to some extent voidable.

The Koranic prohibition of the game of hazard (*maisir*) was extended to gambling in general, and Islamic law insists that the terms of a contract must be clearly stated. This requirement applies with especial strictness to objects that can be weighed or measured and are thus subject to *riba*, no unspecified quantity being permitted.

A characteristic feature of Islamic law is the elaborate body of rules governing *sarf*, the exchange of precious metals, especially in the form of coins. 'The Prophet said, "Sell Gold for Gold, from hand to hand, at an equal rate according to weight, for any inequality in point of weight is usury".'[29] The sale of gold for silver at an unequal rate according to weight is, of course, permitted, but here too the exchange must be from hand to hand. It was generally held that any number of dirhems might be exchanged for a dinar, though learned opinion was not unanimous on the point. The transfer of money by *suftaja* was viewed with suspicion, since it was in the nature of the contract that the two quantities could not be exchanged 'from hand to hand'.

Just as the Islamic laws against usury were more far-reaching and pettifogging than the Judaic, so were the methods evolved to circumvent them more ingenious and elaborate than the Jewish evasionary devices. Moslem commercial practice was brought into line with the theory of the religious law by the *hiyal* or body of well-recognised legal fictions which enabled their users to observe the letter of the law while safely contravening its spirit. It was the task of the learned *hiyal* lawyer to reconcile the activities of his client with the rulings of the Islamic judge, and in course of time hundreds of devices, or 'transactions', as they were euphemistically called, were evolved for the purpose.

The earlier *hiyal* were simple. Several traditions are directed against the double contract of sale, called in Arabic *mukhatara*. We have seen the contract described in the Talmud and in the *Code* of Maimonides. Works on Moslem law describe it in similar terms.[30] The fact that the *mukhatara* was known in Medina as early as the eighth century[31] suggests that the Islamic merchants might have borrowed it from their Jewish colleagues.

Other early evasionary devices used by Moslems were the sleeping partnership, and the giving of land or a house as security for a debt and allowing the creditor to enjoy the fruits, the usufruct representing concealed interest on the loan. These contracts are mentioned in the Talmud. It was natural enough, in a world where Jews and Moslems lived and worked side by side for centuries, and struck countless bargains together, that the Moslems should have adopted some of the hoary but effective methods of the Jews in evasion of the common stumbling-block to commerce, the laws against usury that characterised both religions.

As time went on and the first religious zeal began to fade, the *hiyal* lawyers took pride in working out for their clients, the merchants, small masterpieces of legal construction which could not be upset by the *kadi*, who was bound to the sacred law.

The Koran enjoins Moslems that when they contract a debt, be it large or small, they are to go before a notary and instruct him to take careful note of the terms, more particularly the date of repayment. And, accordingly, written documents often formed an essential element of *hiyal*. The more complicated *hiyal* normally consisted of several transactions between the parties concerned, each of which was perfectly legal in itself, and whose combined effect produced the desired result. Each 'transaction' was recorded in a separate document. The documents were finally deposited in the hands of a trustworthy intermediary, together with an unofficial covering document which set out the real relationship between the parties, and the real purpose of their agreement. Such a covering document is called *muwāta'a*, 'understanding'.[32]

Ibn Asim

Jurisprudence was a favourite profession in Moslem Spain, since it offered the advantage of leading up to the higher posts of state. The Malekite code was introduced in the first half of the ninth century, and thereafter the Andalusian jurists devoted most of their energies to commentating Malik's *Muwatta'* and the *Mudawwana* of his principal follower, Ibn Sahnun. We need not proceed to list here the numerous Andalusian writers who dealt with the subject of commercial contracts,[33] but rather illustrate the above remarks on usury in Islamic law by glancing at the work of one of them alone: Ibn Asim (1359–1426), chief *kadi* of Granada and an influential jurist. In his best-known treatise, the *Tuhfa*, Ibn Asim devotes twenty-three chapters to the subject of sale, eight to contracts of rent and hire, four to partnerships, companies and trusts and two to loans, deposits and guarantees.[34]

In general, Ibn Asim follows the usual practice of Moslem jurists in leaving the parties to a contract free to arrange their own terms, except where usury is concerned. Here our author is uncompromising 'To lend', he says, 'is legal; it is an act commonly practised in all things except women A loan must not produce a profit If this is to be its consequence it is unanimously forbidden '[35]

Ibn Asim pays great attention to money-changing, insisting on the rule that immediate delivery must be made by both parties, and that the exchange of gold for gold or silver for silver is permissible only in equal quantities (when measured by weight) or numbers (when by number).[36] Furthermore, he expressly forbids 'transactions' in matters involving the exchange of precious metals, especially where credit deals are concerned, or where the amounts exchanged are unequal.[37] Ibn Asim is thus a stern upholder of the purity of Islamic tradition But we may doubt how far he succeeded, when he sat in judgement at Granada, in frustrating the arrangements of the local merchants and money-lenders.

CHRISTIAN TEACHING

The New Testament and Tradition

The history of the Christian doctrine of usury is more complex than that of the Jewish or Islamic, since we have to consider not only the sacred writings – in this case, the New Testament – and tradition, but both canon and civil law, which were sometimes at variance on questions concerning usury.

In view of the importance the subject of usury was to assume in the eyes of medieval Christians, it is noteworthy that (apart from the story of how Christ overturned the tables of the money-changers in the

Temple) the New Testament contributes only one significant text to the debate: Luke VI: 35, 'but love ye your enemies, and do good, and lend, hoping for nothing again'. Nor did the first Christians evince the same eager interest in the niceties of the usury doctrine as had been shown by the early rabbis. Prospective martyrs, one supposes, lose much of their zest for hair-splitting.

True, the fathers of the Church whose writings constitute our Christian tradition allude with abhorence to usury. Saint Clement of Alexandria (c. 150–211) reminds us that the Mosaic law forbids lending at usury to a brother, and extends the prohibition to Christians by calling brother not only a man born of the same parents as the lender, but belonging to the same tribe, sharing the same sentiments, and partaking of the same Logos.[38] Saint Jerome (347–419) remarks that the Old Testament forbids usury only between brothers, but that the prophet Ezekiel regards a just man as 'he that hath not given forth upon usury', whether to a brother or a stranger, and that Saint Luke sets an even higher standard when he commands us to 'lend, hoping for nothing again'. Saint Jerome adds that usury may arise in the loan of corn, oil, wine and other agricultural products, as well as in that of money.[39] Saint Basil (330–79) describes the humiliation of the borrower in such convincing terms that we feel sure he must, at some time, have found himself in that uncomfortable position.[40] Saint Gregory of Nicea (c. 335–94),[41] Saint Leo the Great (c. 390–461),[42] Saint John Chrysostom (344–407),[43] Saint Ambrose (339–97)[44] and Saint Augustine (354–430),[45] all condemn usury as a sin against charity or justice, or both. But, as a general rule, the fathers wrote with the indignation of moralists, not the objectivity of legislators.

The Eastern Church and Roman Law

The canon law of the eastern Church did not forbid usury. A widely-used Syrian code of the late fifth or early sixth century allows usury on loans of corn up to a maximum rate of 25 per cent a year, and on loans of money up to 1 per cent monthly.[46] Jesubocht, Archbishop of Persia, who probably lived in the second half of the eighth century, says that 'as rich men do not know how to pass on their possessions to others unless they make a profit, and as the poor cannot live without loans, the fathers of the Church have ruled that the rate of usury is not to exceed 1% monthly'.[47]

The Emperor Justinian, therefore, when in 528 he appointed a committee of jurists to sift and codify the vast mass of legal literature left by the Roman jurists, was acting in harmony with the rules of the eastern Church in drawing up a series of enactments that regulated but did not forbid usury.

The traditional classification of loans embodied in the *Corpus Juris Civili*, the fruit of Justinian's labours, lay at the heart of the medieval Christian doctrine of usury. Four classes are distinguished. A *mutuum* is the free loan of a good that is consumed in use and may be weighed, counted or measured (in legal parlance, a fungible). Since the borrower needs the thing in order to consume it he obviously will not be able to return it, and instead must return another good of the same kind, quantity and quality. Wine and corn are examples of fungibles, and money is formally regarded as a fungible. Wine must be returned for wine, not wine for corn or money, or the contract would no longer be a *mutuum* but a barter transaction or a sale.

In a contract of *mutuum* the ownership of the good lent is transferred to the borrower, and with it the risk of loss or damage. A *mutuum* may be accompanied by a stipulation that interest be paid by the borrower. In this case the contract is no longer called a *mutuum* but a *foenus*. Justinian allows a rate of interest of $12\frac{1}{2}$ per cent a year, except for loans made to farmers, when the maximum legal rate is $4\frac{1}{2}$ per cent. Compound interest is forbidden, and simple interest ceases when the amount paid equals that of the principal.

The second type of loan, the *commodatum*, is the converse of the *mutuum*. It is the free loan of a non-fungible good, such as a house, animal or slave. The debtor must return the identical good he has borrowed, and only its use, not its ownership, is transferred to him for the period of the loan. Risk of loss or damage is born by the lender. When a charge is made for a *commodatum* the contract becomes one of rent or hire.[48] Security for a debt may take the form of a pledge or mortgage, and the debt be guaranteed by a surety.

Gratian's 'Decretum'

As time went on, the western Church gradually stiffened her attitude to usury.[49] Gratian's *Decretum*, compiled between 1139 and 1141, included several early canons that forbid the taking of usury by clerics.[50] The Council of Elvira, held about the year 300, prescribed that lay usurers as well as clerics be reprimanded and, if persistent, expelled from the Church. This disposition was confirmed by later councils; and, in a letter to the bishops of Campania, Pope Leo the Great (*c.* 390–461) also condemned usury for laymen.[51] Included in Gratian is the *palea Ejiciens*, formerly attributed to Saint John Chrysostom but now thought to have been written by an unknown author of the fifth or sixth century, and incorporated into the *Decretum* about 1180. In it are found in embryo many of the arguments that were used by the later medieval scholastics. The passage reflects the standpoint of a holy man who feels only contempt for the things of this world. According to

the writer, 'a merchant can seldom or never be pleasing to God'.
And,

> of all merchants the most accursed is the usurer; for he sells a thing
> given by God, not bought as a merchant buys, and in addition to the
> interest he demands the return of his own thing, taking away the
> other man's with his, whereas a merchant does not ask for the return
> of the thing he has sold.

By 'a thing given by God' is generally understood 'time'. The rest of
this utterance is explained by the principle of Roman law by which the
ownership of a thing lent in a *mutuum* passes to the borrower.

The *palea* proceeds:

> It may be asked whether a man who lets a field in return for the fruits,
> or a house for the rent, is not in the same position as one who lends
> money at usury. Not so. Firstly, because money was not meant to be
> used in any way except for purchasing; secondly, because the owner
> of a field, by cultivating it, obtains the crop, and the owner of a house
> can use it as a dwelling. Thus, a man who lets a field or a house
> appears to give up the use of it in return for money, and in a certain
> manner almost seems to exchange profit for profit; but for hoarded
> money he gets no use; and, thirdly, a field or a house deteriorates in
> use, but money lent in a *mutuum* does not deteriorate or diminish.[52]

This is the most elaborate discussion of usury included in the *Decretum*: we find nothing to compare with the careful expositions contained
in the Talmud or in the writings of Maimonides, or with the detailed
chapters that Moslem authors allotted to the subject. Up to the time of
Gratian, then – that is, up to about the middle of the twelfth century –
the Roman Church in condemning usury did not go beyond simple,
general recommendations. Evasionary devices were not considered at
all.

The *Decretum* became the standard textbook for the study of canon
law, first at Bologna and then at Paris and other universities where the
subject was taught. It inspired a large number of abridgements, often
preceded by an introduction. Among the earlier commentators were
John of Spain, Lawrence of Spain, John of Petesella and Bernard of
Compostela, all of whom wrote in the late twelfth or early thirteenth
centuries.

The 'Decretals'
Nearly a century passed between the compilation of Gratian's *Decretum*

(1139–41) and that of the *Decretals* of Gregory IX (1234), which add to Gratian the papal canons and decretals issued during that period. We may follow in the *Decretals* the growth and maturing of the Catholic doctrine of usury, which tended, on the whole, towards an ever-increasing severity. From the vague disapproval shown in Gratian we pass, in the *Decretals*, to a lively abhorrence of usury, and to an attempt to define the practice more precisely, the better to expunge it from the Christian community.

This stiffening of the Church's attitude toward usury coincided with the increasingly severe persecution and resulting impoverishment of the Jews that had begun at the time of the first crusade, and with the waning of Moslem power and prosperity in the Mediterranean and the transfer of economic leadership from its southern to its northern shores and from east to west. It was natural that Christian merchants should, at about this period, have taken over some of the methods of eastern commerce and banking, and equally natural that the Church should have opposed the adoption of business customs that were not only contrary to the spirit of Christian teaching but tainted with Judaism, Mohammedanism and heresy. Dislike of Jews, fear and hatred of Saracens and disquiet at the deepending absorption of Christians in their business affairs, all perhaps played a part in the intensification of the Church's campaign against usury.

The first of the canons on usury included in the *Decretals* was issued by Alexander III in 1163: it prescribes that where land or other property is held in pledge, and the lender enjoys the fruits, these must be taken into account in the final settlement of the debt.[53] It had been customary for ecclesiastical bodies to invest their surplus funds in this way, which was now closed to them as well as to laymen.

The Fourth Lateran Council, held in 1179, deplores the spread of usury in all countries, and decrees that Christian usurers are to be excommunicated and denied Christian burial.[54] Usurers must make restitution even for usury practised in the past, and their heirs must do likewise.[55]

Alexander III, in a letter to the Archbishop of Genoa, accepts as not necessarily usurious a practice common in that city. This was

> when merchants buy pepper, cinnamon, or other merchandise which at the time of the contract are worth not more than five *libras*, and promise in a public instrument to pay the vendor six *libras* at the end of a stated term. While this contract is not exactly usurious the vendor is nevertheless blameworthy, unless there is a possibility that the value of the goods may have varied by the time payment is due.[56]

Urban III (1185-7) quotes the words of Christ, 'and lend, hoping for nothing again',[57] stressing the word 'hope'. If the *mutuum* is made in the hope or expectation of profit, then the lender must be regarded as a usurer. The same criterion of intention also applies to credit sales.[58]

The decretals of Innocent III (1198-1216) are concerned not so much with doctrine as with the means of enforcing the already existent canon law. The pope enjoins Christian princes to force Jews to restitute usury taken from Christian debtors, and invites the community of Christians to abstain from all relations with Jewish usurers.[59] Usury must be restituted even when the debtor has sworn to waive his right to restitution.[60] Public usurers may be convicted and sentenced by the ecclesiastical courts, whether or not the accuser chooses to appear in court.[61] In a conciliar decree, Innocent denounces Jews who extort 'heavy and immoderate' usury.[62] He specifically condemns fictitious sale and resale agreements made in concealment of usury.[63]

The important decretal, *Naviganti*, issued in a letter from Gregory IX (1227-41) to his Spanish chaplain, Raymond of Peñafort, himself the compiler of the *Decretals*, falls into two parts. The first appears to refer to the sea-loan, a contract that goes back to Greek and Roman antiquity. Money was advanced on a ship or cargo, to be repaid with a premium if the voyage prospered but not repaid at all if the cargo were lost. Some modern scholars, rightly I think, regard the contract as a primitive form of insurance. The decretal runs: 'A person who lends a certain sum of money to a merchant travelling by sea or going to the fairs is to be considered a usurer if he does so on the understanding that he is to receive some addition to the principal on the ground that he is taking over the risk.'

This utterance, taken at its face value, strikes not only at the sea-loan but at every form of risk-bearing partnership, and the commentators performed prodigies of ingenuity in their efforts to reconcile the canon with the legitimate claims of commerce.

The second part of *Naviganti* is more permissive. It takes up the view of Alexander III that a possible alteration in the value of a commodity sold may justify the repayment of more than was received:

A person who pays ten shillings and contracts to be repaid a certain measure of corn, wine, or oil at some future date, even if the merchandise be worth more at that date, is not on that account to be considered a usurer, provided there is a genuine doubt at the time of payment as to what may be the value of the goods at the time of delivery. Similarly, a person who sells cloth, wine, oil, or other goods in order to be paid more than their present value at some future date is also to be excused.[64]

The *Sextus* and *Clementinae*, two compilations of canon law that bring us to the end of the pontificate of Clement V (1305–14), include several enactments on usury that were practically panic measures. They reflect the powerlessness of the Church to stem the tide of credit transactions in which usury played its inevitable part, and attest the growing use of legal fictions as a cover for the various forms of loan contract.

The Council of Lyons (1274) confirms the severe treatment prescribed for usurers by the Fourth Lateran Council, adding some further measures that worsened their lot still more and virtually turned them into outcasts,[65] while the Council of Vienne (1311) threatened with excommunication any civil ruler or magistrate who condoned usury or forced debtors to comply with usurious contracts. Since such contracts – so runs the decree – are generally hidden under 'diverse colours' and by means of 'exquisite frauds', money-lenders are required to submit their books to the inspection of the ecclesiastical authorities. Civil laws protecting usurers are to be repealed within three months, and anyone who presumes to deny the sinfulness of usury is to be tried as a heretic.[66]

These canons complete the bare skeleton of the Church's official teaching on the subject of usury. No important modification in the canon law was made until well on into the nineteenth century. But, beneath this apparently firm surface, many canonists and theologians were working out the implications of the Church's doctrine, and, in the course of their activities, opening cracks that contributed to an eventual weakening of the fabric. Thus, no sooner had the usury doctrine formed and crystallised than the very intransigence of the Church's attitude forced her most faithful sons to seek some measure of compromise with the activities of the commercial world. In fulfilment of this task they followed the same path as had been trodden by their forerunners in the Jewish and Islamic communities.

USURY IN SPAIN

Saint Raymond of Peñafort

A key figure in the history of usury in Spain is that of Saint Raymond of Peñafort (1180–1278), the compiler of the *Decretals* and the patron saint of canon-lawyers. A member of a noble Catalonian family, as a young man Raymond taught philosophy at Barcelona. So far as it is known, he did not leave Catalonia until he was 30, when he went to Italy, studying and later teaching law at Bologna. Raymond entered the newly-founded Dominican Order in 1219, and in that year returned to Barcelona.

Raymond's life-work was closely bound up with the detection and suppression of heresy, which since the second half of the twelfth century had been widespread in southern Europe. The stronghold of the Albigensian heretics was at Toulouse, and there was a danger that the anticlerical movement might spread into the neighbouring territories of Catalonia and Aragon. Raymond's zeal in the Church's cause attracted the attention of Pope Gregory IX, who in 1232 called him to Rome as his chaplain and secretary. At Raymond's request, inquisitors were sent into Aragon. But this early attempt to found the Inquisition in Spain met with only moderate success, partly for lack of funds and partly because of the public hostility it aroused, culminating in the murder of the chief inquisitor.

Raymond returned to Barcelona for the second time in 1236, and two years later was appointed general of the Dominican Order. He was active in its proselytising work, and established a school of Hebrew studies, probably in Murcia, and of Arabic studies in Tunis, for the training of missionaries. In connection with this aspect of Raymond's work, we may remember that it was at his request that St Thomas Aquinas wrote his *Summa contra Gentiles*.

In Raymond's day Barcelona was a busy Mediterranean seaport. Hence, perhaps, his interest in questions of commercial morality, attested by the inclusion among his writings of a manual for the spiritual guidance of merchants.[67] The problems of usury engaged Raymond's anxious attention. In a book of instructions for archdeacons, probably written in Barcelona, he enjoins the latter, on arriving in a parish on a visit of inspection, to inquire before anything else whether there are any notorious usurers among the parishioners, and, if so, what form of usury they practise. Among other 'manifold shifts and stratagems' Raymond condemns the following: profiting from the fruits of a pledge; taking horses in pledge and over-charging for their fodder; forestalling; usury cloaked as a partnership, 'as when a man lends money to a merchant on condition that he is to share in the profits but not in the losses'; usury disguised as a penalty for failure to return the principal by a certain date; and usury charged through a third party.[68] Of these devices we have seen that the first and fourth were condemned by the Talmud and classed by Maimonides as mere quasi-usury, and that the fifth and sixth were also among the stock Jewish subterfuges.

There is nothing in Raymond's instructions to show that they reflect conditions peculiar to Spain. The devices he mentions were, on the contrary, in common use among the Christians of southern Europe in his day.[69] Yet the inclusion in his list of several traditional Jewish devices suggests that Raymond may well have come across them in Barcelona, the city where he spent most of his life, and the home of a flourishing Jewish culture as well as of a thriving commerce.

In an influential treatise on canon law, probably written on his return to Barcelona from Italy in 1236, Raymond deals more fully with the subject of usury.[70] His remarks are of considerable interest in so far as he belonged to the first generation of scholars who sought to reconcile the legitimate needs of commerce with the severity of the Church's attitude. In this attempt Raymond, together with others among his contemporaries, drew upon the Roman law which, at the time when he was working at Bologna, was in process of being rediscovered and intensively studied. Usury was not forbidden under Roman law, and it was desirable to harmonise the permissiveness of the admired Roman system with the strictness of the Church's prohibition.

A solution to the problem was found ready to hand in the Roman concept of *interesse*, 'that which is between' the amount due under a contract and the amount actually paid, or damages arising from the default of one of the parties. This concept offered a neat and intellectually respectable way round an awkward dilemma. Full use was made of it. Henceforth the Catholic analysis of usury may be seen as a gradual but steady widening of the field of 'compensatory' or legitimate interest, as contrasted with the 'lucrative' or forbidden variety, until today any additional payment beyond the principal of a loan is regarded as 'interest' and not 'usury', so long as it does not too grossly exceed the customary limits.

Among the titles to *interesse* approved by Raymond, provided they are genuine and not a mere cloak for usury, are the following: expense incurred in caring for pledged property; loss suffered by the lender owing to the borrower's failure to return the loan on the agreed date; and loss of the profit the lender might have been expected to make if, instead of letting himself be persuaded into lending his money, he had used it for the purpose of his business (e.g. to buy merchandise for subsequent sale).[71]

Raymond confirms the meaning we have given to the controversial decretal, *Naviganti*, directed against the sea-loan. As he was the Pope's secretary and the person to whom the decretal was addressed, we may assume that he understood its significance perfectly. Some commentators, Raymond says, hold that the sea-loan is not a *mutuum* and therefore not a source of usury, on the ground that in a *mutuum* the ownership of the thing lent and the risk of loss always passes to the borrower. In the sea-loan the risk remains for the lender, and so the contract is really one of hire. Raymond regards this argument as of doubtful validity. Such contracts, he thinks, are usually made in fraud of usury, and are best avoided, since 'the thoughts of men cannot be hidden from the Almighty'.[72]

In so far as a sea-loan, when made for the outward voyage only, sometimes entailed repayment in a currency other than that originally lent, it partook of the nature of an exchange transaction. Raymond asks 'If a man lends 1000 [silver] shillings in Barcelona, bargaining that 100 gold shillings be returned to him in Ceuta, and he knows or believes the said gold shillings to be worth more [in Ceuta than the silver shillings in Barcelona] but he nevertheless assumes the risk, is he committing usury?'[73]

In this case, Raymond replies, the contract cannot possibly be one of hire, because money by its very nature is not susceptible to hire. We should do well to regard the contract as usurious, especially since those who make such a *mutuum* do so in the hope of pecuniary gain. This is the first reference to an exchange-contract made in any of the scholastic treatises that I have read.

Raymond was familiar with the double contract of sale and resale used as a cloak for a loan, a favourite device, as we have seen, among Jews and Moslems. He permits a genuine sale with the right of redemption, but 'it is to be understood that the contract be not made in concealment of usury'.

The Castilian Civil Law

In the earlier Middle Ages, though the usurer was seldom mentioned without being called accursed, usury was not forbidden by the civil law of Castile. The most important code during this period was the Visigothic *Liber Judiciorum*, compiled in the seventh century. The history of this code is remarkable. Its authority was maintained among the mozarabs or Christians who fell under Moslem rule and who were allowed to govern their internal affairs according to their own laws. After the tenth century, when many Christians fled from Islamic territory to settle in Leon, the *Liber* took root there also. In Catalonia the *Liber* prevailed until about the eleventh century, when it was largely replaced by other codes. After the Christian conquest of Toledo in 1085 the *Liber* was found to be still current among the Christian population, and it was eventually adopted as the general law of the newly-won kingdom of Toledo. Finally, in the thirteenth century the *Liber*, now known as the *Fuero Juzgo* or *Fuero de Toledo*, was given by Ferdinand III of Castile as a municipal law to Cordova (1241) and Seville (1250), and by Alphonso X to Murcia (1266). Thus, for one reason or another, the old Visigothic code sprang up anew over a large part of reconquered Spain.

The *Fuero Juzgo* maintains the half-permissive attitude of the early Church, and that of Justinian, towards usury. Dealing with sale, it prescribes that if the price of a good sold is partly paid, and the rest is not settled on the day appointed, the bargain must stand provided the purchaser pays the usury due on the amount that is still owing.[74] This clearly takes the payment of usury for granted. The *Fuero* limits the rate of usury to $12\frac{1}{2}$ per cent a year on amounts of 8 *sueldos* or more. If the lender charges a higher rate he is to be repaid the principal but must forfeit the usury,[75] a mild punishment that is in striking contrast to the severity of later legislation. A higher rate – 3 measures for 2 – is permitted on loans of corn, oil, or wine.

In the *Fuero Viejo de Castilla*, a collection of laws probably made in 1212 by Alphonso VIII of Castile to regulate the rights and privileges of his nobles, there is a section on the pledges that were given by noblemen to Christian as well as Jewish money-lenders. Anything seems to have been pledged. Houses, orchards, vineyards, clothing bedclothes, stuffs, silver, arms, animals – all are mentioned in that connection.[76] The readiness of the Castilian nobleman to pawn even his bedclothes seems at first sight surprising. But this was the great period of the reconquest. In many cases, no doubt, the *hidalgo's* desire for a loan arose not so much from love of idleness and luxury as from eagerness to take part, properly equipped, in whatever profitable expedition was on hand.

In 1254 Alphonso X of Castile, called 'the Learned', issued the *Fuero Real*, a code chiefly based on the law of Justinian but which also preserves to some extent the general character of Visigothic law and of the customary law evolved in Castile during the earlier centuries of the reconquest. The usury laws included in this code reflect the teaching of the *Digest*. The distinction between the *mutuum* and the *commodatum* is explained in simple terms, and there are the usual sections on guarantors and pledges. Money-lenders, whether Jewish, Moorish or Christian, are permitted to charge the 'three for four' ($33\frac{1}{3}$ per cent a year) on their loans, usury being no longer payable when it exceeds the principal. The penalty for over-charging is again mild: the money-lender must repay double his illicit gain.[77]

In the later Middle Ages the hardening of the Church's attitude towards usury placed the Castilian monarchs in an awkward predicament. Many Jews were bankers and money-lenders. To comply with the ecclesiastical ban on usury would diminish Jewish fortunes, and with them the revenues of the Crown. Nevertheless, as faithful sons of the Church, the Castilian princes followed, after long delay, her teaching in their legislation.

The famous legal treatise of the *Partidas* (late thirteenth century) opposes earlier Castilian tradition by repeating almost word for word the already long-established canon law on usury. To lend at usury is forbidden to both clerics and laymen.[78] If an object pledged (for example, an orchard, estate, or slave) bears fruit, the holder must discount the value of the product from that of the pledge itself, reducing the loan by the corresponding amount.[79] Fictitious contracts made in evasion of usury are invalid, especially one that was a general favourite:

> ... and this will be when the money-lender in reality takes some hereditament as a pledge and outwardly feigns that the pledger is selling it to him, drawing up a deed of sale for this purpose so that he may enjoy the fruits without being prosecuted for usury. We therefore say that this sort of fraud is not to be upheld if it can be proved that the said contract was really a loan, and that the deed of sale was a mere cloak for it.[80]

This is the earliest reference I have found in a Spanish legal code to a fictitious contract made in concealment of usury.

Alphonso XI of Castile, after solemnly proclaiming the *Partidas* at the cortes of Alcalá in 1348, immediately published a short but important code of his own, the *Ordenamiento de Alcalá*, in which the laws against usury are so severely tightened as to constitute a definite break with earlier policy. Much heavier penalties than had hitherto been customary were imposed on Christian usurers, who were now to lose all their illegal profit and to pay a fine equal to that amount, a third of which was to go to the informer and two-thirds to the Crown. A second offender was to forfeit half of his entire possessions and a third to lose everything he had, the proceeds being divided in the same way.[81] Furthermore, the absolute veto on usury was now to apply to Jewish and Moslem lenders as well as Christians:

> Because [says the king] usury is found to be a great sin, forbidden as much by the law of nature as by those of scripture and grace, and a thing very grievous to God, and because evil and tribulations come to the land where it is practised ... we think proper to forbid any Jew or Jewess or Moor or Moorish woman to presume to lend at usury, either on his or her own account or on that of another.[82]

These measures proving ineffective, later Castilian monarchs went to even more extreme lengths to foil the machinations of 'those who do not lend directly at usury but enter into other contracts in concealment of it', as Alphonso XI had said. In 1377 Henry II of Castile decreed that any bonds taken by Jews or Moors from Christians were to be invalid, except such contracts as related to cash transactions,

> because, in defiance of the law and in concealment of usury ... the

said Jews and Moors . . . invent and conceive diverse forms of contracts, sales and malicious obligations, we forbid any Jew or Moor, either in his own name or in that of another, to take a bond from any Christian person, council, or community, in terms of money, corn, wine, wax, wool, or anything else, by reason of a loan, sale, purchase, safe-custody, deposit, rent, or any other contract whatsoever, which may render the Christian person, council or community liable to pay any quantity of the above commodities to a Jew or Moor, or a Jewess or Moorish woman. Furthermore, all sales must be paid for when the good sold is delivered.[83]

But all measures were useless. No sooner was one loophole closed than another was opened, and usury flourished as never before, more vigorously in Castile than in any other part of Spain

Now, what exactly were the malicious and fraudulent contracts to which the Castilian legal texts repeatedly refer? They were not, I suggest, evasive devices that each Jewish or Moorish money-lender thought up for himself, but, on the contrary, the time-honoured contracts used by Jews and Moors, with the hard-won approval of their religious leaders, in order to circumvent the Jewish and Islamic prohibition of usury. Among Jews and Moslems such contracts had long since become a matter of business routine, and they were ready to hand when, from the twelfth century onward, an increasingly determined attempt was made to repress usury in the Christian community. A series of mozarab documents from Toledo, dating from the second half of the thirteenth century, show that the Toledan Jews of this period were making use of various evasive devices in their dealings with Christian borrowers.[84]

It is well known that in the course of the Middle Ages a growing class of Christian financiers took over to some extent the functions of the Jews. Many of these were New Christians, Jews who had accepted baptism in order to escape the persecution that darkened the life of Spanish Jewry in the closing centuries of the reconquest. These New Christians did not desert their old professions but carried on their work as counsellors, doctors, ambassadors, tax-collectors, bankers, shopkeepers and artisans. In due course the descendants of rabbis became monks and friars, bishops and cardinals and even inquisitors. It is suggested that after the pogroms of 1391, in particular, as many as half the community of some 200,000 Jews in Castile were converted to Christianity, and that these converts, together with the Jews who refused baptism, 'were the motive-force of money and craftsmanship in Castile'.[85] An example of such converts was the rich Don Alvar García de Santa María (brother of Don Pablo, born Salomon Halevi, once chief rabbi of Burgos and later bishop of that city), who did not allow his conversion to prevent him from making loans to King John I of Navarre, the Prince of Viana and many private persons. We cannot doubt that other converts did the same.

It may be asked why I seem to lay more stress on the Jewish than on the Moorish use of contracts that were common to the law of both religions. The Castilian legal texts do indeed allude repeatedly to the evil devices of both Jews and Moslems in evasion of the Christian laws that regulated usury, and we may suppose that Moorish as well as Jewish money-lenders made use of the classic devices. But there is a good reason for attributing the survival of the evasive devices in Castile primarily to Jewish influence. As the reconquest progressed, and one Andalusian city after another was won for the Crown of Castile, the Moors were expelled in great numbers, first from the towns and later from the countryside, whence they emigrated to Africa and to the Moorish kingdom of Granada. Even so, by the middle of the fifteenth century the Moorish community still probably amounted to about a tenth of the population and was larger than the Jewish and ex-Jewish elements together. But it was nothing like as rich and powerful, and played a steadily declining part in the business life of Castile.

In the fifteenth century the rigidity of the usury laws was somewhat modified. True, in 1434, King John II of Castile issued a decree enjoining the justices to enforce the regulations. But four years later, at the request of the Cortes, he dispensed the Jews from observing the absolute prohibition of usury, while limiting the rate to 25 per cent.[86]

Another petition of the Cortes, made to Henry IV of Castile in 1462, pointed out the injustice of the existing laws that forbade the Jews to enter into any form of contract, whether usurious or not. Mindful, no doubt, of the simultaneous decline in Jewish fortunes and in the Crown revenues, the king agreed to allow the Jews to contract freely, provided their dealings were neither usurious nor in evasion of usury.

In 1480 we find the Catholic kings confirming the usury laws directed against Christian lenders:

Though by divine and human law usury is forbidden and severely punished, this does not suffice to restrain it, nor the greed that moves usurers to possess themselves of other men's goods by cunning and evil means. . . . We decree that any Christian who lends at usury or enters into any contract to conceal it should incur the prescribed penalties.[87]

In 1492 came the fateful decision to expel from Castile and Aragon all Jews who refused baptism. Henceforth the usury laws could apply only to Christians and, for a few years longer, to Moslems, until they too were offered the choice between exile and conversion. After 1502 the Castilian and Aragonese monarchs no longer ruled over men of different faiths. In name, if not always at heart, their subjects were all Catholics.

Usury in Aragon

The Aragonese princes were even slower than those of Castile in adopting measures prejudicial to the interests of their Jewish subjects.

In a statute of 1241 James I of Aragon limits usury on loans made by Jews and Moors to 20 per cent a year, and on those made by Christians to 12 per cent. At first the loan-contract was supposed to state the principal and interest separately, but from 1262 onwards the same king on various occasions permitted the Jews of certain towns to lump the two items together. This concession was to the advantage of the money-lender, since it enabled him to charge interest on the interest due during any period when the loan was in default, as well as on the principal.

As in Castile, the punishment at this period for infringing the regulations was mild: the offending money-lender merely forfeited the usury, and in grave cases the principal also. Money forfeited by usurers was an important source of revenue to the Crown; when James II granted pardons for exceeding the maximum legal rate to the Jews of Lerida, Saragossa, Valencia, Gerona, Majorca and other places, the measure brought him in the tidy sum of 164,300 shillings.

Research has disclosed much interesting information about the practice of usury among the Jews of Perpignan in the thirteenth century.[88] Perpignan, which was among the possessions of the Aragonese Crown until 1278, was at this period a thriving commercial centre and the meeting-place of merchants from France and Spain.

Money-lending seems to have been the chief occupation of the Perpignan Jews. Those most active in the business were the leading members of the community. The fact that rabbis, scholars and poets were eager to invest their money in this way accords with talmudic doctrine, which, as we have seen, recommends money-lending as especially appropriate for such persons, since they are less likely than the common run of mortals to be corrupted by the contact with Gentiles that is unavoidable in these activities.

The Perpignan Jew travelled regularly through the countryside, making the greater number of his loans to villagers. Then came loans to townsmen, knights and nobles, the clergy and the royal officers. The word *usura* occurs in hundreds of documents recording loans made by Jews, for whom it clearly carried no moral slur. The Perpignan registers also contain many loan-contracts between Christians, but they never mention *usura*, although such charges were certainly hidden in their terms.

Towards the end of the thirteenth century, in Aragon as in other parts of western Christendom, an increasingly bitter conflict arose between civil and religious authorities over this matter of usury. James I of Aragon had issued repeated orders to his officials to enforce the loan-contracts entered into by Christian debtors, provided their terms accorded with the legal limits. But by 1275, if not before, Christians were citing Jewish creditors before the ecclesiastical courts for the very practices permitted by the king. In that year the Aragonese monarch ordered his officers in the Rousillon to collect substantial fines from any Christian layman who presumed to cite a Jew before a church court, provided only that the Jew stood ready to answer the charge before a royal tribunal. If a cleric should do so, the royal officers were to prevent other Christians from trading with the plaintiff, lending him money, lodging him in their houses, working his land or aiding him in any other way.

Even in the fourteenth and fifteenth centuries the Aragonese kings were still far from desiring the impoverishment of their Jewish subjects. They were well aware that the hard-working Jewish communities were their main source of wealth. Alphonso III remarked in 1328 that 'our predecessors ... have tolerated and supported the Jews in their kingdoms and lands, and the Church of Rome tolerates them still, because the Jews are the very coffers and treasuries of kings'. In 1391 John I condemned a pogrom at Huesca on the ground that the Jews 'constitute our royal revenues and treasure'. In 1417 Alphonso V thought it necessary to restore the Jewish community of Saragossa after an outburst of popular persecution because its disappearance would bring 'great harm and damage to ourselves and to our royal revenues'. And even Ferdinand the Catholic, who, together with his consort, expelled the Jews from Aragon and Castile in 1492, was, as late as 1481, still calling them 'our coffers and patrimony'.[89]

Yet it would seem that the prudent policy of the Aragonese Crown towards its Jews, which combined royal protection with moderate exploitation, was unable to arrest the decay in Jewish prosperity that marked the later Middle Ages in Aragon. Towards the end of the fourteenth century an economic and financial crisis, whose causes have not yet been fully elucidated but for which the ravages of the Black Death would seem to offer a sufficient explanation, sowed ruin throughout the kingdom. Popular anger was, as usual, vented on the Jews, and culminated in the massacres of 1391. The failure of many Jewish bankers forced the Aragonese kings to place the credit of the Crown in the hands of Italian financiers and of the New Christians of Jewish origin whose numbers increased so greatly during this period.

An important instrument of State and personal credit in Aragon was the *census* or rent-charge. The contract is unknown to Roman law and seems to have arisen in various parts of Europe in the course of the twelfth century, perhaps, as Noonan seems to think, in answer to the increasingly strict control of usury.[90]

It will be recalled that among the Jewish evasionary devices mentioned in the Talmud is the enjoyment by the money-lender of the fruits of property given in pledge for a loan or sold with the right of redemption. Some early commentators[91] jocosely connected the *census* with the 'iron flock', as the Jews called a partnership in which the partner who supplied the capital ran no risk of loss. This lends a certain colour to the hypothesis that the *census* originated as a Jewish evasionary device.

The *census* is, in essence, an obligation to pay an annual return from fruitful property. For example, a farmer might sell for ready cash the right to certain produce for so many years to come. Landowners found the sale of *census* on their property a convenient way of raising money, and kings financed themselves by the sale of *census* on their lands, monopolies and tax-receipts. The *census* instalments were sometimes paid in cash instead of in kind, and the transaction then became the sale of a right to money secured on property.

Great attention was paid to the *census* contract by the theologians of the thirteenth and fourteenth centuries, and there was much doubt and controversy as to whether it was licit. An effort was made to keep loan-theory and *census*-theory apart, and we generally find the *census* discussed under the heading of sale and the just price. As time went on, ever finer distinctions were drawn between the various types of *census*, some being generally approved and others (such as the personal *census* by which a man sold his future labour for ready cash) universally condemned. On the whole, the real *census* on fruitful property was held to be lawful, despite the difficulty of distinguishing between this type of contract and a loan.

Aragonese practice played a significant part in the later development of *census*-doctrine. In 1452 Alphonso V of Aragon represented to Pope Nicholas V that in his domains the goods of many borrowers were consumed by voracious usury, but that individuals, corporations and churches had found a more convenient way of raising funds by selling annuities redeemable by the seller, founded on their 'houses, possessions, and properties, especially or even generally on all their goods, returns, emoluments, rights and things'. Now, however, the rich hesitated to invest in this way for fear of committing usury, and the poor had fallen a prey to the common money-lender. In answer to this plea, the pope determined that in Aragon and Sicily (at this date among the possessions of the Aragonese Crown) such *census*-contracts as the king described were licit, provided they paid not more than 10 per cent.[92]

Despite the king's lament that in Aragon usury was rife, it appears to have been a somewhat less heavy scourge there than in Castile. The greater commercial experience of the Aragonese, and their more advanced banking system, which in some places dated back to the early Middle Ages, helped to provide credit, and perhaps to protect them from the more rapacious demands of the private money-lender.

OLD DEVICES IN A NEW WORLD

The year 1469, which saw the marriage of Ferdinand, heir to the throne of Aragon, and Isabella, heiress to that of Castile, may conveniently be taken as marking the end of the Middle Ages in Spain. The union of the two young people, who in 1474 and 1479 assumed their crowns, announced the opening of a new era. True, we cannot yet speak of a united Spain. The two kingdoms were to retain their separate parliaments, laws and systems of taxation until the time of the Bourbons. Still, the concept of 'Spain' was coming to replace that of 'the Spains' in the minds of the people. The last decades of the fifteenth century brought a series of great achievements and innovations that combined to make that concept a reality. The conquest of Granada severed the last political link with the Maghreb, and the imposition of religious unity throughout Castile and Aragon confirmed the place of Spain among the kingdoms of the Catholic West. The voyages of discovery and the winning of a vast colonial empire, the final union of the Crowns of Castile and Aragon under Charles I, and the coming of the new and foreign dynasty of Habsburg, were further steps that helped to bring Spain into the modern world and transform her into a great European power.

And yet, running through the new Spain like veins in marble, the traces of her multi-racial, religious, linguistic and cultural past were not to be effaced. Even today they are clear enough, in many branches of the national life. How much more evident must they have been in the sixteenth century!

In our own little field of economic thought and its reflection in business practice, the above remarks may be illustrated.by showing how some of the age-old evasionary devices lingered on into the new era, the 'age of mercantilism', as it is sometimes called. Their survival is of greater importance for the history of economic doctrine than may appear at first sight. As Schumpeter says, 'the very high level of Spanish sixteenth-century economics was due chiefly to the scholastic contributions'.[93] And the Spanish scholastics devoted much of their effort in this field to examining the permissibility or otherwise of the evasionary devices that still flourished in the commercial world. Thus, the old game of handball that had for long centuries been carried on between rabbis, *kadis*, priests and merchants was played out in Spain with a virtuosity unequalled since the days of the Babylonian rabbis. In my third chapter I shall describe some of this scholastic work, and contrast it with that of the political economists who wrote at the same period. Here I wish merely to show that certain of the traditional evasionary devices not only survived in the new Spain but took on fresh life and vigour there.

Dry Exchange

Perhaps the most striking feature of the economy of Spain in the sixteenth century is the increase in her supplies of gold and silver caused by imports of the precious metals from the recently discovered Indies.

Small quantities of gold and silver began to reach Spain in the first decades of the century. The exploitation of the 'silver mountain' of Potosí from 1545 onward greatly increased the supply of silver to Spain, and imports attained their greatest volume between 1581 and 1630, after which they began to decline.

The first half of the sixteenth century saw a dramatic rise in the Castilian price level, which continued until the end of the century. The increase in prices began in Seville, home port of the treasure fleet, and spread through Andalusia and New Castile, and thence to Old Castile and Valencia. Since the curves of treasure imports and of prices do not correspond exactly (the former rising more rapidly in the second half of the century, and the latter in the first half), the phenomenal increase in Spanish prices and wages – a fourfold growth between 1501 and 1600 – cannot be explained, as contemporary observers often explained it, by the simple application of the quantity theory of money. But, while opinions differ as to the precise effect of treasure imports on the Spanish price level, no historian has gone so far as to doubt that the influx of precious metals helped in some measure to inflate prices.

A vivid picture of the inflationary economy of the period, and of business life in Seville, has been left us by the Dominican friar, Tomás de Mercado, whose celebrated handbook of commercial morality was first published in 1569. The city of Seville, he says, 'is on fire with all manner of business. There are great real-exchanges for all fairs, within and without the kingdom, sales and purchases on credit and for cash, and for huge sums, great shipments, and *baratas* for many thousands and millions, such as neither Tyre nor Alexandria in their day could equal.'[94]

In this whirlpool of commerce there could not fail to be sin and fraud, sometimes committed in ignorance of the Church's teaching. Mercado proposes to light the merchant's way by offering him a guide in his own vulgar tongue.

Credit, continues Mercado, is the Seville merchant's most pressing requirement: 'Merchants and money-changers live in such a confusion of contracts that a rich merchant is no longer content to buy and sell, but tries to deal on the exchanges, so as to find ready in every place the money he so direly needs.'[95] The business of the exchanges, Mercado goes on to explain, 'embraces East and West, and takes in both the Poles'. It is a gentlemanly occupation 'not like usury, though indeed the two are closely related (but people do not generally admit to following an evil way of life)'.[96]

'Real exchange', the bona fide exchange of a sum of money in one place for an equal sum elsewhere, is permissible. But the practice has arisen of lending money at usury and disguising the contract as an exchange-deal. Such a usurious contract is called 'dry exchange'.

Dry exchanges [continues Mercado] are exchanges that exist not, nor have being, but are imaginary, and bear a blank space for a name. They are scarcely to be numbered. Firstly, the gentlemen and princes take out a great quantity of bills drawn on Naples, Antwerp, or Coimbra. Where they have no money, nor expect to have it except on paper, but only to gain time, they draw a first bill of exchange on some person in that place, and mostly there is no such person. The bill does not so much as leave the changer's desk until it matures. Then, when it does, he draws another in the name of his factor [in the distant place, of course] and says that, having no funds for that payment, he has taken it on exchange at so much per cent. And in the six months of pretended coming and going the gentleman has to pay for his pomp at the rate of 25%.[97]

Sometimes a little more subtlety was employed:

Occasionally, being somewhat scrupulous, and thinking the fault lies in not sending off the bill, the changer actually does remit it to Flanders, instructing his correspondents to protest it and rechange it at the market rate.

But these scruples were rare:

Others, to spare themselves such vain work, if the customer says he has no one to answer for him, offer to do so for a commission of 2%.

46

All these frauds, first, second, and third are steps that lead straight to hell.

The subject of the 'exchanges' has been thoroughly investigated in recent years.[98] However, a short commentary on Mercado's text may perhaps be called for.

The transfer of money by some kind of document, avoiding the necessity of transporting the coins themselves, must go back to the very beginnings of long-distance trade. I have already mentioned one or two of the instruments used by Jewish and Islamic traders to convey money from country to country. We have also seen that the transfer of debt was long frowned upon by the orthodox of both religions, and that money-changing was suspect (in Islam, highly so), since usury could easily be hidden in the exchange-rates.

The exact mechanics of an exchange-transaction do not matter for the purpose of this study. Whether the instrument used to perform the exchange was called by a Hebrew, Arabic or Latin name, or took the form of a notarial contract, bill of exchange or informal private letter, the effect was the same. Money present was exchanged for money absent, as the medieval phrase had it, and if the two amounts were in different currencies, as was usually the case, they were exchanged at the market rate.

The exchange-contract was known to Roman law and was probably common in the earlier Middle Ages. The oldest bills of exchange that have come down to us date from the twelfth century. One of the earliest records of an exchange-contract concerns an Islamic city: in 1157 a Genoese businessman mentions '£10 Genoese taken in exchange against a promise to repay in Tunis'.[99] In a bill of 1156 a certain Soliman, probably the Jew, Soloman of Salerno, promises to repay in Alexandria money and goods received in Italy. Other bills of about the same period refer to advances made in Genoa in local money and repayable in Provisine currency at the next fair of Champagne. Sometimes the contract stipulates that if the payment is not duly made the debt must be settled in Genoa on the return of the caravan bringing home the Genoese merchants from the fair.[100] Such a contract is the prototype of the 'exchange and rechange' of a later period. It may have been a genuine transfer of funds, or it may have been a straight loan disguised as an exchange transaction. If the latter, it is an early example of the 'dry exchange' we are here concerned with.

As the rates of exchange between the different coinages fluctuated continually, as well as the rate at which bills could be bought and sold, a broker could make a profit by speculating on the exchanges, 'giving' money where it was scarce and dear, and 'taking' it where it was plentiful and cheap.

It would seem, too, that the changer, or broker, commonly charged a commission for his services. Here the concept of *interesse*, derived from Roman law, came into play. In 1311 and 1349 the French Crown authorised the payment of *interesse* on bills payable at the fairs of Champagne and Brie, which were held six times a year. Up to 15 per cent could be charged on bills payable at the next fair 'because at these fairs large loans have of necessity to be made, and credit is given from fair to fair'. In 1419 the fairs of Lyons were granted similar privileges.

In Flanders, in the sixteenth century, the exchanges functioned in much the same way. Merchants made loans carrying *interesse* to other merchants who were travelling to a distant country, justifying their profit on the pretext of *lucrum cessans*. It was argued that, as money was the merchant's tool, he had a right to compensation when he deprived himself of it in order to make a loan. This usage was sanctioned by Charles V in an Act of 1540, in which '*interesse* is allowed to good merchants according to the profit they could reasonably expect to make, up to 12%'.[101]

But lenders were not content with this relatively moderate rate of *interesse*, or with whatever profit they could make by speculating on the exchanges. They made loans not only to merchants who genuinely needed money for trading purposes but to all-comers, charging exorbitant *usura* made up of *interesse* where it was permitted and the proceeds of a fictitious rate of exchange fixed in advance. This, broadly speaking, was the 'dry exchange' condemned by Mercado.

From the twelfth century onwards 'dry exchange' was widely used in Catholic countries as a cloak for loans at usury. In the sixteenth it was widespread throughout Castile where it seems to have become a favourite device for evading the civil and ecclesiastical prohibition of usury. The popularity of 'dry exchange' was no doubt owing to the difficulty of distinguishing between a dry and a real exchange contract.[102]

The Mohatra

In the shadow of the dry exchange favoured by 'gentlemen and princes' there flourished in Castile another ancient device, one less genteel, perhaps, but better suited to the needs of humbler folk. This was none other than the *mohatra*, or double contract of talmudic times, a device which, as we have seen, was half-approved by the Babylonian rabbis, fully sanctioned by Maimonides, and often woven by the Islamic lawyers into their elaborate webs of legal fiction.

The contract is condemned in a manual for the use of confessors, published in Saragossa in 1552. The priest is instructed to ask the penitent: 'Have you sold any merchandise to a person who could not pay for it immediately, and, having done so, have you bought it back at a lower price, paying at once? If so, you have committed usury.'[103] Nine years previously the author of a similar manual, published at Medina del Campo, had observed that:

> At the fairs there is scarce any business but the borrowing of money at usury and the taking of *mohatras*. All is done through the brokers, which ill-fated wretches are left with the lesser part of the profit and the greater part of the guilt, for they run after these customers, importune those, and deceive them all with their lies, promises, and perjuries.[104]

The double contract was condemned not only by the Church but also by the State. It is clearly described in a law of 1543 directed against '*mohatras and trapazas*'.[105]

> On account of the many dealers and money-lenders who travel through the Adelantamientos,[106] the farmers and the very poor suffer great distress. They enter into contracts and fraudulent schemes by which they bind themselves for large sums and receive much less than the amount they promise to repay, buying goods on credit and immediately afterwards selling them for cash, sometimes to the very same merchants who have sold them the goods.[107]

Furthermore, instead of hunting down and punishing these 'traders and usurers who by such wiles and deceits destroy the poor', the local authorities turn a blind eye to their activities, 'being more mindful of their own interests than of the public weal'.

It was not only at the fairs, then, that the double contract flourished. In certain districts of Castile, namely the Adelantamientos, it was the common resort of poor people in 1543. The Adelantamientos included Leon and Burgos, both of which had been important centres of Jewish commerce throughout the Middle Ages. It seems reasonable to suppose that the *mohatra* or double contract, which I have shown to be of Jewish origin, was among the devices used by medieval Jewish money-lenders to conceal usury, and that after the expulsion of the Jews in 1492 it continued to be used among Christians, especially those of Jewish antecedence, in the parts of Castile where it had been most firmly rooted.

The use of the *mohatra* (or *barata*, as the double contract was often called) was by no means confined to the poorer borrower, We have seen that Tomás de Mercado, writing in 1669, mentions '*baratas* for many thousands and millions' as familiar features of the Seville business world. He describes the contract in several passages:

Another ocean of fraud are the *baratas* that are here in use. . . . The origin of this business was and remains the want of money in which many find themselves. They cannot borrow in exchange, because the term allowed for repayment is very short and they desire it to be long.[108] They fear that by dealing in exchange and rechange from fair to fair they will lose more than if they take a *barata*, and so they arrange one in which they can get whatever they need for the present.'[109]

The *barata*, then, was the resort of those who needed long-term credit. Mercado goes on to explain that there are two kinds of *barata*, one being permissible and the other forbidden. We may call them 'real' and 'dry', perhaps.

The first sort of *barata* consists 'in buying a quantity of clothing on credit and selling it immediately for cash, at so much less than it is worth. The cheapness of the merchandise invites everyone to buy, and so, by losing 25 or 30%, the borrowers are able to raise ready cash.'

Mercado regards the contract as permissible for the borrower, provided he sells the merchandise openly. Indeed, he is performing a public service by selling his goods cheaply. But the merchant who sells him the clothing on credit is to be looked on with suspicion. He has probably charged too high a price for his merchandise, given bad or unsaleable goods or otherwise 'thrust in the dagger up to the hilt' because he sees that 'the poor man is in desperate need, with the rope round his neck, as they say'.

The second kind of *barata* is called 'infernal'. This is 'when the very same merchant who sells the clothing on credit buys it back again for cash, paying 25 or 30 per cent less than the price he sold it for, though often the goods have not even left his house or shop'. Mercado disapproves of this type of *barata*: 'Even the common people, without much philosophy and only by the light of their natural reason, think ill of the lender who buys the merchandise back again. They hold him in no good opinion, though they do not condemn or reprove anyone else who may buy the goods.'[110]

As Saravia had observed twenty years before, dealings in *baratas* were largely in the hands of *corredores* – those brokers or commission-agents without whose services, even today, it is difficult to transact the smallest piece of business in certain parts of Spain.[111] According to Mercado, the brokers were often parties to the deal. Touts were sent out to fish for customers:

A broker arrives from the market and says: 'Fifty bales of satin or a hundred boxes of cocoa are being sold cheap. If you want to make a thousand pieces over the deal, give me the money', and he only wants it so that the borrower may have the use of it. Then he makes out a receipt for the satin or the cocoa, though generally he has never even seen them, nor ever could, except in the land of Cockaigne. But they all understand one another and turn a blind eye to the fraud.[112]

Occasionally there would come forward some simple-minded person who was unfamiliar with the device:

I once saw a broker offer the business to a rich blacksmith in so bold and care-free a manner that the smith took him at his word. He handed over two thousand ducats, no little pleased at the prospect of earning two hundred in each thousand. But when he found out the truth he undid the contract like a good Christian, being unwilling to take *interesse* arising out of such a diabolical fraud.[113]

Few were so ingenuous. The hoary double contract was, as a rule, recognised by all. We have already noted its use in medieval Italy. A scholar who studied the contract observed, however, that it was particularly widely diffused in Spain, and in view more especially of its Arab name, suggested that the Christian peoples of Europe 'all took it from a single source: the Moslem practice of contracts, with which they had become acquainted through their own relations with the Arabs'.[114] While I do not dispute the use of the *mohatra* among Moslems in Spain and elsewhere, I think that the contract may be regarded as primarily Jewish. The correspondence between the talmudic, Maimonidean and modern descriptions of the *mohatra* leaves, it seems to me, little doubt on that score. As regards the name, *mohatra*, I have been unable to find any instance of its use in Spain before 1543, though I cannot believe that the word was not in use before that date.

The double contract was to keep its popularity for many years to come. Some theologians began tentatively to condone it, calling down the contempt of their opponents. Among the latter was Pascal, who, in his attack on the Spanish Jesuit Antonio de Escobar, made skilful use of Escobar's rather half-hearted disapproval of the *mohatra*.[115] As late as 1679, Pope Innocent XI renewed the Church's condemnation of the contract, and threatened with excommunication any who should venture to defend its legality. We may suppose that in the course of the eighteenth century the *mohatra* fell gradually out of use together with other evasionary devices, the merging of the once well-separated concepts of *interesse* and *usura* having by that time rendered them superfluous.

The Census

As for the *census*, which may reasonably be surmised to have originated in reply to the prohibition of usury, it had long since become the general and respectable recourse of the Spanish capitalist. Nevertheless, it did not escape the attention of the Spanish doctors, many of whom devoted chapters, and even entire treatises, to the subject.[116]

Tomás de Mercado defines the *census* as 'the pension and tribute that one person binds himself to pay to another in particular', and tells us that there are two kinds of *census*, the 'reservative, customary between ecclesiastics', and the 'consignative', in common use among the laity. A reservative *census* is

> when one party gives the other a benefice or a dignity, or some vineyards, olive-orchards, pastures, or houses, reserving to himself a certain quantity of such fruits and rents as the property may bring in. We see this continually in the benefices and prebends of the Church; it is a thing so widely introduced that a man rarely acquires a benefice without it.

Mercado approves the contract on the ground that it is the sole concern of ecclesiastics, to whom it is fully familiar.

The consignative *census*, 'the contract the vulgar engage in, and which is somewhat suspicious', does not seem to differ in any material point from the reservative. It occurs 'when one party gives the other, let us say, 1,000 ducats on houses, hereditaments, or other property, on condition that the latter pays him a certain annual rent, either in money, which is usual, or in wine, wheat, scarlet grain or fruit'. Some *census* were perpetual and others redeemable. The contract, says Mercado, is very confusing to the ignorant, who are apt to mistake it for a *mutuum*, but essentially it is the sale of a right to a yearly payment of money or produce, secured on real estate.[117]

This old evasionary device (as we may suppose it to be) enjoyed great popularity in sixteenth-century Spain. González de Cellorigo was to lament in 1600 that:

> All the ills of Spain proceed from shunning what naturally sustains us and turning to what destroys republics, when they place their wealth in money and in the income derived from *census*-contracts, which like a general plague have reduced these realms to abject poverty, since all or most men have desired to live by this means, on the interest they get from their money, without considering where they are to find what they require for such a way of life. This is the thing that has so obviously ruined this republic and the *census*-

holders, because, thinking only of getting an income, they have renounced the virtuous processes of the crafts, commerce, husbandry, and all that naturally sustains mankind.[118]

The Mosaic prohibition of usury, then, presented the same dilemma to the members of the three religious communities of medieval Spain. Should the taboo be observed in its original purity or circumvented to suit the facts of business life? Jews, Moslems and Christians in turn chose the second course, but, in each case, only after a tenacious, centuries-long struggle.

What effect, we may wonder, did the attempt to abolish usury have on the life of medieval Spain? It is difficult to agree with those who hold that the civil and ecclesiastical laws against usury greatly hampered the economic development of the Peninsula. In the first place, many lenders were Jews and Moors, and it was not until the middle of the fourteenth century that these were forbidden to lend at a moderate rate of usury. Secondly, Christian lenders found ways of evading the ban (we have examined only a few of them). In the words of the Catholic kings, though by divine and human law usury was forbidden and severely punished, this did not suffice to restrain it, nor the greed that moved usurers to possess themselves of other men's goods by cunning and evil means. We can probably take this pronouncement at its face value.

It was perhaps fortunate that the anti-usury laws could not be fully enforced. One of their chief aims was to protect the needy peasants from the depredations of the money-lender. Yet, speaking as one who has farmed in Spain for many years, I am sure that without some means of getting credit to tide him over the bad years – and bad years, in Spain, have always been frequent – it could no more have been possible for the medieval Spanish farmer to scratch a living from the soil than it is for his modern successor.

This conclusion is borne out by the experience of a fifteenth-century magnate, Don Pedro Fernández de Velasco, Count of Haro, who actually succeeded in repressing Jewish usury throughout his vast domains. The result was disastrous. The vassals complained that it was far worse to get no credit at all than to pay usury, since they were now obliged to sell their cattle, wool and corn in advance of the crop, and begged the count to restore the old state of affairs. Being unwilling to do so, Don Pedro was forced to furnish three of his towns with stocks of money and grain that could be borrowed by the farmers. But, so far as is known, there were few such public granaries in Spain at this period. We may safely assume that if the rapacity of the medieval money-lender brought ruin to some, the provision of credit saved others from that fate.

53

We may perhaps venture to ask another question, one that is more far-reaching in its implications. Spain, it has often been said, is a difficult country to govern. Her people are – have always been – individualists, mistrustful of authority, indifferent to the public good, united only in the evasion of any law that does not suit their purpose. And it must be confessed that this criticism (a commonplace among travellers in Spain from the sixteenth century onwards, as well as among Spaniards themselves) is not entirely unfounded. Can the last of these alleged defects, the light-hearted flouting of tiresome regulations – the observance, let us say, of the letter, not the spirit, of the law – be yet another legacy of the complex Spanish past? Could it be that the Jewish and Moslem custom of evading outworn taboos by the use of legal fictions (a habit by no means confined to usury but extending to many other walks of life) and the adoption, in turn and for similar reasons, of evasive devices by Christians, have helped in some measure to bring law itself into contempt? Legal fictions, it is true, were far from being unknown to Roman law. But their function was the relatively minor one of providing the legal framework for current practice with a minimum of innovation and disturbance: in Jewish and Islamic law it was that of evading a positive and solemn commandment of religion.

NOTES

1 *Las siete Partidas del rey D. Alfonso el Sabio*, in *Los códigos españoles* (Madrid, 1847–51), Vols 2, 3 and 4, partida 2, tit. 20, laws 6 and 7.

2 *The Babylonian Talmud*, ed. J. Epstein (London, 1938–52), Vol. (not numbered) *Baba Mezi'a*, 60b–64b. The square brackets used in the quotations from the Talmud are the translator's.

3 Miles Mosse, *The Arraignment and Conviction of Usurie* (London, 1595). Reprinted in *Tudor Economic Documents*, ed. R. H. Tawney and Eileen Power (London, 1924), Vol. 3, pp. 377–86.

4 Blaise Pascal, *Lettres Provinciales* (1656). The eighth letter discusses various devices used to evade the charge of taking usury, and allegedly sanctioned in current manuals of moral theology. Among them is the *mohatra*, 'quand un homme qui a affaire de vingt pistoles achète d'un marchand des étoffes pour trent pistoles, payables dans un an, et les lui revend à l'heure même pour vingt pistoles comptant'.

Pascal's chief victim, Antonio de Escobar, in his *Universae Theologiae moralis receptores* (Lyons, 1652), similarly defines the *mohatra* contract as 'celui par lequel on achète des étoffes chèrement et à crédit, pour les revendre au même instant a la même personne argent comptant at à bon marché'. Escobar admits that the *mohatra* is forbidden by the canon law, but adds that it is permissible 'encore même que celui qui vend et rachète ait pour intention principale le dessein de profiter, pourvu seulment qu'en vendant il n'excède pas le plus haut prix des étoffes de cette sorte, et qu'en rachetant il n'en passe pas le moindre; et qu'on n'en convienne pas auparavant en termes exprès ni autrement'. The French version of the Latin original is Pascal's.

Some theologians went further, and ruled that the illicit profit made in a *mohatra* need not be restituted. But, as we shall see later in this study, with respect to the *mohatra* the Christian theologians of the seventeenth century had still some way to go before reaching the completely permissive position of the Spanish Jew, Maimonides, in the twelfth.

Pascal also cites a passage from a French manual in which loans at usury are approved provided they are made in the form of a partnership agreement. This was the Jewish 'iron flock', forbidden by the Talmud but condoned by the medieval rabbis.

5 *Baba Mezi'a*, 64a–64b.
6 ibid., 70b–72b.
7 J. Schacht, *An Introduction to Islamic Law* (Oxford, 1949), p. 149, and bibliography, pp. 274–5. Jewish business practice in talmudic times is discussed by J. Neusner, *A History of the Jews in Babylonia* (Leyden, 1969), Vol. 4, pp. 220–8.
8 S. D. Goitein, *A Mediterranean Society* (Berkeley, Calif., 1967), Vol. 1.
9 S. W. Baron, *A Social and Religious History of the Jews* (New York, 1952–65), Vol. 4, pp. 212–13.
10 Werner Sombart, *Die Juden und das Wirtschaftsleben* (Leipzig, 1911), p. 73.
11 *The Code of Maimonides* (Yale, 1941–51), Book 13, *The Book of Civil Laws*, tr. I. J. Rabinowitz (1949), treatise 3, ch. 4, laws 2 and 3.
12 *Code*, Bk 13, tr. 3, ch. 5, laws 2 and 3.
13 ibid., law 16.
14 ibid., law 15.
15 ibid., law 8.
16 ibid., law 15. In his description of the double contract or *mohatra*, Maimonides follows the Talmud:

There are things that are permissible in themselves, yet one is forbidden to do them because they constitute a device for the evasion of the Law of Usury. How is this to be understood? If one said to another, 'Lend me a *mina*', and the other said 'A *mina* I have not, but wheat at a *mina* I have', and he gave him wheat at a *mina* and thereafter purchased it back from him for 90 *zuz* it is permissible. But the Sages have forbidden this, because it is a device for the evasion of the Law of Usury, the lender giving only 90 *zuz* and receiving a *mina*. If the lender, transgressing the prohibition, does some such thing, this is not even quasi-usury, and he may recover the full 100 *zuz* at law.

17 Baron, op. cit., Vol. 4, p. 203.
18 A. Neuman, *The Jews in Spain* (Philadelphia, 1942), Vol. 1, p. 211.
19 Baron, op. cit., Vol. 4, p. 200.
20 loc. cit.
21 ibid., p. 201.
22 *Code*, Bk 13, tr. 3, ch. 6, law 8.
23 Goitein, op. cit., Vol. 1, pp. 229–37.
24 Neuman, op. cit., Vol. 1, pp. 223–4.
25 *The Koran*, translated by J. M. Rodwell, in Everyman's Library, No. 380 (London, 1909), Sura 3 (The Family of Imran), v. 125.

26 ibid., Sura 74 (The Enwrapped), v. 6.
27 ibid., Sura 2 (The Cow), vv. 276–7.
28 *The Encyclopaedia of Islam* (Leyden, 1936), article 'Ribā' by J. Schacht.
29 *The Hedaya of Ali ibn Bakr*, translated by C. Hamilton (London, 1791), Vol. 2, pp. 551–66.
30 E. Sachau, *Muhammedanisches Recht* (Stuttgart, 1897), p. 281.
31 Schacht, *Introduction to Islamic Law*, pp. 79, 153.
32 ibid., pp. 79–83.
33 A list is given in E. Lévi-Provençal, *Histoire de L'Espagne musulmane* (Paris, 1953), Vol. 3, pp. 470–6.
34 *Traité de Droit Musulman, La Tohfat d'Ibn Acem*, translated by O. Houdas and F. Martel (Algiers, 1882). There is another translation, *Al-Acimiya ou Thu'fat*, by I. Bercher (Institut d'Études Orientales, University of Algiers, 1958), which I have not been able to consult.
35 Ibn Asim, op. cit., v. 1305.
36 ibid., vv. 716–17.
37 ibid., p. 155, note.
38 St Clement, *Stromata*, 11, 18, in J. P. Migne, *Patrologiae cursus completus* series graeca (Paris, 1857–66), Vol. 8, p. 1024. Spanish translation in R. Sierra Bravo, *Doctrina social y económica de los Padres de la Iglesia* (Madrid, 1967), para. 66.
39 St Jerome, *Com. in Ezek.*, Lib. VI, cap. XVIII, 5 and 6, in Migne, op. cit., series latina (Paris, 1844–55). Vol. 25, pp. 174–6. Spanish translation in Sierra Bravo, op. cit., paras 1513, 1514.
40 St Basil, *Homil. 11 in Psalm XIV*, in Migne, op. cit., s.g., Vol. 29, pp. 265, 280. Spanish translation in Sierra Bravo, op. cit., paras 151–8.
41 St Gregory *Contra Usura*, 11, in Migne, op. cit., s.g., Vol. 46, pp. 433, 436. Spanish translation in Sierra Bravo, op. cit., paras 507–10.
42 St Leo, *Sermon XVIII*, cap. 111, in Migne, op. cit., s.l., Vol. 54, p. 181. Spanish translation in Sierra Bravo, op. cit., para. 1835.
43 St John Chrysostom, *In Mattaeum*, V, 5 and *Hom. LVI*, 5 and 6. Spanish translation in Sierra Bravo, op. cit., paras 765, 766, 812–15.
44 St Ambrose, *Lib. de Tobias*, 7–11, in Migne, op. cit., s.l., Vol. 14, pp. 798 *et seq.* Spanish translation in Sierra Bravo, op. cit., paras 1403–6.
45 St Augustine, *Psalm 36*, Sermon 3, 6, in Migne, op. cit., s.l., Vol. 36, p. 386. Spanish translation in Sierra Bravo, op. cit., para. 1605. *Sermon 239*, 5, in Migne, op. cit., s.l., Vol. 38, p. 1128. Spanish translation in Sierra Bravo, op. cit., para. 1708.
46 Leges Constantini, Theodosii, Leonis, in E. Sachau, *Syrische Rechtsbücher* (Berlin, 1914), Vol. 1, p. 129.
47 *The Corpus Juris of Jesubocht, Archbishop of Persia*, in Sachau, op. cit., Vol. 3, pp. 167–9.
48 *Codex*, 4:32:3; *Institutions*, 3:14:2; *Digest*, 12:1:2:1; 13:6, f.3, n.6 and f.4; 44:7:1:4; 50:16:121; See J. T. Noonan, *The Scholastic Analysis of Usury* (Cambridge, Mass., 1957), pp. 39–41.
49 The development of the Church's doctrine of usury may conveniently be followed in any edition of the *Corpus Juris Canonici* issued before 1918.
50 *Decretum*, P. 1, dist. 46, caps 9 and 10; P. 1, dist. 47, caps 1–5.
51 ibid., P. 2, cap. 14, Q. 4, cap. 8.
52 ibid., P. 1, dist 88, cap. 11. The idea that money is not 'meant' to be anything but a medium of exchange, and that it is therefore sterile by nature, is generally held to be Aristotelian. However, we find it cropping up from

time to time in the early Middle Ages, well before Aristotle's *Politics* and *Nicomachean Ethics*, the principal works in which his monetary theory is developed, reached the West. An important source of these early echoes of Greek theory was the Roman jurist Julius Paulus, in a pronouncement that was widely quoted in later economic literature. Discussing price, Paulus briefly summarises the account given by Plato and Aristotle of the inconvenience of barter and the invention of money to serve as a means of exchange, adding that the stamped material of which money is made derives its utility not so much from its substance as from its tale.

In our next chapter we shall see how these celebrated doctrines, with which our elementary textbooks of economics are still accustomed to open, reached the Christian West in more elaborate form in the twelfth century. Meanwhile, we note that they were preserved, through this text of Paulus's, in the *Lex Romanum Visigothorum* (promulgated in 506), and in the *Digest* of Justinian.

53 *Decretals*, Lib. 5, tit. 19, caps 1 and 8.
54 ibid., cap. 3.
55 ibid., caps 5 and 9.
56 ibid., cap. 6.
57 Luke VI: 35.
58 *Decretals*, Lib. 5, tit. 19, cap. 10.
59 ibid., cap. 12.
60 ibid., cap. 13.
61 ibid., cap. 15.
62 ibid., cap. 18.
63 *Decretals*, Lib. 3, tit. 17, cap. 5 and Lib. 3, tit. 21, cap. 4.
64 *Decretals*, Lib. 5, tit. 19, cap. 19.
65 *Liber Sextus Decretalium*, Lib. 5, tit, 5, cap. 1.
66 *Clementinarum*, Lib. 5, tit. 5, cap. 15.
67 'Modus iuste negotiandi in gratiam mercatorum', published in *Analecta Sacri Ordinis Praedicatorum*, (1899) Vol. III.
68 'Raimundi de Penna-forti Summa Pastoralis', in Ravaisson, *Catalogue Géneral des MSS des Bibliothèques publiques des Départements, 1849,* Vol. I, pp. 621–3. Partly translated into English by R. H. Tawney, *Religion and the Rise of Capitalism* (London, 1925), ch. 1, note 69.
69 An early (if judged by Christian standards, 'late' if by Jewish) example of the false sale or *mohatra* contract is included in R. S. Lopez and I. W. Raymond, *Medieval Trade in the Mediterranean World* (New York and London, 1955), Document No. 143. A citizen of Nîmes claims annulment of a contract drawn up in 1287, by which two Florentine merchants made him a loan of £200 Tournois, payable in Lucca. The loan was disguised as a sale of silver plate and gold cloth. The routine was the following: the goods were formally shown to the borrower, so that he could not later use the legal exception that they had not been delivered. The borrower agreed to buy them for £280 Tournois payable within four months. He did not, however, take possession of them, and in consideration of this the money-lenders caused the sum of £200 to be paid to him immediately.
70 *Summa ad manuscriptorum fidem recognita* (Verona, 1744). In earlier editions this work bears the title of *Summa de poenitentia* or *Summa casuum conscientiae*.
71 ibid., 2:7:2; 2:7:5.

72 ibid., 2:7:5.

73 loc. cit.

74 *Fuero Juzgo*, in *Los códigos españoles* (Madrid, 1847), Vol 1, Lib. 5, tit. 4, law 5.

75 ibid., tit. 5, laws 8 and 9.

76 *Fuero viejo de Castilla*, in *Los códigos españoles*, Vol. 1, Lib. 3, tit. 5 and 7.

77 *Fuero real de España*, in *Los códigos españoles*, Vol. 1, Lib. 3, tit. 16, law 1; tit. 18 and 19; Lib. 4, tit. 2, law 6.

78 *Las siete Partidas del rey D. Alfonso el sabio*, in *Los códigos españoles*, Vols 2, 3 and 4, partida 1, tit. 6, law 45.

79 ibid., partida 5, tit. 13, law 2.

80 ibid., tit. 11, law 40.

81 *Ordenamiento de Alcalá*, in *Los códigos españoles*, Vol. 1, tit. 23, law 1.

82 ibid., tit. 32, law 51.

83 *Ordenanzas reales de Castilla*, in *Los códigos españoles*, Vol. 1, tit. 9, laws 17 and 23.

84 An account of Jewish usury in Castile and Aragon is given by Claudio Sanchez-Albornoz, *España, un enigma histórico* (Buenos Aires, 1956), Vol. 2, pp. 190–206.

85 J. Vicens Vives, *Manual de historia económica de España*, 4th edn (Barcelona, 1965), p. 225. English translation: *Economic History of Spain* (Princeton, NJ, 1969).

86 Manuel Colmeiro, *Historia de la economía política en España* (Madrid, 1863), 2nd edn (Madrid, 1965), 2 vols, ch. 43, p. 471.

87 *Novísima recopilación*, Bk 12, tit. 22, law 4.

88 R. W. Emery, *The Jews of Perpignan in the Thirteenth Century* (New York, 1959), pp. 26–108.

89 A. Castro, *España en su historia* (Buenos Aires, 1948), pp. 516–17.

90 J. T. Noonan, *The Scholastic Analysis of Usury* (Cambridge, Mass., 1957), p. 155.

91 ibid., p. 160, note 29.

92 ibid., pp. 160–1.

93 J. A. Schumpeter, *History of Economic Analysis* (New York, 1954), p. 165.

94 Tomàs de Mercado, *Tratos y contratos de mercaderes* (Salamanca, 1569), fol. 1. A revised and extended edition of the book appeared at Seville in 1571, under the title of *Suma de tratos y contratos*. Modern edition (Madrid, 1975), with an introduction by R. Sierra Bravo.

95 ibid., fol. 4.

96 ibid., fol. 75.

97 ibid., fol. 96.

98 W. Endemann's fundamental study, *Studien in der romanisch-kanonistischen Wirtschaftslehre* (Berlin, 1874–88), 2 vols, is valuable from the doctrinal point of view. The mechanism of the 'exchanges' is explained in R. de Roover, *Gresham on Foreign Exchange* (Cambridge, Mass., 1949); *L'Évolution de la lettre de change, XIVe–XVIIIe siècles* (Paris, 1953); 'Le marché monétaire au Moyen Age et au début des temps modernes', *Revue historique*, No. 495, July–September 1970. Also useful are G. Mandich, *Le Pacte de Ricorsa et le marché italien des changes au XVIIe siecle* (Paris, 1953); and Lopez and Raymond, op. cit., pp. 162–6. On the Spanish exchanges, the best studies are A. E. Sayous, 'Observations d'écrivains du XVIe siècle sur les changes', *Revue économique internationale*, Vol. 4, November 1928,

pp. 289–320; and, especially to be recommended, H. Lepeyre, *Une famille de Marchlands, les Ruiz* (Paris, 1955), pp. 243–335.

99 Endemann, op. cit., Vol. 1, p. 82.

100 De Roover, *L'Evolution de la lettre de change*, pp. 27–9.

101 *Dictionnaire de Droit Canonique* (Paris, 1950), article 'Interêt et usure'.

102 A model contract under the heading of 'Exchange with Pledges' is included by Fernando Diaz de Valdepeñas, public scrivenor of Granada, in his *Summa de notas copiosas*, published in 1543, a collection of specimen contracts censored and approved by the Mercedarian friar, Juan de Medina, himself a leading authority on commercial morality. The terms of the contract may be summarised as follows:

I, the taker [or borrower] agree to repay in another place whatever sum I take [or borrow] by drawing a bill of exchange on my agent in that place. If, upon its maturity, the bill is not duly met, then you, the giver [or lender] are empowered to take in exchange the said sum wherever and from whomsoever you chose, at whatever rate of *interesse* you may arrange, and rechange it upon me and my goods, and I bind myself to repay the said principal debt, together with such changes and rechanges and *interesse* and postal charges and other expenses as you may incur, your declaration on oath being sufficient to justify seizure of my person and goods.

It is clear that a contract drawn up in this form provided an excellent cloak for dry exchange, since only the parties concerned could know whether it was genuine or not.

103 Bartolomé Lucala, *Baculus Clericalis* (Saragossa, 1552), fol. 14.

104 Luis Saravia de la Calle Veroñense, *Instrucción de mercaderes muy provechosa* (Medina del Campo, 1544), fols. 103–6. The whole of ch. 11 is devoted to 'Exchange-brokers and *mohatras*'.

105 The word *trapaza*, a banker's 'wangle', is derived from the Greek word for the table on which the money-changer placed his piles of coins. *Mohatra*, from the Arabic *mukhatara*, 'wager' or 'speculation', was used in Spain in the sixteenth century to designate the double contract of sale, as well as in the wider sense of 'fraud' in general. What of *barata*, another word used in Spain to denote the double contract? It seems strange that there should have been two terms in common use for this contract. The adjective *barato*, the Spanish word for 'cheap', is of uncertain origin. The etymology of the word is discussed by J. Coromina, *Diccionario crítico etimológico de la lengua castellana* (Madrid, 1954). The nouns *barato* and *barata* were used in the twelfth and thirteenth centuries in the sense of 'fraud, confusion, mix-up', and the verb *baratar* meant, among other things, 'to reduce the price of a good in order to settle a debt'. In Catalonia, at about the same time, a *baratador* was a person who engaged in shady business. Hostiensis (*d.* 1271) in his *Summa* (V. de usuris, N. 8) allows a resale agreement but believes that many such contracts are tainted. Usurers, he says, 'make *baratos*, and they are truly *baratae*, since they lead straight to *barathrum*'. *Barathrum* is the Latin word for 'pit' or 'hell'. This little piece of word-play met with immense success, since it continued to be repeated by writer after writer for the next four centuries. The municipal loans raised by the city of Seville at the end of the fourteenth century were known as *baratas*. R. Carande, *Sevilla, fortaleza y mercado* (Seville, 1972), pp. 182–9, discusses the Sevillian *baratas*.

106 The Adelantamientos were former frontier districts governed by a member

of a judicial or military Order, and retaining certain of their ancient judicial privileges.

107 *Novísima recopilación*, Bk 12, tit. 22, law 5.
108 The 'usance', or period in which a bill of exchange fell due, varied according to commercial custom and was closely linked to the calendar of the fairs.
109 Mercado, op. cit., p. 154 verso.
110 ibid., p. 69 verso.
111 The prominent part played by the *corredor* in the commercial life of Spain, and the reasons for it, are discussed by J. A. Pitt-Rivers in his sociological study of an Andalusian township, *People of the Sierra* (London, 1954).
112 Mercado, op. cit., p. 154 verso.
113 ibid., p. 154.
114 E. Bussi, 'Contractus Mohatrae', in *Rivista di storia del diritto italiano*, Vol. 5 (1932), p. 498.
115 See note 4.
116 Feliciano de Solis, whose treatise *De Censibus*, published at Alcalà in 1594, was reprinted at Frankfurt in 1605, cites Domingo de Soto, Diego de Covarrubias, Miguel de Palacio and Francisco García, as among the authors who dealt with the subject.
117 Mercado, op. cit., pp. 127–9 verso.
118 Martín González de Cellorigo, *Memorial de la política necesaria y útil restauración de la República de España* (Valladolid, 1600), p. 4.

2

Greek Economics in Spain

In the first chapter I chose the subject of usury as an example of economic thought governed by religious principles. The view that all the activities of life, even the trivial haggling of the market-place, are subject to the commands of God, for ever valid and immutable, was that taken by the three religions of medieval Spain. It may be contrasted with the attitude of the Greeks, whose economic teaching rested chiefly on ethical principles, and who appealed to reason, and not to any form of revealed truth.

This second type of doctrine gained a footing in Spain at a period when the first was still in its heyday. The transmission of Greek economics to the West was the joint work of Christians, Moslems and Jews, who collaborated in harmony. It is paradoxical that this lofty task should have been performed by men who in their private affairs may well have been busy evading the usury laws by some such sordid device as those I have described. But human life is made up of light and shade. Up to now I may seem to have taken rather a cynical view of the intellectual activities of our medieval Spaniards. It is more than time that we watched them follow a more elevated purpose.

GREEK ECONOMIC THEORY

We shall begin by considering what were the economic doctrines whose passage through Spain we are able to trace, and later show the way in which they were transmitted.

For the purpose of this study Plato and Aristotle overshadow all other Greek authors. Their importance for later theory can hardly be exaggerated. The first five chapters of the *Wealth of Nations* simply develop the line of reasoning laid down by Aristotle, and, even today, textbooks of economic theory generally open by recapitulating the ideas that we are about to examine.[1]

Plato's 'Republic'
In the second book of the *Republic* Plato considers the problem of justice within the community. He paints for us a state 'coming into being

before our eyes', so that we may watch the growth of justice or injustice within it'. A state, according to Plato, comes into existence because no individual is self-sufficient. We all have many needs. To satisfy these needs we seek each other's help, and when we have collected a certain number of helpers or associates together in one place we call the resulting settlement a state.

Plato next examines the nature of commercial exchange. If a man exchanges his product for that of another, it is because the transaction is to the advantage of both parties. To satisfy the primary demands of even the smallest settlement we shall need at least a farmer, a builder, a weaver and one or two other specialised producers. More things will be made, and the work will be easier, if each man devotes himself entirely to his own trade. As our little state develops, other workers will be needed. Farmers must have ploughs, and builders, weavers and shoemakers their necessary tools. There will have to be merchants to fetch the things that are needed from other countries. And, since they must carry back in return the goods those countries require, home production has to be increased by adding to the number of farmers and craftsmen employed. We shall also need ship-owners and others skilled in foreign trade.

In our own city we shall want a market-place, and, to avoid wasting time in barter, a currency 'to serve as a token for purposes of exchange'. There will be shopkeepers 'to take goods for money from those who want to sell, and money for goods from those who want to buy'. There will also be a class of hired labourers to do the heavy work.[2]

This short discussion is full of ideas that were taken up and developed by many later writers. The fact that Plato considers them in relation to the concept of justice helps to explain why, up to the end of the eighteenth century at least, it is in juridical treatises that we find some of the best discussions of such topics as the division of labour, demand, utility, and money as a medium of exchange.

Plato continues his description of the economic growth of the state by showing how an unhealthy demand for luxury and unlimited wealth may lead to aggression and war. Demand is for Plato morally neutral having a good and an evil side.

Plato now launches into his famous disquisition on the qualities and education that best befit the 'Guardians' or rulers of the state, who are the most important of the workers prescribed by the principle of the division of labour. Finally he returns to that principle, and shows its intimate connection with the problem of justice. He goes so far as to say that 'it may be that the minding of one's own business, when it takes a certain form, is actually the same thing as justice', and concludes that 'when each order – tradesman, Auxiliary, Guardian –

keeps to its own proper business in the commonwealth and does its own work, that is justice and what makes a just society'.[3] For Plato, then, the principle of the division of labour is of supreme importance, since he goes so far as to say that it is synonymous with justice itself.

Aristotle's 'Nicomachean Ethics'

The economic teaching of Aristotle is found chiefly in his *Politics* and *Nicomachean Ethics* and to a small extent in the *Rhetoric* and *Topics*. As we shall here be considering Aristotle in connection with Hispano-Moslem thought we shall have to disregard the *Politics*, since this work was not well known to the Arabs and was certainly quite unknown to Averroes, the principal transmitter of Aristotle's economic doctrines to the Latin West.

The *Nicomachean Ethics* is not a particularly easy work. Indeed, certain key-passages in this treatise have puzzled even Schumpeter,[4] and we are forced to do a certain amount of 'interpreting' if we are to make sense of them at all.

Aristotle's economic teaching, like that of Plato, is a by-product of his judicial doctrine. In the fifth book of the *Nicomachean Ethics* he begins by considering the general nature of justice and its various branches. Commercial justice depends on the attainment of equality between the parties to a transaction. When a dispute arises it is the business of the judge to add to, or take away from the shares currently held by the contending parties until he is satisfied that he has made them equal. The line, as it were, being unequally divided, he takes from the greater part that by which it exceeds the half, and adds it on to the lesser. Then he divides the whole into two equal portions and gives each man his own.

Now, he could not do this in a barter economy. Take the case of a builder and a shoemaker. How are we to decide how many shoes are worth a house, having regard to quantity and quality? In other words how are we to compare the value of things diverse in nature? Aristotle answers this question by saying that we do so by reducing them to mathematical terms. For this reason, he says, money was invented: so that we might be able to compare everything that is capable of being exchanged. Money is the measure of all things, and with its help our imaginary judge can set up his 'line', add to or subtract from the two halves and find the middle point or mean.

All this is simple enough, though it is not obvious or banal. But now comes a difficulty. Having just stated that money measures all things, Aristotle proceeds to say that the measure of all things is really the demand for them. Demand, it now appears, is the common bond of commercial dealings. If the parties were not in want 'at all', or at least 'not similarly', of one another's wares, there would not be any exchange, or 'at least, not the same'.

Aristotle resolves the apparent contradiction between his two statements, that the measure of all things is first money and then demand, by going on to say that money by general agreement has come to be a 'representative' of demand. This seems satisfactory when we consider what has gone before. Our first 'line', which represented the material things that had to be cut into equal halves by the judge, may also be regarded as representing the parties' demand for them. We may perhaps be permitted to go a little further and say that it now represents the utility the goods have for the contendants – that is, the total amount of utility involved in the deal. By expressing this utility in mathematical or monetary terms the judge can assign an equal amount of utility to each party.[5]

Aristotle proceeds to remark that the Greek word for money, *nomisma* is derived from *nomos* (custom or law), and this, he says, implies that money is not a natural thing but arose out of custom, so that it rests with us to change its value or to make it wholly useless. This is quite consistent with the rest of the discussion. For the purpose of equal division it does not matter what substance our imaginary line represents (though it does matter for other reasons, such as ease of transport).

Aristotle further adds that money has another use. It is a store of value. Of course, money is liable to depreciation, for its purchasing power varies. Still, at least it is more durable than the goods themselves. Money, therefore, enables us to compare and measure goods that are not only of a different nature but that also exist at different times.

These few pages of Aristotle's are probably the most formative that have ever been written on monetary theory, and their influence on theory of value has been no less far-reaching.[6]

A few other significant ideas on value may be gleaned from Aristotle's *Topics* and *Rhetoric*. For instance, he says that demand, and hence exchange-value, is increased by the difficulty of acquiring an object, that is, by its rarity, and in one passage he seems to have glimpsed the famous 'paradox of value' that was to play such an important part in later theory.[7] But it was a fleeting glimpse, no doubt, and nothing more.

GREEK ECONOMICS IN ISLAM

Our next task will be to show how these ideas were absorbed into the writings of Islamic authors, and how they passed through the Maghreb, into Spain, and thence into the Christian West.

Arabs as Heirs to Greece

main source of the social sciences in Islam was what was known as
k or peripatetic philosophy. Of course, the subject-matter of the
l sciences formed only a small part of the scientific legacy that the
s took over from Greece. The realistically minded Arabs attached
rtance to those disciplines that yielded immediate practical results,
ınyone versed in Greek philosophy was expected to cover, in addi-
to metaphysics, ethics and politics, such diverse subjects as math-
ics, astronomy, medicine, physics, psychology and all the rest that
to make up the study of 'natural philosophy' throughout the
ıle Ages and into modern times, and that still, for the man in the
t, constitute 'science'.

ıere were good reasons why the medieval world of Islam knew
: about Greek science than did western Christendom. The Latin-
king peoples of the Roman Empire had long since forgotten Greece;
n the eastern provinces, which were those first conquered by the
s, the usual liberal education was an education in Hellenistic
ıric, while the tradition of Greek scientific (and especially medical)
ıing was still unbroken. Such teaching was still alive in Alexandria,
nstance, when that city fell to the Arabs in 639, and also in the
ır centres of Palestine, Syria and western Mesopotamia.

ıe Greek language did not die out suddenly in the provinces that
: under Moslem rule, but survived at least until the middle of the
ı century. This was the greatest period of translation from Greek
Syriac and Arabic. The translator, Hunain ibn Ishaq (809–73).
presided over the school of translation that flourished in Baghdad
ıe time of Harun-al-Rashid, was thus in touch with Greek as a
g language. Hunain was a Nestorian Christian, well versed in
:k, Arabic and Syriac. It was through the versions produced in
chool that the bulk of the scientific work of classical antiquity
me known to the Arabs.

ıe Arabs eagerly absorbed all this Greek learning and carried it into
ɣ part of their empire. They were soon able to surpass the true
of Greek civilisation, the Byzantines, so decidedly that by the
:nth century Arabic works on medicine and other subjects were
ʒ translated into Byzantine Greek instead of vice versa. Yet the
:otelian and other Greek writings were also preserved and to some
ıt used in Byzantium throughout the Middle Ages; and at the end
.e medieval period these two streams of Greek thought, the Arabic
the Byzantine, met together in western Europe, carrying with them
eeds of the Renaissance. Moslem Spain was the principal (though not
ınly) channel by which the former of these streams, the Islamic,
:d into western Christendom.[8]

65

Some Early Islamic Economists

One of the earlier Moslem philosophers who introduced the teaching of Plato and Aristotle into Islamic political thought was al-Farabi (*d*. 950), for Moslems 'the second teacher', the first being Aristotle. His *Fusal al-Madani* is a book of advice for princes and their counsellors. Such 'Mirrors for Princes' or mirror-books, as they are often called, were brought into Arabic literature from the Persian in the eighth century. They sometimes included discussions on taxation and other economic subjects, as well as moral exhortation and general remarks on the art of government. The Platonic flavour of al-Farabi's style may be recognised in many parts of his mirror-book. As a sample we may take a passage in which he compares the city to the human body, a simile that has been sadly overworked by writers of every age but is here used to rather good effect.[9] Al-Farabi was steeped in the teaching of Aristotle, and wrote a commentary on the *Nicomachean Ethics* which is unfortunately lost.

Another well-known mirror-book is that of al-Ghazali (1058–1111), one of the greatest of Islamic philosophers. This consists chiefly of moral precepts adorned with anecdotes. Another work of al-Ghazali's, an encyclopedia of religious, philosophical, political and economic theory, holds more interest for us. Al-Ghazali here follows Plato in describing how the diverse institutions of mankind – industry, government, money, and so on – are successively established in order to meet man's ever-increasing needs, and develops on Aristotelian lines Plato's brief remark that money was invented as a 'token of exchange', bringing in the concept of money as the common measure of value and pointing out the advantages of unencumbered trade. In his condemnation of usury al-Ghazali follows the Koran. The same may be said of the passages in which he condemns the two extremes of luxury and avarice, counselling moderation in the acquisition of wealth, and charity once it is acquired.[10]

Also based on the doctrine of Plato and Aristotle is the work of Abul-Fadl al Dimashqi, an author whose biography is unknown to us. He was formerly thought to have lived in the twelfth century but is placed by more recent scholars as early as the ninth. Like al-Ghazali, Abul-Fadl reproduces Plato's pseudo-historical account of the origin of the state, the growth of a barter economy, its inconveniences, the need for specialisation and the division of labour, and the invention of money to serve as a 'common measure' and a store of value. This is followed by an elaborate discussion as to what substance money should be made of, in which Abul-Fadl anticipates some of the tritest passages in the nineteenth-century textbooks.

More interesting is Abul-Fadl's attempt to grope after a theory of value. Price, he says, is relative, varying from place to place and depending on many factors, of which cost of transport is particularly important. To arrive at the average price of a commodity the merchant should ask experienced people what is the usual price determined by long custom. Then he should note, first, the 'ordinary' fluctuations in this price, and second, the 'extraordinary' ones that are caused by unusual circumstances such as the scarcity or abundance of the goods and the state of war or peace in the place where they are traded. Finally, he should combine all these factors and thus be in a position to estimate the average value of the commodity in question.[11]

The writings of al-Farabi and al-Ghazali were certainly, and those of Abul-Fadl probably, studied in Spain, and the political and economic theory of Plato and Aristotle became known there through their work and that of other authors.

In the eleventh century the best-known Hispano-Moslem writer on politics and economics was Abu Bakr Muhammad al-Turtushi (1059–1126). Born at Tortosa, he studied law and mathematics at Saragossa, and the humanities at Seville. After making the pilgrimage to Mecca and visiting Baghdad, he settled as a teacher in Damascus and later in Alexandria, where he died. Although much of al-Turtushi's life was spent out of Spain his influence there was considerable. We know the names of three of his disciples, scholars of Spanish birth, who studied under him in Alexandria and returned respectively to Valencia, Jaen and Majorca to disseminate his doctrine.

In addition to Greek sources al-Turtushi drew upon Persian and Indian models for the mirror-book that he wrote in the hope of outshining his great contemporary, al-Ghazali. Though not, perhaps, of the highest intellectual quality, it is full of sensible advice and may be enjoyed for its colourful style.

Al-Turtushi regards agriculture as the chief source of wealth. The sultan must encourage farmers and refrain from taxing them too heavily, for if he oppresses them he will be like a man who whittles away his own tent-poles. Once farmers are impoverished they will no longer care for their land, the revenue derived from taxation will fall, the troops can no longer be paid and the sultan will finally be conquered by his enemies. Taxes of every kind should be just, and their proceeds employed on objects that will benefit the ruler's vassals. They should be collected without fuss or violence: 'the leech, without hurting or making a sound, can suck more blood than the mosquito, for all the latter's painful sting and annoying whine'.

Al-Turtushi exhorts the sultan not to seek to amass treasure but to spend it on the state, and more especially on the army. 'Treasure', he says, 'is the enemy of the sultan, and troops the friends.' A sultan who hoards treasure resembles a bird that plucks out its own feathers to enjoy the taste of the marrow, and so weakens himself that at last he falls to the ground. Instead, the sultan should imitate the prudent owner of a palm-grove whose money is like the fertilising water that flows from a spring.

Al-Turtushi does not, of course, suggest that money should be spent on the army alone. He quotes at length, giving many figures and details, from a Coptic history of Egypt which describes how the pharaoh spent the money that Joseph collected for him. He 'invested 800,000 dinars in agriculture, opening a canal and building dykes and water-channels, making free allowances of fodder to the poorer farmers so that they might be able to keep some working animals, bringing more land into cultivation, providing tools, and paying extra labour to help with the sowing and general farm-work'. In short, al-Turtushi advocates a heavy programme of capital investment and stresses the futility of accumulating treasure as an end in itself.[12]

AVERROES

As well as being woven into the original work of Islamic writers, the doctrines of Plato and Aristotle reached Spain in the form of Arabic paraphrases and commentaries. No direct translations from Greek into Arabic were made in Spain itself. The author of a great series of commentaries on many of the scientific writings of Aristotle was a younger contemporary of al-Turtushi's, also of Saragossa, known to the Christian West as Avempace (c. 1085–1138). Avempace did not leave any work on the social sciences, an omission that was repaired by his disciple and admirer, Averroes.

Muhammad ibn Ahmad, called Ibn Rushd in Islam and Averroes in the Christian West, was born in 1126 and came of a distinguished Cordovan family. His grandfather was *kadi* or chief judge of that city and famous for his wise decisions. They were gathered into a vast compilation so highly esteemed among the Arabs that Averroes, whose renown in the Christian West came to rival that of Aristotle himself, is for his co-religionists merely 'the Grandson'. Averroes's father also held the same important post of *kadi* in Cordova.

As a boy Averroes studied medicine, law and philosophy with the best teachers and enjoyed the society of the most distinguished men of his time. In 1153 we find him at Marrakesh, where he was presented to the *emir* Abu Ya'qub Yusuf, a learned prince who loved to discourse on the Greek philosophers, using his great powers of memory to expound the arguments of the Moslem theologians against them. It was probably this *emir* who suggested to Averroes that he should continue Avempace's work of commentating Aristotle.

In 1169 Averroes was appointed *kadi* of Seville, returning in 1171 to Cordova, where he probably composed his commentaries on Aristotle during the years that followed. In 1182 Yusuf recalled him to Morocco as his chief physician, and later made him *kadi* of Cordova, as his father and grandfather had been.

Under Yusuf's successor, Ya'qub al-Mansur, Averroes at first enjoyed great favour but later fell into disgrace. It is said that in one of his writings he left out the diacritic signs that in Arabic distinguish the flattering phrase, 'King of the two continents', from the contemptuous 'King of the Berbers'. And, apart from this unlucky slip, Averroes had come under the suspicion of religious unorthodoxy. Greek philosophy, with its obvious rationalism, was the object of attack, and the *emir*, bowing to the storm, condemned its study and ordered that all books on the subject should be destroyed, except for those on medicine, arithmetic and elementary astronomy. Together with other scholars who had become associated with Greek philosophy, Averroes was banished to Lucena. But his life had a happy ending. Four years later, when the current wave of opposition to Greek philosophy had spent its force, the caliph recalled him and restored him to favour. Averroes died at Marrakesh in 1198.[13]

Averroes's Commentary on Plato's 'Republic'
The corpus of Averroes's work is enormous and its bibliography beset with pitfalls. It includes treatises on philosophy, theology, jurisprudence medicine, astronomy, grammar and other subjects. Among the more readily accessible writings on politics and economics the commentaries on Plato's *Republic* and Aristotle's *Nicomachean Ethics* must take first place. Both were probably composed at Cordova in the year 1177. Averroes tells us that, Aristotle's *Politics* not having come into his hands, he regarded the *Nicomachean Ethics* and the *Republic* as two complementary works on the same science of politics, the former providing the theory of the subject and the latter the practical instruction.

In his commentary on the *Republic*, Averroes is careful to define the scope of social science. It differs essentially, he says, from the speculative sciences in dealing entirely with matters dependent on free will and choice. Whereas the aim of the speculative sciences is theoretical knowledge alone (the practical application of such knowledge being accidental), the aim of political and economic science is action alone.

Averroes's views on the democratic State are of some interest. He takes a rather more positive view of democracy than Plato, and even thinks on philosophical grounds, that out of it an ideal State might be born. But he also points out the dangers inherant in democracy. In such a State, he says, every kind of man is to be found. The rule of law will probably be maintained, though in a haphazard fashion, and this rule will be equal, favouring no one. But the excessive quest for freedom in a democratic State, which leads to a man ruling himself and his affairs just as he wishes, and having no civic duties to perform, will turn many of the people into drones. However, since in a democracy a man will be free to work as well as to be idle, there will arise a class whose members seek wealth alone. These people will serve to make honey for the drones. And there will be a third class, of men who go about their business but are not property owners. The first and third classes will plunder the money-making class and hate them. After that, one of two things will happen. Either the only active class in the State will disappear, or its members gain power and the State become a tyranny.

Averroes accepts Plato's plea that women should share the same work and civic duties as men, and enjoy the same rights. Moreover, he applies this doctrine of Plato's to the position of women in his own time and civilisation, thus venturing to run counter to Islamic teaching and practice.

Commenting on Plato's cursory observation that the embryo State will require a currency 'to serve as a token for purposes of exchange', Averroes makes use of Aristotle's more carefully developed ideas, introducing the latter's definition of *nomisma* and his concept of money as a common measure 'between separate things, so that equality prevails in business between things where it is difficult to measure equality in [real] existence'. Averroes also mentions that money is needed 'because of the difficulty of transacting business [in a barter economy]', thus defining the first and most obvious function of money, which is to serve as a medium of exchange.[14]

Averroes's Commentary on the 'Nicomachean Ethics'

For Averroes, as we have seen, the *Nicomachean Ethics* provided the theoretical basis for Plato's practical treatise. I have already summarised the passages that chiefly concern us here. Averroes's commentary is a fairly free paraphrase which reproduces Aristotle's teaching fully and with reasonable accuracy, while adding little that is original. Averroes does make one rather significant omission. Aristotle had observed that the Greek word for money, *nomisma*, was derived from *nomos*, law or custom, and that it lies with us to alter the value of money or even to make it wholly useless. Averroes keeps the wordplay but passes over the statement that it rests with us to alter the value of money, perhaps wishing to reject any approval of debasement.[15]

Averroes's original contribution to theory is very small. Yet he is of importance in the history of economic thought owing to the part he played in the transmission of Greek economics to the Christian West. The rest of our discussion of Averroes will concern this aspect of his work.

THE TRANSMISSION TO THE CHRISTIAN WEST

Averroes wrote in Arabic and commentated an Arabic text. Manuscripts of his writings in Arabic are rare, Hebrew translations plentiful and Latin versions to be found in all important libraries.

The Latin Translations of Averroes

At about the beginning of the twelfth century the Christian West began to awaken to the superiority of Islamic culture – or, perhaps we may better say, of Islamic technology, since the desire of western Christians was not so much to enrich their intellectual heritage as to improve their performance in such practical activities as medicine, mathematics, arithmetic, astronomy, astrology, botany, torture and magic, in all of which the Arabs were known to be exceptionally proficient. It was also realised that the key to this knowledge lay in the mastery of Arabic. But a reading acquaintance with Arabic is not to be acquired in a day, and a single glance at an Arabic manuscript must have discouraged all but the most ardent seekers after fame. Clearly, the best way to get over this difficulty would be to travel to the nearest place where Arabic manuscripts were plentiful, and where assistants knowing Arabic and another language understood by the foreign scholar could be found to help in the work of translation.

Two places in Europe fulfilled these requirements. One was Sicily, under Arab rule from 902 to 1091, where there remained a considerable Moslem population protected by the Norman conquerors, who had themselves become Islamised to an extent that shocked the rest of Christendom. The other was Spain, which offered a wider scope than Sicily and was more congenial to the orthodox mind. At first the work of selecting and translating suitable Arabic texts was carried on at different cities in the Peninsula, but it soon came to be centred on Toledo, which had been regained by the Christians in 1085. Here the would-be investigator found a powerful and enthusiastic patron in Raymond, Archbishop of Toledo and Chancellor of Castile (d. 1150), and a still greater one in the scholar-king, Alphonso X of Castile, called 'the Learned' (1221–84), who gathered Christian, Moslem and Jewish scholars round him and himself took an active part in their labours.

The method commonly used in Toledo and other Spanish centres was for one person to put the text from Arabic into Spanish and for his collaborator to turn it from Spanish into Latin, the latter being the more important partner and putting his name to the completed work. We know the names of several of these pairs of translators. They include the converted Jew, John of Seville, and the Segovian, Dominic Gundisalvo; the Jew, Andrew, who translated from Arabic into Spanish for Michael Scot and Hermann the German; Gerard of Cremona and the mozarab, Galippus; and Hermann of Carinthia with his English friend, Robert of Chester, both of whom, after 'long vigils', learned enough Arabic to be able to turn their joint translations directly from Arabic into Latin.

From Spain, then, in the course of the twelfth and thirteenth centuries, an enterprising body of translators sent out to the rest of Europe the Latin versions of Aristotle, Ptolemy, Euclid, Galen and Hippocrates, and their Moslem expositors, abridgers and commentators, thus laying down for several centuries to come the basis of study and teaching in the universities of western Christendom.[16]

A considerable part of Aristotle's writings had been translated into Latin by the end of the twelfth century. The work of Averroes began to penetrate the Christian West about thirty years after his death in 1198. Latin versions of his commentaries on Aristotle's *De Caelo et Mundo* and *De Anima* were made by Michael Scot, either when he was at Toledo in 1217, or, more probably, between 1228 and 1235, while he was at the court of Frederick II, King of Sicily. Unfortunately for the good name of Averroes, Michael Scot was an accomplished astrologer. His sinister reputation for being on familiar terms with the Devil helped to surround the person and writings of Averroes with an aura of sorcery and heresy that was to be long in fading.

A very different figure from the sophisticated Scot was one of his fellow-scholars at Frederick's court. Perhaps encouraged by Michael Scot's success, Hermann the German made up his mind to follow his example and seek new material in Toledo. But he came rather late on the scene. By the time he reached Spain the more important scientific works of Aristotle had already been turned into Latin, together with many of Averroes's commentaries on them. Hermann decided to begin his work by translating Averroes's commentary on the *Nicomachean Ethics*. As we have seen, the commentary includes what is practically a paraphrase of the fifth book of the *Ethics*, the only part of the treatise that is concerned with economics. Hermann tells us that he finished his translation on the third Thursday of June 1240, in the chapel of the Holy Trinity at Toledo. He also says that he had translated an Arabic version of the *Nicomachean Ethics* itself, but that his labours had been rendered vain by Robert Grosse-Tête, who at Oxford, in 1243, had translated that treatise directly from the Greek. Hermann is almost certainly referring to a shortened version of the *Nicomachean Ethics*, called the *Alexandrine Compendium*, which had circulated among the Arabs during the Middle Ages and which he is known to have translated in 1243–4. This abridgement also covers the fifth book in which alone we are interested.

Hermann stayed on in Toledo for many years, eventually becoming Bishop of Astorga. In 1250 he translated Averroes's commentary on Aristotle's *Rhetoric*, and, in 1256, his paraphrase of the *Poetics*. We have noted one or two passages in the *Rhetoric* that concern our study. In course of time quite a large number of translations were circulating under Hermann's name, but, with admirable candour, he admits that he had played only a small part in their production. For once the humble Jew, Andrew, is saluted from afar, even though he is not specifically named as co-translator.

Hermann's translation of Averroes's commentary on the *Nico-machean Ethics* enjoyed great success and was never superseded. It has been used in all the editions of Aristotle that are accompanied by Averroes's commentaries, and has remained, almost into modern times, one of the main sources of Aristotelian economics.[17]

The Hebrew Translations of Averroes
For the first four centuries of Arab rule the Jews found in Spain a second homeland. But, with the conquest of the greater part of Islamic Spain by the fanatical Berber sect of the Almohades, in the twelfth century, the climate of religious opinion grew harsher and was no longer propitious to a flourishing Jewry. Many Jewish families sought refuge in Provence and in course of time lost their knowledge of Arabic, though not their appreciation of Arab learning. They felt the need for Hebrew versions of the chief works of Arab science and philosophy. Medical books, especially, were needed by the many Jews who were physicians. This work of translation into Hebrew, which continued throughout the thirteenth century and the first half of the fourteenth, was largely performed by the Tibbonides, a family of Andalusian Jews who had established themselves at Lunel.

The two commentaries of Averroes with which we are concerned, on Plato's *Republic* and the *Nicomachean Ethics* of Aristotle, were put into Hebrew about the year 1321 by Samuel ben Yehuda, a Jew of Marseilles. Like Averroes, Samuel regarded them almost as parts of a single work, and wrote an epilogue to serve for both commentaries. Other Hebrew translations of Averroes's commentary on the *Nico-machean Ethics* were made by Joseph ben Caspi in 1330, and by Todros Todrosi, of Arles, in 1337.

Samuel ben Yehuda's Hebrew version of Averroes's commentary on the *Republic* presented this work of Plato's for the first time to the Christian West as well as to the Jewish world, no Latin translation having as yet been made. In assessing the importance of Samuel's work we should bear in mind that a reading knowledge of Hebrew was not a Jewish prerogative but a fairly common accomplishment among educated people of all religions. A Latin translation of the Hebrew version was made by the Spanish Jew, Jacob Mantinus of Tortosa, in 1539, and is included in the great eleven-volume edition of Aristotle with Averroes's commentaries that was published by order of the Venetian senate in 1550–3. Thus, the two commentaries were at last brought together in Latin, as they had been in Hebrew and Arabic.

Averroes in the West
The infiltration of Greek science into the Christian West at the end of the Middle Ages was mistrusted by many Christians, as it had been by pious Moslems and Jews. We need not here discuss the doctrinal controversies that centred on Aristotle and his Cordovan commentator in the thirteenth century. They were not concerned with economics, and interest us only in so far as the misgiving aroused among conservative theologians by a part of Aristotle's work, and that of Averroes, reflected upon the whole. It is enough to say that by the beginning of the fourteenth century the earlier suspicion of Aristotelian science had faded, and the authority of Averroes as his commentator come to be acknowledged. When in 1473 Louis XI of France undertook to regulate the teaching of philosophy in the universities he felt able to recommend the doctrine of Aristotle and Averroes as 'long-recognised to be wholesome and safe'.

This was the signal for an eager swarm of commentators to fall upon the Commentator. Many questions remained to be settled: how far Averroes differed from Aristotle, whether the translations of Aristotle that by then had been made directly from the Greek coincided in all important points with those made from Arabic and Hebrew, and a hundred other matters that occupied the learned world for several generations. Index followed index, abridgement abridgement, commentary commentary. One of the busiest centres of Averroism was the University of Padua, which was closely linked with that of Bologna. Here the tough-minded of northern Italy – the physicians, astrologers and natural philosophers in general – grouped themselves round Averroes, leaving the poets and men of letters to seek, through the study of Greek and of Greek literature, a beauty of form and expression as yet unfamiliar to Europe.

Up to the end of the sixteenth century the editors of Averroes had continued to use the old translations made from Arabic into Latin in the thirteenth. These texts were often deficient and in some parts unintelligible, and new Latin versions were now made from the Hebrew translations.

In Venice, the printing centre for the universities of Padua and Bologna, some fifty editions of Aristotle with Averroes's commentaries appeared between 1480 and 1580, fourteen of them being complete. Complete editions were also published at Padua (1472-4), Bologna (1501, 1523 and 1580), Rome (1521 and 1539), Pavia (1507 and 1520), Strasbourg (1503 and 1531), Naples (1570 and 1574), Geneva (1608) and Lyons (1517, 1524, 1531, 1537 and 1542).

By the last quarter of the sixteenth century the editions had become less frequent, though the study of Averroes was still pursued at Padua. Probably the last professor to allot him an important place in his lecture-course was Cesare Cremonini, with whose death in 1631 we may regard the old Hispano-Arabic Aristotelianism as virtually ended.

It was, then, on Spanish soil, at Cordova and at Toledo, that the economic teaching of Plato and Aristotle first gained a foothold in western Europe. In view of the great influence exerted by the Greek authors on the whole course of economic theory, I hope that this fact may be judged worthy of note in a book on early economic thought in Spain.

There is one remarkable feature of the story. Our beturbanned Aristotle was led westward by a German and a Spanish Jew. Nor, so far as is known, did Aristotle's social and economic teaching arouse the same interest in Christian Spain as it did, almost immediately, abroad. A few years after the rediscovery of Aristotle's *Ethics*, St Albert the Great and St Thomas Aquinas made use of the work in order to reach a synthesis between Greek social science and Christian tradition and learning. They were followed by other commentators, but there is no outstanding Spanish name among them, although the scholars of Christian Spain were distinguished in other branches of learning, including Aristotelian logic. Not until the sixteenth century, in the Indian summer of scholasticism, did the Spanish Doctors assume the lead in further elaborating the political and economic thought of Aristotle.

NOTES

1 In his *Economic Analysis Before Adam Smith* (London, 1975), pp. 21–69, Barry Gordon gives a general account of the economic teaching of Plato and Aristotle, and summarises recent research on the subject.

2 *Republic*, 367e–372a.

3 ibid., 431–4.

4 J. A. Schumpeter, *History of Economic Analysis* (New York, 1954), pp. 60–5.

5 This, at least, seems to be the interpretation put upon Aristotle by St Thomas Aquinas, who, in his commentaries on Peter Lombard's *Sentences* (quoted by R. de Roover, 'Joseph A. Schumpeter and scholastic economics', *Kyklos*, Fasc. 2, 1957) says that money is a 'measure of the utility of other things'.

6 The continuing influence of Aristotle's ideas on value has been well traced by E. Kauder, 'Genesis of the marginal utility theory from Aristotle to the end of the 18th century', *Economic Journal*, Vol. 63, September 1953, pp. 638–50; and in his *A History of Marginal Utility Theory* (Princeton, NJ, 1965). B. Gordon, 'Aristotle and the development of value theory', *Quarterly Journal of Economics*, Vol. 78, February 1964, pp. 115–28, shows that there is a traditional labour or cost-of-production theory of value, as well as a subjective or 'utility' theory, which stem from Aristotle and link him with St Thomas Aquinas, Davanzati, Bernoulli and Galiani.

7 *Topics*, 117b, 28–30. *Rhetoric*, 1364a, 24–30.

8 Interesting discussions of the role of the Arabs as the cultural heirs to Greece are included in the following works: G. Barton, *Introduction to the History of Science* (Washington and Baltimore, 1929–48), 5 vols, Vol. 1, p. 18; C. H. Haskins, *Studies in the History of Medieval Science* (Cambridge, Mass., 1924) Vol. 24 of Harvard Historical Studies; A. Mieli, *La Science Arabe et son rôle dans l'évolution scientifique mondiale* (Leyden, 1938); R. R. Walzer, *The Arabic Transmission of Greek Thought to Medieval Europe*, reprinted from the *Bulletin of the John Rylands Library* (Manchester, 1945); De Lacy Evans O'Leary, *How Greek Science Passed to the Arabs* (London, 1951); G. E. von Grunebaum, *Medieval Islam* (Chicago, 1953); M. A. Faris, *The Arab Heritage* (Princeton, NJ, 1946); Sobhi Mahmassani, *Les Idées Économiques d'Ibn Khaldoun, Essai historique, analytique et critique* (Leyden, 1932), ch. 3 (on Moslem thought before Ibn Khaldun); E. I. J. Rosenthal, 'Some aspects of Islamic political thought', *Islamic Culture*, Vol. 22, No. 1, January 1948 (Hyderabad); F. Rosenthal, *A History of Muslim Historiography* (Leyden, 1952), especially pp. 102–4.

9 Al-Farabi, *Fusul al-Madani. Aphorisms of the Statesman*, ed. D. M. Dunlop (Cambridge, 1961), in University of Cambridge Oriental Publications, p. 37:

> Just as the body is composed of different parts of a determinate number, some more, some less excellent, adjacent to each other and graded, each doing a certain work, and there is combined from all their actions mutual help towards the perfection of the aim in the man's body, so the city and the household are each composed of different parts of a determinate number, some less, some more excellent, adjacent to each other and graded in different grades, each doing a certain work independently, and there is combined from their actions mutual help towards the perfection of the aim in the city or household, except that the household is part of the city and the households are in the city, so the aims are different.

> Al-Farabi adds that just as a doctor treats any sick member only in such a way as will benefit the whole body, so must the ruler of the city treat each part of the city (whether small, like a man, or big, like a household) only in a way that will benefit the whole.

10 The mirror-book is *Ghazali's Book of Counsel for Kings*, translated by F. R. C. Bagley (Oxford, 1964), in University of Durham Publications. The encyclopedia is *The Book of Knowledge*; the main ideas developed in this work are resumed by Mahmassani, op. cit., pp. 64–7, and by W. Heffening in his article 'Tidjara' in the *Encyclopedia of Islam* (Leyden, 1936).

11 Abul-Fadl Al-Dimashqi, *The Book of Knowledge of the Beauties of Commerce and of Cognizance of Good and Bad Merchandise and Falsifications*, partially translated into German by H. Ritter, 'Ein arabisches Handbuch der Handelswissenschaft', in *Der Islam*, Vol. 7 (1917). English translation of two short passages in Robert S. Lopez and Irving W. Raymond, *Medieval Trade in the Mediterranean World* (New York and London, 1955; repr. 1961), pp. 24–7 and 412. The Platonic and Aristotelian economic theory that reappears in Abul-Fadl's work is resumed by Mahmassani, op. cit., pp. 72–90.

12 Abu-Bakr Muhammad al-Tirtushi (Abu-Bequer de Tortosa), *Lámpara de los príncipes*, translated into Spanish and edited by M. Alarcón (Madrid, 1930), 2 vols. See especially Vol. 2, *passim*.

13 Books and articles on Averroes are legion. *Averroès et l'Averroïsme* (Paris, 1852), the study with which the youthful Renan first made his name, is still indispensable. Certain aspects of the work are criticised by M. Asín, 'El Averoismo teológico de Sto. Tomás de Aquino', in *Homenaje a D. Francisco Codera en su jubilación del profesorado, Estudios de erudición oriental*, ed. E. Saavedra (Saragossa, 1904). Carra de Vaux, in *Les Penseurs de l'Islam* (Paris, 1923), Vol. 4, pp. 65–93, discusses the importance of Averroes for the history of Arab scholasticism, as does E. I. J. Rosenthal in his contribution to the social sciences in 'The place of politics in the philosophy of Ibn Rushd', *Bulletin of the School of Oriental and African Studies*, University of London, Vol. XV, pt 2, June 1953.

14 E. I. J. Rosenthal, *Averroes' Commentary on Plato's Republic*, ed. with an introduction, English translation and notes (Cambridge, 1965).

15 There is no modern edition of Averroes's commentary on the *Nicomachean Ethics*. I can, however, recommend the edition published in Venice, 1489, in 2 vols. The Latin version of Aristotle's *Nicomachean Ethics* made by Leonardo Bruni of Arezzo, 'Aretinus' (1369–44), is placed in the middle of the page, with Hermann's translation of Averroes's commentary surrounding it, the type being exceptionally clear and the title-pages charmingly (though distractingly) adorned with wild flowers.

The only discussion of this commentary that I know of is by C. Miller, *Studien zur Geschichte der Geldlehre*, Münchener Volkwirtschaftliche Studien, Stück 146 (Stuttgart, 1925), pp. 68–73.

16 C. Sanchez-Albornoz, *La España musulmana según los autores islamitas y cristianas medievales* (Buenos Aires, 1946), includes a description of Toledo as a centre of translation.

17 C. Marchesi, *L'Etica Nicomachea nella tradizione latina medievale* (Messina, 1904). Sybil D. Wingate, *The Medieval Latin Versions of the Aristotelian Scientific Corpus* (London, 1951).

PART TWO

The Age of Mercantilism

3

The School of Salamanca

In this chapter and the next we shall follow some part of the development of economic thought in Spain from the end of the Middle Ages to the beginnings of *laissez-faire*; that is to say, from the end of the fifteenth century to the middle of the eighteenth. For most historians this period constitutes the 'age of mercantilism'. And certainly, in Spain as elsewhere, mercantilist doctrine was preached by many writers. But for the historian of economic thought it does not, perhaps, represent the most interesting work of the period. The high level of Spanish sixteenth-century economics noted by Schumpeter was largely the achievement of the late scholastics – the School of Salamanca, as they have sometimes been called. These writers were, in the main, theologians and jurists in whose thought the social and economic order played an important though secondary part.[1]

Among the topics of an economic character discussed by the Spanish Doctors we may include the nature of private property; taxation; poor relief or 'welfare'; commerce; the 'just price' and usury; and money, banking and foreign exchange. I shall mention some of this late scholastic work in my last chapter, together with the contributions of the 'political economists', as I shall call the writers who made the interests of the Spanish economy their first concern. Here I shall consider such part of our Doctors' teaching as would seem to approach most closely to economic 'analysis', as distinct from description or the formulation of policy.

Notable features of 'Salamancan' doctrine were the adoption of a subjective or utility theory of value, inherited, it is true, from medieval times, but applied in a living and clear-sighted manner to contemporary events; the realisation of the relation between the quantity of money in circulation and the price-level; and the development of certain other ideas on money and banking, including a theory of foreign exchange based on the quantity theory.

SOME EARLY SOURCES

To some extent we have already cleared the ground. In connection with the subject of usury we have mentioned the Old and New Testaments, the fathers of the Church, and the Roman, canon and earlier Spanish codes of civil law. We have also seen how Greek economic teaching was brought into the Christian West at the middle of the thirteenth century, in the first place through Averroes's commentaries on Plato's *Republic* and Aristotle's *Nicomachean Ethics*. At about the same time – the exact date is a matter of dispute – another important source came to enrich the still scanty supply of economic literature available to the Christian West. This was Aristotle's *Politics*, a work unfamiliar if not entirely unknown to the Arabs. The appearance of the first Latin translation, which was probably that made by William of Moerbeke (*d.* 1281), constitutes a landmark in the history of the social sciences in the West.

The 'Politics'

Aristotle begins by distinguishing real wealth from money. The art of administering real property, he says, is alone called economy. Money is a mere tool that serves for acquiring the things that are necessary to domestic and civil economy and the business of money-making is to economy proper as the shuttle to the art of weaving.[2]

Next follows the oft-quoted passage about the uses of every possession being two: its ordinary or natural use, and its use as an object of barter. A shoe, for instance, may be worn, or it may be exchanged for something else. Through barter the use of money was introduced, mainly in order to facilitate trade over great distances. Men looked for some medium of exchange which would be valuable in itself, and at the same time easy to transport, such as iron, silver or some similar material. At first this was measured by weight or size, but later the value was stamped on the coin to save the trouble of weighing.

Once money had been established as the necessary means of exchange, men took to seeking more of it by trading where and in whatever way they could make most profit. Wealth is often supposed to consist of a large quantity of money. But in fact money has only a conventional value which is fixed by general consent, and if the people who use it alter their opinion it will be worth nothing. Therefore, a prudent man will take care also to acquire some other form of property.

Money-making, according to Aristotle, differs from true economy by knowing no bounds. It seeks an unlimited amount of money for its own sake, whereas true economy requires money in order to buy the things that are necessary for life. Money is to be used, not hoarded. It may commendably be used in the service of the household, but not in retail trade, which has not its origin in nature but in men's desire to gain from one another. Of all forms of money-making, usury is the most unnatural and detestable because it uses money as a means of making more money, instead of as a medium for the exchange of real goods.[3]

Other concepts that have been traced to the *Politics* are the distinction between instruments of production and 'instruments of action' or consumption-goods,[4] and the observation that the use-value of an article will at some point begin to decline as the quantity of that article increases.[5]

Medieval Lines of Approach

Before the rise of mercantilism in the sixteenth century, when 'political economy' came into being as a separate subject of study, economic analysis existed only as a by-product of legal, theological and philosophical inquiry. This was almost entirely centred in the 'schools', as the newly-founded universities were called. The teachers or 'Doctors' who occupied themselves with such matters were mainly theologians and jurists, the latter including Roman as well as canon lawyers. There was no conflict between the doctrines held by the various professional groups. Many Doctors were proficient in several subjects, and taught and wrote on them all. When we refer to a Doctor as a theologian or a jurist, therefore, we shall simply mean that he was speaking in that capacity on the occasion that interests us.

The Doctors did not envisage the economic system as a single mechanism made up of interlocking parts. Such economic analysis as they produced was generally developed in commentaries on Aristotle or St Thomas or in the examination of a series of contracts (including some that we met in our first chapter), undertaken in order to determine whether or not they were licit. This method led to a patchwork of theory. However, although the Doctors did not try to formulate any general and consistent body of doctrine, in the course of their inquiries they were bound to meet certain basic problems, some of which persist in modern economics. The most interesting was probably that of value.

The Problem of Value

In the Middle Ages, as now, the correct or 'just' assessment of value was of great practical importance in daily life. It was important to lawyers: the just division of inheritances, the proper compensation of parties injured in unfair transactions and a hundred other matters, all depended on the court's assessment of the value of property under dispute. And it was important to moralists, since it governed the daily business-dealings between men. The principles that ought rightly to guide the determination of value were discussed by the Doctors under the general heading of Sale, and embodied in what is often called the doctrine of the 'Just Price'.

It was generally agreed that a prince had the right and duty of fixing the prices of the commoner necessities of life in the territory under his control. Wherever a legal price existed, that price was accepted by the courts. But the greater number of prices were not fixed in this way. How, then, were they to be determined?

The fundamental Roman position had been that a buyer and seller might strike any bargain they could, and so conclude a valid sale. The *Code* prescribes that a seller may recover the '*justum pretium*' from a buyer who has paid less than half the proper price of the thing in question. The *Digest* declares that 'the prices (values) of things are not to be calculated from the desires or needs of individuals but, rather, commonly', adding that the value of a good is not to be assessed by the price it will fetch at a certain moment of time, or of unusual shortage. These texts, which deal with the assessment of value in a certain type of litigation, guided the medieval Doctors in their search for a general theory of price. The identification of the just price with the market price, which in its turn was settled by 'common estimation', became firmly entrenched in the course of the Middle Ages, and formed the basis of scholastic value-theory.[6]

The introduction of Greek economics to the West in the thirteenth century, and the task of harmonising Greek theory with Catholic doctrine, called forth a large number of works in which Greek teaching was preserved and developed.

St Albert the Great (1193-1280) worked on Hermann's translation of Averroes's commentary on the *Nicomachean Ethics*, and on a Latin version of the *Politics*, probably William of Moerbeke's. St Albert's theory of value shows a certain ambiguity that was reflected in the work of his successors. He accepts the established legal principle that the just price of a thing should accord with the estimation of the market at the time of the sale.[7] Yet he says elsewhere that the arts would be doomed to destruction if the producer did not receive a price that covered his outgoings,[8] and he held with Aristotle that commutative justice requires strict equivalence between what is given and what is received. It is thus possible to trace the source of a labour theory of value, as well as of a subjective or utility theory, in the work of St Albert and his disciples.

St Albert's most distinguished pupil was St Thomas Aquinas, at whose instigation new Latin translations of Aristotle were made from Greek instead of Arabic texts. St Thomas's economic doctrine is scattered through his commentaries on the *Nicomachean Ethics* and *Politics*, and in his *Summa theologica*, *Summa contra Gentiles* and other works. The *Summa theologica*, which ousted Peter Lombard's *Sentences* as the leading university textbook of theology, includes a treatise on

Justice. A long line of scholastic theologians wrote commentaries on this treatise, generally under the titles of *De justitia et jure*, *De secunda secundae* (because St Thomas's treatise is contained in Part 2, 2 of his *Summa theologica*), or, when dealing more specifically with economic problems, *De contractibus* or *De justitia commutativa*. Taken as a whole, these commentaries on St Thomas constitute what is probably the most interesting body of economic literature that was produced before the end of the seventeenth century.

St Thomas's theory of value shows little significant advance on that of St Albert. He reminds us that the contract of sale was instituted to ensure equal utility for buyer and seller, since each possesses what the other wants.[9] Taking up a celebrated dictum of St Augustine's, he explains that want is the true measure of value, since things are not priced according to their rank in the scale of nature (otherwise a mouse, being a living creature, would fetch more than a pearl, which is inanimate), but according to men's need of them for their use.[10] Supply and demand play their part in determining price. The price of bread rises in time of famine, gold is valuable because it is rare and the price of wheat is likely to fall when fresh supplies come on to the market.

These utterances stress the subjective aspect of value. At the same time, St Thomas recognises that labour and costs enter into the determination of price, he holds that 'the arts will be destroyed if the workman who has made one article does not receive in exchange another article similar in quantity and quality. One man's labour must be compared with another's if the exchange is to be just' and that 'justice will be served if as many shoes be given in exchange for a house or for food as the builder or farmer exceeds the cobbler in labour and costs'.[11]

The predominantly subjective theory of value held by St Albert and St Thomas was accepted by most of their contemporaries and by all later Thomists, who included the important theologians of the Dominican Order. In the work of these writers, the argument that the price of a thing should in justice cover the labour and costs employed in its production certainly occurs in the discussion of value, but plays a secondary part.

A somewhat divergent view of value is expressed by the Franciscan theologian, John Duns Scotus (1265–1308). Although in principle his theory remains grounded in utility, Duns Scotus asserts that the merchant performs a necessary function in society and is entitled to sell his wares at a price that will compensate him for his work, cover the risks he has incurred, and enable him to support himself and his family.[12]

This idea that price should be linked to the social condition of the producer was again put forward by Henry of Langenstein (1325–83), who says that each man may reckon for himself the price of his wares by calculating how much money he needs to support himself according to his status.[13] The relevant text has been widely quoted by modern scholars in support of the thesis that the scholastics held a labour theory of value.[14] Yet, in fact, Henry of Langenstein paid great attention to the part played by 'human want' in the determination of price, carefully analysing the subject of 'want', and distinguishing between 'extensive' and 'intensive' demand, the former depending on the number of prospective purchasers and the latter on the scarcity of the merchandise.

In the fifteenth century the outstanding writers on value were two saints of the Church: the Franciscan St Bernardino de Siena (1380–1444), and the Dominican St Antonino of Florence (1389–1459). They may be considered together, since they were contemporaries, shared the same views on economic matters, and were equally well-informed on the business life and customs of their day. Of the two, St Bernardino slightly preceded St Antonino, but the latter is more often cited by later writers.[15]

Our two Italian economists hold a utility theory of value: for them, value is composed of three elements, *raritas, virtuositas* and *complacibilitas*, which may be rendered in English as scarcity, usefulness and pleasingness. An interesting distinction is made between *virtuositas* (the property of satisfying human wants, inherent in the goods themselves) and *complacibilitas*, (the property of appealing to the individual taste of the prospective purchaser).[16]

The 'paradox of value' that had been glimpsed by Aristotle and that was destined to play so prominent a part in the economic literature of a later age was stated by St Bernardino as follows: 'Secondly, the value of a saleable good is assessed by its scarcity ... so that the four elements are less appreciated among us, owing to their abundance, than balsam and gold, though they are more necessary and useful for life.' The 'paradox' is stated by St Antonino in almost the same words.

The more deeply the student immerses himself in scholastic discussions of the 'Just Price', the stronger will be his impression not only that the Doctors believed the free play of market forces to be the principal determinant of price but that they were anxious, on moral grounds, to protect this doctrine from all danger of attack. Why did they set such great store by it?

The answer surely is that they regarded the poor man as breadwinner rather than producer. Dearth and famine were constant threats, and a primary aim of all authorities was to ensure that abundant supplies reached the market as cheaply as possible. Measures were everywhere taken against evil men who hoarded stocks ('engrossers', as they were called in England), bought up goods before they could come on to the market ('forestallers') or formed corners to drive up prices ('regraters')

Middlemen were viewed with suspicion as being naturally given to such practices, and the Doctors feared that a labour or cost-theory of value would encourage merchants to plead high costs as an excuse for charging high prices to the consumer.

A market policy of free competition was not in itself enough to ensure cheapness and plenty. In times of shortage, when prices soared out of reach of the poor man, the authorities were forced to resort to price-control. In general, despite their basic preference for a free market, the scholastics allowed price-regulation in the case of first necessities, such as bread, for which there was no substitute.

Many scholastic writers held that wages should be determined in the same way as other prices, by the play of supply and demand. For St Bernardino, wage differentials are explained by scarcity, because skilled workers are less numerous than unskilled. And St Antonino, who had a close acquaintance with labour conditions in the Florentine textile industry, says quite bluntly that wages are determined by common estimation in the absence of fraud.[17]

It follows from the above remarks that monopoly of any kind was unanimously rejected by the medieval Doctors, and that they tended to regard the trade-guilds with suspicion as cradles of unlawful conspiracy.

The Value of Money

Aristotle's doctrine that the functions of money were to serve as a medium of exchange, a measure of the value of goods and a store of value or 'guarantor against future need' was preserved throughout the Middle Ages. It was also realised that money can hardly serve as a means of exchange, and not at all as a store of value, unless its own value is stable. Yet, though the phrase *valor pecuniae* is often used, we cannot always be sure of its meaning.

Most of the schoolmen seem to have had the metallic content of the coin uppermost in their minds when considering its value. The tale of the coin, which determined its ratio to other coins and stamped it with legal authority, was also an important element in its value. A rather more sophisticated view was that 'money as money' (to borrow a phrase that was often used) had a value derived from its functions, apart from the value of its metallic content or the legal value that was stamped upon it. Some writers stressed one aspect of monetary value, and some another. The matter was succinctly put by John Buridan (1300–58), rector of the University of Paris, who, in his commentary on Aristotle's *Politics*, says that the material cause of money is some rare material, its efficient cause the State, its final cause the need of men to exchange goods and its formal cause the sign set upon it.[18]

As the Middle Ages wore on, it came to be glimpsed that the value of money might fluctuate under the influence of supply and demand, just as that of goods fluctuated. This doctrine appears most clearly in the discussion of foreign exchange. (I use the term 'foreign exchange' in order to distinguish between the exchange of monies and that of goods.)

The Problem of Foreign Exchange

In my first chapter, when considering the scholastic doctrine of usury, I touched upon the development of the exchange-contract and on the increasing use that was made of 'dry' or fictitious contracts drawn up in concealment of usury. We dwelled, however, on business practice rather than theory, and must now sketch out what may perhaps be termed the 'pre-Salamancan' doctrine.[19]

Many of the earlier writers on the 'exchanges' were Italian. In the progressive Italian centres of trade, theory followed practice and in turn modified it, in much the same way that Jewish doctrine and practice had acted upon one another.

Cardinal Hostiensis (d. 1271) considers the following question: can a certain sum be sent on the understanding that it is repaid within a stipulated term in another currency? Not, he replies, if the loan is made in the expectation of profit. Those who lend at one fair in order to be repaid a larger sum at the next are usurers. 'Time cannot justify profit.'[20]

St Thomas Aquinas does not discuss exchange-business in any detail, but says that the exchange-bankers 'commit many frauds'. More tolerant views were expressed by two of St Thomas's disciples. These were the Dominican Giles de Lessines, and Alexander Lombard, at one time provincial of the Franciscan Order.

Giles's treatise on usury, which appeared in 1278, has the distinction of being the first theological work that was devoted exclusively to the subject. The author holds that, although money cannot be bought and sold, the dealers are entitled to some reward 'because of the risk, and by way of *interesse*, since they have to pay the expenses of their servants'. Moreover, a dealer would otherwise be providing the customer with more 'utility' than he received in return. These remarks are, I think, interesting. They show how Aristotle's principle of utility was gaining ground in western Christendom and being applied to different sorts of contracts, and they hint at the fusion of value-theory and usury-theory that was not, however, to be made complete for several centuries to come.[21]

Alexander Lombard (d. 1314), a Piedmontese who seems to have had practical experience of business, defends the bankers in a short but influential treatise. He adopts what was perhaps the most promising line of approach that was open to him, namely, to regard the exchange-contract as a *permutatio*, or barter-transaction, and not a *mutuum*. Alexander condemns the bills-of-exchange currently drawn in Genoa on the fairs of Champagne whenever they brought the dealer a profit by reason of the delay that took place between the original payment and the reimbursement. But he holds that the profit may be justified if it arises not from delay but from a speculation on the future rate of exchange.[22]

The moral theologian Astesanus (*d.* about 1330), the jurists Calderini (*c.* 1300–65) and Baldo (1327–1400), and other Doctors, follow Alexander Lombard in regarding the exchange-contract as a sale or *permutatio*, and not a *mutuum*. Broadly speaking, we may say that by the end of the fourteenth century the exchange of two monies in a single place and at the same time ('from hand to hand', as the Islamic authors said), technically called *cambium manuale* or *cambium minutum*, and that of money in one place for money in another, allowing a reasonable time for the necessary letter of instructions to arrive (*cambium per litteras*), had come to be regarded as licit by most Doctors. It was generally admitted, also, that the exchange-dealer might lawfully make some charge that would compensate him for his services. When a particular transaction came under scrutiny, the paramount problem was whether it was a genuine exchange-contract or a *mutuum* disguised as such (*cambium siccum*), the latter being universally reprobated.

In the course of the fifteenth century these basic principles were worked out more fully. In 1403 the Florentine jurist, diplomat and university professor, Lorenzo de Rodulfis (*c.* 1360–1442), produced a more detailed work on usury than had so far appeared. On the exchange-contract, however, he says little that is novel. When trying to define what he means by the 'value' of a coin he does not get beyond distinguishing between its 'intrinsic' and its 'extrinsic' value; that is to say, the metal content of the coin in question and the tale or legal value. Like all the other writers of the period that I have read, Lorenzo fails to take the purchasing-power of money into account.[23]

St Bernardino and St Antonino agree that the exchange-contract is licit and even useful, unless it is misused to conceal a loan. St Bernardino goes so far as to say that the exchange-banker performs a valuable service by facilitating the foreign trade that is necessary for the support of human life, and by transferring funds from country to country, thus doing away with the need to transport specie. Like his teacher, Alexander Lombard, St Bernardino objects to exchange by bills if a profit is charged merely because there is a delay in repayment, but sanctions such a profit if there is a doubt as to the future course of the exchange-rate.[24]

St Antonino accepts *cambium per litteram* when the banker sells drafts of letters-of-credit payable elsewhere, but looks askance at those transactions in which the banker is the purchaser of foreign currency: that is, when he 'lends' or pays out money in one place in order to be repaid a larger sum elsewhere. Although, as our author admits, the banker might lose if the foreign currency declined in value, the risk involved was small, and such business was nearly always profitable. Both writers are severe in their denunciation of dry exchange.[25]

At once the summarisers of earlier scholastic work and the immediate forerunners of the Spanish school of the sixteenth and seventeenth centuries were Thomas de Vio (1468–1534, generally cited as Cajetan), and Sylvester of Prierio (1456–1523), professor at Bologna and Padua. In his short treatise on the exchanges Cajetan declares that the art of banking is useful and honourable, and that an exchange-transaction is not in itself unjust. Profit on the exchanges is licit, if approved by common custom.

One contention of Cajetan's was to prove especially fruitful for later doctrine. He says that a dealer who advances money in Milan against a bill in Lyons may licitly give a lesser sum in Milan for a greater in Lyons because 'money absent is always worth less than money present'. This was commonly accepted doctrine. But Cajetan goes further. He realised that the price of money might be determined, like that of commodities, by the laws of supply and demand, and that the rate of exchange would vary accordingly, a larger sum being given in a place where the demand for bills was small, and a smaller where demand was great. Cajetan even proceeds to say that a smaller sum may licitly be paid now in exchange for a larger sum at a future date, if demand is thought likely to increase in the interval between payment and reimbursement. Such a profit, he maintains, does not arise from the time-lag that must necessarily separate the two operations, but solely from the alterations in the state of the money-market that take place within the period in question.

Cajetan does not define what he means by saying that one money may be 'worth' more than another. He was probably alluding to the value of one currency (generally silver) in terms of another (generally gold). If he had the concept of purchasing-power in mind, he did not express it. Cajetan is cited frequently by our Spanish Doctors. His work consolidated that of earlier writers provided a solid base for further advance.[26]

Another Dominican theologian, Sylvester of Prierio, was among the last of the summists and, together with Cajetan, an immediate predecessor of the School of Salamanca.[27] The two writers held similar views in the matter of foreign exchange. According to Sylvester, money has a dual value: as a commodity, and as a means of exchange. The commodity-value of money may fluctuate. Money absent is worth more than money present, because it is subject to risk. Therefore, the banker or merchant may licitly pay a smaller sum in his own city in exchange for a larger sum in a distant place.

If distance of the place of repayment is a valid reason for reimbursing more than was originally paid, does the same consideration apply to distance in time? Sylvester is not quite clear on this crucial point, but seems to agree with Cajetan that if the rate of exchange varies between the time of payment and that of reimbursement the dealer may ask to be reimbursed a larger sum than he paid. By the 'value' of money Sylvester clearly means the tale, or price of a coin in terms of other coins. Thus, he remarks that in Milan the gold *scudo* had a 'value' of 28 groats and in Lyons of 30 groats. If, let us say, a banker paid 60 *scudi* or 168 groats in Milan, bargaining to be reimbursed in Lyons, he would receive 60 Lyonese *scudi* or 180 groats, making a profit of 12 groats on the deal. Such a transaction, Sylvester seems to hold, may be genuine and licit. But when the time-element comes into play it may also be a form of 'dry exchange' or concealed *mutuum*, and of course illicit, unless the ratio between the *scudo* and the groat varies during the period that elapses between payment and reimbursement.

It may well seem to the reader that exchange-doctrine was entering a maze of doubt and confusion through which the only sure guide was a firm insistence on the criterion of intention. Some writers did indeed rely on this criterion.[28] But the future of economic theory did not lie in their hands.

THE SCHOOL OF SALAMANCA

We now come to the main purpose of the present chapter, which is to examine the theory of value and the ideas on money, banking and foreign exchange held by the Spanish scholastic writers of the sixteenth and seventeenth centuries. Before we can do so we must see something of the circumstances that helped to call up their teaching.

We have already mentioned the salient features of the 'age of mercantilism' in Castile. At the end of the fifteenth century Castile was a poor kingdom, recently emerged from the long struggle of the Reconquest, and but newly allied to her more prosperous neighbour, Aragon. Her economy depended on subsistence farming, on the wool trade and on the shipping that made use of the Cantabrian and Mediterranean ports. Her sons were farmers, cattle-owners, soldiers, sailors and priests.

It was to this dour kingdom of Castile that fate assigned the riches of El Dorado. In the Indies the Spaniards found gold and silver in quantities undreamed of a few years before. American treasure began to reach Spain at the beginning of the sixteenth century, and in larger quantities from 1535 onwards. The richest mines were opened between 1545 and 1558, and the flood of treasure continued unabated during the rest of the sixteenth century.

What were the effects on Spain of such extraordinary and unexpected good fortune? They may be briefly summarised as follows. Castile entered a period of inflation caused by the demand in the New World for the products of the mother-country, and by the influx of gold and silver that was shipped to Spain in compensation for her exports to the colonies. Seville, the home-port of the treasure-fleet, became a magnet for the merchants of all Europe. A trade-boom set in. Prices rose, first in Seville, then throughout New Castile, and later in Old Castile, Valencia and the rest of Spain, doubling themselves in the first half of the sixteenth century and again in the second.

Such a rise in prices may seem moderate to us today, but from contemporary observers it evoked prophecies of doom that were all too soon to be fulfilled. Spain found herself increasingly unable to sell her products abroad, and increasingly threatened by foreign competition in both her home market and her Indian trade. The government followed a vacillating policy, now (in 1552) trying to supply the shortage of goods by throwing open the Spanish market to certain foreign manufactures, now (in 1558) reversing this policy with a view to preventing the outflow of the precious metals.

In addition to a lack of goods, an excessively high price level, and a crushing burden of taxation, there were other factors that helped turn the tide of Spanish fortunes. Agriculture declined after the expulsion of the Moors who had tended the land so lovingly. The world of industry and commerce did not gain by exchanging the Jews, who had looked on Spain as their ancestral homeland, for Italians whose links with the country were weaker. The Spanish merchant families, when once their fortunes were established, showed in succeeding generations a tendency to sell their businesses, buy land with the proceeds and retire to the tranquil pleasures of their estates. In every sphere of the national life there was a lack of skilled and experienced leadership.

The internal problems of Spain were grave enough. Yet they might, perhaps, have found solution had it not been for the heaviest of all the drags that hampered Castilian progress – Spain's close political links with Europe, and her involvement in the wars to which the Habsburgs were committed.

The influx of silver lessened at the beginning of the seventeenth century, and fell off abruptly after 1650, the Indian trade passed almost entirely into foreign hands and the population of the Castilian cities declined. Spain, to whom the conquest of the Indies might have brought lasting progress, entered a long period of economic stagnation, and became in the later seventeenth century as she had been in the Middle Ages, a poor, a 'backward' country, inferior to her neighbours, if in no way culturally, yet in all the benefits that material prosperity can bring.

The sixteenth and early seventeenth centuries were in every sense a golden age for Spain. How far, if at all, that great flowering of art and literature was stimulated by the inflow of American treasure can only be a matter for conjecture. It is otherwise in the case of learning, where the more notable Spanish achievements were closely related to the conquest of the Indies and all that followed from it.

Since the completion of the Reconquest, the Spanish universities had come to occupy a foremost place among those of Europe. In particular, the University of Salamanca was famed for the brilliant teachers who were attracted to its chairs: grammarians, poets, historians and, above all, theologians, philosophers and jurists.

At the beginning of the sixteenth century the old scholastic tradition, though threatened and to some extent modified by the 'new learning', was still very much alive. Indeed, important scholastic treatises would continue to be written in many countries for another century and a half. Scholasticism was outwardly unchanged. In form there is little to distinguish, let us say, a sixteenth-century commentary on St Thomas's doctrine of the Just Price from one written in the fourteenth, except that it will probably be longer and more elaborate. Questions, Articles, Objections, Distinctions, Solutions and Conclusions follow one another in dutiful procession, and the most trivial statements are supported by a heavy apparatus of citations.

In contrast to their unbending rigidity of form, the Spanish treatises display considerable flexibility in the development of their themes. To begin with, their authors did not shrink from the task of defining the relations that were in process of creation between the Spanish Crown and the recently won kingdoms of the New World. It was urgently necessary to find a juridical order that would govern this new colonial association, and, in their search for the principles on which it might be established, the Spanish theologians and jurists laid the foundation of the science of international law as we know it today.[29]

In addition to the moral and juridical problems that confronted the Spanish Crown in its relations with the conquered peoples of the Indies, the economic condition of the country was causing general concern. The inflation provoked in Spain as a result of the American enterprise could not fail to sow dismay and perplexity. The Church's warnings against the sin of avarice passed unheeded when opportunities for enrichment offered themselves every day. Usury flourished, often in the guise of legitimate commerce. Indeed, it was hard to distinguish between the two things, and in such deep matters, where even the Doctors differed, how could a simple priest be expected to guide his penitents? Our Spanish writers, building on the work of their predecessors, made what proved to be the last great attempt to tackle the problem of usury, and in so doing developed various concepts that have passed into modern economic theory.

As the sixteenth century advanced, the conflict between business practice and the Church's teaching grew ever more acute. In 1517, and again in 1532, the Spanish merchants of Antwerp sent to Paris to obtain a ruling on the legitimacy of exchange-transactions from the learned doctors of the Sorbonne.[30] The second Reply includes an opinion given at Salamanca by Francisco de Vitoria. It is now time for us to make Vitoria's acquaintance, and that of the other scholars who lived and taught in Spain.

Vitoria, the founder of the School of Salamanca, was born at Burgos in 1492 or 1493. He joined the Dominican Order while still a boy, and in 1506 went to Paris, where he studied and taught at the Sorbonne until 1522. In 1512 Vitoria helped to bring out the first modern edition of the second part of St Thomas's *Summa theologica*, and in 1522 an edition of St Antonino of Florence's *Summa*. We have seen that both these works are important landmarks in the history of economic thought.

In 1522 Vitoria returned to Spain. After teaching for four years at Valladolid, he obtained a chair of theology at the University of Salamanca, where he remained until his death in 1546. Vitoria's fame rests on the brilliant lectures in which he sought to reconcile Thomist doctrine with the manifold legal, political, ethical and economic problems that arose in the government of the far-flung Spanish Empire. Vitoria wrote no book of his own – or, at least, none that has come down to us. We know his work only through the lecture-notes taken by his students. Yet his influence on his own and later generations was great: it is not too much to say that the science of international law originated in his lecture-room at Salamanca.[31]

Among the founders of the School of Salamanca, probably the most thorough and systematic exponent of its philosophy was Domingo de Soto (1495–1560). Of humble origin, Soto studied at Alcalá and later in Paris, where he attended Vitoria's lectures. In 1520 he returned to Alcalá to occupy a chair of metaphysics. In 1525 he entered the Dominican Order and in 1532 was appointed to a chair of theology at Salamanca. In 1545 he was named by Charles V as his representative on the Council of Trent in succession to Vitoria, who was in failing health. In 1548 Soto became confessor to the emperor, but two years later he gave up this influential post in order to return to his work at Salamanca.

Soto's fame rests chiefly on his treatise *De justitia et jure*, which went through no less than twenty-seven editions in fifty years.[32] In this work Soto pays careful attention to economic problems and even goes so far as to say that his desire to discuss the subjects of usury, contracts, exchange-business and simony was his main motive for assuming the burden of writing it. Soto devotes chapters to the place of commerce within the State, the fixing of the just price, the fluctuations of that price and their cause, rent-charges, commercial companies and the propriety of investment in them by Christians, and the nature of insurance, illustrating his doctrine with copious descriptions of the business life of his day. Particularly valuable is his account of the Spanish and Flemish fairs, which were held in conjunction with one another and which together constituted one of the main channels by which American treasure flowed from Seville across the Pyrenees. As Soto truly remarks, 'an author who seeks to reprehend the customs of the exchanges must note the practice of merchants with his own eyes'.

Another founder-member of the school was Martín de Azpilcueta, generally called Navarrus (1493–1586). He, too, after a brief period in Cahors and Toulouse, came to occupy a chair at Salamanca, where he introduced a new method of teaching civil law, combining its exposition with that of canon law. This innovation, and Azpilcueta's vast learning, drew large audiences to his lecture-room.

In 1538 Azpilcueta was sent by Charles V to the newly-established University of Coimbra, where for some years he continued to expound and develop the principles of international law that had been laid down by his friend and colleague, Vitoria. Azpilcueta spent his last years in Rome, becoming the trusted counsellor of Pius V, Gregory XIII and Sixtus V. Admired and consulted even in extreme old age, he was generally regarded as the most eminent canon-lawyer of his day.

For economists Azpilcueta must ever be notable as having made the first clear and definite statement of the quantity theory of money. The passage in question is included in a commentary on foreign exchange which is often printed, together with four other commentaries, as an appendix to a manual of moral theology which Azpilcueta dedicated to his friend and patroness, the Princess Juana, sister of Philip II. Originally written in Portuguese, the manual enjoyed great success, going through edition after edition and being translated into Spanish, Latin and Italian before the end of the sixteenth century.[33]

These three writers – Vitoria, Soto and Azpilcueta – were born within a year or so of each other and, though Soto and Azpilcueta acknowledged Vitoria as their leader, were of equal eminence and seniority. Another distinguished expert on economic questions was Juan de Medina (1490–1546), who, however, taught not at Salamanca but at Alcalá. Medina's best-known work, a treatise on penance which includes chapters on usury and the exchanges, was published in 1550. Medina is often cited by later writers on that branch of moral theology with which we are concerned.[34]

Among the minor writers of this first phase of Spanish pre-eminence in moral theology are three authors of handbooks for merchants, published in 1542, 1543 and 1544 respectively, in which the doctrines of greater theologians are succinctly explained for the benefit of confessors and their penitents: Cristóbal de Villalón,[35] Luís de Alcalá[36] and Luís Saravia de la Calle.[37] Their little treatises are frequently cited by later writers. Saravia, in particular, enjoyed considerable influence, since his work was translated into Italian in 1561 and found at least one close imitator in Italy.[38]

We now come to rather younger men who nevertheless were contemporaries of Vitoria. Diego de Covarrubias y Leiva was the greatest jurist among them. A pupil of Azpilcueta's, he spent ten years at Salamanca as professor of canon law. In 1548 the emperor named him auditor of the Chancellery of Castile, in 1560 he became Bishop of Ciudad Rodrigo and in 1564 Bishop of Segovia. In 1572 he attained to the supreme magistrature of Castile, but in 1577 his death deprived Spain of a learned jurist and a sagacious statesman. Covarrubias was a man of remarkably wide culture. His writings are not confined to legal problems but relate to many aspects of theology, history, philology, numismatics and other branches of learning.[39]

Among other Doctors of Covarrubias's generation there were many who followed and developed the teaching of the School of Salamanca. Especially to be mentioned are Domingo de Bañez, Tomás de Mercado, Francisco García and Luís de Molina, but I am far from wishing to defend this selection as definitive. My only reason for omitting the Jesuit, Diego Lainez, for example, is the trivial one that his writings circulated in manuscript and were not printed until 1886. Many other writers of the period, whose work has been forgotten, would repay study.

The Dominican Domingo de Bañez (1527–1604), who for some years taught theology at Salamanca, is remembered as the friend and confessor of St Theresa. His doctrine of grace was opposed by Molina, and a polemic ensued which troubled the whole cultural and religious life of Spain during the closing years of the sixteenth century. The pope finally imposed silence on the contending parties, but the writings of Bañez and Molina passed into Belgium and France, bearing with them the seeds of Jansenism. In his commentary on St Thomas Bañez closely follows the plan of the *Summa*, which he discusses question by question and article by article, demonstrating yet again how firmly the teaching of the School of Salamanca remained anchored in that of the 'Angelic Doctor'.[40]

We have already had occasion to glance at the work of Tomás de Mercado. Little is known of his life, except that he was born in Seville, went as a young man to Mexico, where he entered the Dominican Order, spent some years at Salamanca and in Seville, and died at sea while on his way back to Mexico. In the course of his travels, and in Seville, Mercado acquired a thorough knowledge of the business practice of the day. His handbook of moral guidance for merchants, based on the doctrines of the leading theologians, stands out as a model of penetrating observation and realistic counsel, expressed in a pithy and often humorous style. Mercado is frequently cited by later writers.[41]

Francisco García was a Dominican, born in Valencia and professor of sacred theology at Tarragona. In his little treatise of popularisation García explains the ideas of the Doctors in a clear, thoughtful and sometimes original manner, referring frequently to the business customs of his day.[42]

The Jesuit Luís de Molina (1535–1601) was not only a theologian of great repute and authority but also an excellent civil lawyer. His treatise on commutative justice provides a wealth of information on every branch of contemporary economic life.[43]

Among the numerous younger men who continued in the tradition of the School of Salamanca may be mentioned the Augustinian friar Miguel Salón (1538–1620), and the Jesuits Juan de Salas (1553–1612) and Francisco Suárez (1548–1617).

Miguel Salón, as his name suggests, came of a New Christian family. He was born and died in Valencia, and in his treatise on commutative justice gives much curious information about the commercial life of that city.[44]

Juan de Salas taught at Salamanca. His commentary on St Thomas is divided into five parts, which treat of buying and selling, usury, rent-charges, exchange-transactions and gambling. Sala's work is detailed but lucid, and he lightens our task by placing at the head of each section of his work a bibliography of the subject he is about to discuss.[45]

Francisco Suárez was a celebrated theologian and jurist who taught successively at Segovia, Rome, Alcalá, Salamanca and Coimbra. In Rome Suárez was the teacher of Leonard Lessius, the Belgian theologian who closely followed the doctrines of the School of Salamanca and helped to propagate them in the Netherlands. Suárez's writings exercised a marked influence on Grotius and Pufendorf. His importance for us lies more in his eminence as a theologian than in any novelty that may be shown in his economic doctrine.[46]

The Jesuit cardinal Juan de Lugo (1583–1660) was the last great Spanish follower of the School of Salamanca,[47] whose doctrine may thus be said to have flourished in full vigour for some hundred and twenty years. By the middle of the seventeenth century this vigour was almost spent, and the Indian summer of scholasticism had begun to pass away. True, the second half of the seventeenth century still yields the names of many Spanish theologians. But few of them are much more distinguished than that of Antonio de Escobar (1589–1669), author of a popular handbook for confessors that served as a target for Pascal's wit and endowed the French language with a new word, *escobarderie*, to denote what were generally held to be the quibblings of the casuists.[48]

We shall later see in some detail that the economic teaching of the School of Salamanca had, by the middle of the seventeenth century, passed far beyond the confines of moral theology. Embodied in treatises of natural law and of the law of nations, as well as in the writings of political economists, it had, well before the death of scholasticism, become part of the common cultural heritage. For the present, however, let us examine some of the ways in which the Spanish late scholastics modified and developed medieval economic doctrine.

Theory of Value

The Spanish Doctors made a useful contribution to the progress of value-theory. In their doctrine of the Just Price they consolidated and popularised the advances made by their predecessors, tested accepted theory against contemporary events and transmitted to later economists a more complete and better elaborated theory of value.

We have seen that by the end of the fifteenth century it was generally accepted that the value or price[49] of a thing was justly to be assessed according to the abundance or scarcity of the object in question and its suitability for serving man's needs. It was also held that value is not to be measured by the need or demand of a single individual but by that of the community as a whole. The 'common estimation' or market assessment of value was thus the chief determinant of the just price. Labour and costs were also allowed to play some part in the determination of value.

We may begin our account of the theory of value held by the Spanish scholastics by glancing at the teaching of Francisco de Vitoria, founder of the School of Salamanca. Our information is drawn from the lecture-notes of a course of lectures given by Vitoria at Salamanca between 1534 and 1537.[50]

Vitoria's theory of value was based on the principles I have just summarised. He considers two main classes of goods: those whose price is fixed by the State; and, those whose price is not so fixed.

Vitoria has not much to say about the value of things whose price is fixed by the State. Like the generality of the moralists and jurists who preceded him, he assumes that the legal price is also the just price, and as such to be upheld.

On the subject of things whose price is not fixed by the State, however, Vitoria would seem to depart some way from traditional doctrine. He makes a careful distinction between things that are necessary for human life and things that are not. In the case of necessities, the just price is the market price, which reflects the 'common estimation' based on utility, supply-and-demand and so on, without regard to cost of production. But it sometimes happens that a thing has no market value; as, for example, 'in the case of wheat which in time of dearth has come into the hands of one or a few sellers'. In this situation the price must be settled between the parties themselves, and cost of production may be taken into account. Vitoria adds that luxuries, such as lutes or precious stones, may be sold for what we should call a 'fancy price', because the buyer is under no compulsion to pay the high price demanded, and does so of his own free will.

Thus Vitoria accepts, in principle, the law of supply and demand as the main determinant of price, but only in conditions of perfect competition.[51]

A neat discussion of value is included by Juan de Medina in his treatise. If, he says, a new kind of merchandise is brought into a place, and there is no law to determine its price, then we should consider the factors proceeding from (a) the vendor, (b) the purchaser and (c) the thing itself. Under (a) we include costs, labour, care, industry and risk; under (b) the need felt for the good, the fewer or greater number of prospective buyers, and *complacibilitas* or taste; and under (c) the rarity or commonness of the thing, its fertility, the advantages it offers its owner and its condition.[52]

An extreme form of utility theory was expounded by Saravia de la Calle, who does not adopt Vitoria's distinction between luxuries and necessities: 'In order to determine the just price we need only consider these three things: abundance or scarcity of goods, merchants and money – of things that people want to barter or exchange for money. This doctrine is founded on Aristotle's dictum, *pretium rei humana indigentia mensurat*, "the price of things is measured by human need".'[53]

Saravia denies, and with considerable vehemence, that cost of production can play any part in the determination of price. Like his medieval predecessors, he views the poor man not as producer but as consumer, and clearly fears that any relaxation of this tenet will give merchants an excuse for raising prices on the pretext of recouping their expenses:

> Those who measure the just price by the labour, costs, and risk incurred by the person who deals in the merchandise or produces it, or by the cost of transport or the expense of travelling to and from the fair, or by what he has to pay the factors for their industry, risk and labour, are greatly in error, and still more so are those who allow a certain profit of a fifth or a tenth. For the just price arises from the abundance or scarcity of goods, merchants, and money, as has been said, and not from costs, labour, and risk. If we had to consider labour and risk in order to assess the just price, no merchant would ever suffer loss, nor would abundance or scarcity of goods and money enter into the question.

The same view is expressed by Covarrubias:

> The value of an article does not depend on its essential nature but on the estimation of men, even if that estimation be foolish. Thus, in the Indies wheat is dearer than in Spain because men esteem it more highly, though the nature of the wheat is the same in both places.[54]

In assessing the just price, Covarrubias continues, we are not to consider how much the article originally cost, nor the labour its acquisition cost the vendor, but only its common market-value in the place where it is sold. Prices fall when buyers are few and goods and vendors many, and rise when the contrary conditions prevail.

A modified version of the same utility-theory of value was held by Domingo de Soto:

> The price of goods is not determined by their nature but by the measure in which they serve the needs of mankind . . . Aristotle says that want is the cause and measure of human commerce. If no one needed the goods or labour of his fellows, men would cease to exchange their products. We have to admit, then, that want is the basis of price.[55]

Soto, however, differs from Vitoria, Saravia and Covarrubias in holding that, although the demand that exists for the article in question, and its abundance or scarcity, are the first things to be considered in the assessment of price, we have also to bear in mind the 'labour, trouble, and risk' that the transaction involves.

Much the same ideas on value and price are expressed in most of the late scholastic treatises that I have read. Some authors deny that the cost of production should be allowed any part in the determination of price, others allow that it may be taken into account, but it is generally agreed that the most important factors to be considered in assessing the 'natural' or uncontrolled price of a commodity are the 'estimation' in which that commodity is commonly held (such estimation reflecting the utility of the thing in question), and the forces of supply and demand.

As time went on, this predominantly subjective theory of the Just Price was elaborated a little further. Francisco García, for instance, analyses the concept of utility rather more deeply. He suggests that a thing may be used in a way that is necessary for the preservation of human life, for pleasure, as an adornment, or to delight our curiosity, and also that the utility or value of a thing may vary because (1) one object may have many uses and serve more purposes than another, (2) it may render a more important service than another and (3) it may perform a given service better than another.[56]

A little-known author, Bartolomé de Albornoz, develops these concepts at length, and tells the story of King Tarquin and the Sibylline books to illustrate the principle that price, as the expression of estimation, increases with rarity.[57]

Coming into the seventeenth century we find our scholastic doctrine of the Just Price continuing to flourish in the work of the Spanish theologians. Juan de Salas, professor of theology at Salamanca, whose treatise on contracts appeared in 1617, remarks that the price of goods depends on their utility. The price will vary according to the abundance or scarcity of the goods and money, the newness or antiquity of the goods, 'the common utility of the article and the need felt for it', and the manner of sale (whether wholesale, retail, in bulk or by auction). Salas adds that 'goods sold in the warehouse are cheap, because this mode of sale indicates abundance of goods and scarcity of buyers and money, and suggests that the articles possess only slight utility for the vendor'.[58]

Juan de Lugo, a learned and influential Jesuit theologian, whose treatise *De justitia et jure*, published in 1642, was reprinted several times during the seventeenth, eighteenth and nineteenth centuries, observes that price fluctuates

not because of the intrinsic and substantial perfection of the articles – since mice are more perfect than corn, and yet are worth less – but on account of their utility in respect of human need, and then only on account of estimation; for jewels are much less useful than corn in the house, and yet their price is much higher. And we must take into account not only the estimation of prudent men, but also that of the imprudent, if they are sufficiently numerous in a place. This is why our glass trinkets are in Ethiopia justly exchanged for gold, because they are commonly more esteemed there. And among the Japanese old objects made of iron and pottery, which are worth nothing to us, fetch a high price because of their antiquity. Communal estimation, even when foolish, raises the natural price of goods, since price is derived from estimation. The natural price is raised by abundance of buyers and money, and lowered by the contrary factors.[59]

There are exceptions to every rule. The celebrated jurist, theologian, philosopher and classical scholar, Pedro de Valencia, took a different view. In his *Discourse on the Price of Wheat* (1605) he defends the *tasa* or fixed maximum price on wheat, which he suggests should be assessed in terms of labour rather than money. We should consider only how many working days ought in justice to be paid for a measure of wheat, allowing the labourer sufficient for his needs, and calculate the price accordingly.[60]

Money, Banking and Foreign Exchange
Our Spanish Doctors form an important link in the long chain of economists who have handed down Aristotle's doctrine of the origin and functions of money. The idea of money as a medium of exchange, measure of value and store of value (or, as it was put, a 'guarantor against future need') reappears constantly throughout their work.

We have seen that in the course of the Middle Ages some attempt was made to bring goods and money under a single theory of value. Though in general the medieval writers were metallists, the utility of money was occasionally mentioned, and a supply-and-demand theory of value was applied, by Cajetan at least, to money as well as goods.

We have also noted that the more interesting statements about the value of money occur in the discussion of exchange-transactions. The exchange-banker's use of money in order to make a profit was, by the end of the Middle Ages, generally acknowledged to be legitimate, even though it could not easily be reconciled with Aristotle's doctrine of the functions of money, and still less with his explicit disapproval of money-making for its own sake. The matter was summed up by Azpilcueta as follows:

Now, Aristotle disapproved of this art of exchange and of trading in money: it seemed to him to be both unnatural and unprofitable to the republic, and to have no end other than gain, which is an end without end. St Thomas, too, condemned all business whose main object is gain for gain's sake. But even St Thomas allows that the merchant's trade is lawful, so long as he undertakes it for a moderate profit in order to maintain himself and his family. After all, the art of exchange benefits the republic to some extent. I myself hold it to be lawful, provided it is conducted as it should be, in order to earn a moderate living.

Nor is it true that to use money by changing it at a profit is against nature. Although that is not the first and principal use for which money was invented, it is none the less an important secondary use. To deal in shoes for profit is not the chief use for which they were invented, which is to protect our feet: but that is not to say that to trade in shoes is against nature.[61]

If, then, money may be bought and sold like any other commodity, how is its just price to be assessed? We have seen that the greatest advance in medieval monetary theory had been made in the attempt solve this problem, and have followed the process by which the utility concept of value, derived from Aristotle and elaborated in discussions of the Just Price, eventually came to be used, though as yet tentatively, in order to modify the taboo on usury inherited from the Mosaic law and converted by the Church into the complex usury-doctrine of the later Middle Ages. This tendency to harmonise the theory of the Just Price with usury-doctrine, and to bring both goods and money under the governance of a single theory of value, was continued and confirmed by our Spanish Doctors.

In 1553 Domingo de Soto applied the teaching of St Antonino, Cajetan and other earlier writers to contemporary conditions in Spain, observing that

The more plentiful money is in Medina the more unfavourable are the terms of exchange, and the higher the price that must be paid by whoever wishes to send money from Spain to Flanders, since the demand for money is smaller in Spain than in Flanders. And the scarcer money is in Medina the less he need pay there, because more people want money in Medina than are sending it to Flanders.

Just as one measure of wheat delivered in a place where the price of wheat is high may lawfully be exchanged for two in a place where it is low, so will it be with money.

It is lawful to exchange money in one place for money in another, having regard to its scarcity in the one and abundance in the other, and to receive a smaller sum in a place where money is scarce in exchange for a larger where it is abundant.[62]

When the two sums are exchanged by reason of a divergence in place, not time, the transaction is not a loan but 'the true exchange of two things present that are of equal value'.

Soto was among the first scholastic writers to describe and approve the credit creation of the banks. It is customary, he says, 'that if a merchant deposits cash with a bank, the bank will guarantee to repay a larger sum. If I deliver 10,000 to the banker, he will repay me 12 or perhaps 15 thousand, because it is very profitable for a banker to have cash available. There is no evil in this.'[63]

In 1556 Azpilcueta de Navarro makes two notable advances in a single passage of his commentary on *Naviganti*. Discussing the 'exchanges' he improves on Cajetan and Soto by basing the value of money not merely on its abundance or scarcity but, more specifically, on its purchasing-power. Furthermore, he makes the first clear and definite statement of the quantity theory of money that is known to us. Supporting the commonly held view that the value of money, like that of goods, varies according to supply and demand, Azpilcueta argues that

other things being equal, in countries where there is a great scarcity of money, all other saleable goods, and even the hands and labour of men, are given for less money than where it is abundant. Thus we see by experience that in France, where money is scarcer than in Spain, bread, wine, cloth and labour are worth much less. And even in Spain, in times when money was scarcer, saleable goods and labour were given for very much less than after the discovery of the Indies, which flooded the country with gold and silver. The reason for this is that money is worth more where and when it is scarce than where and when it is abundant. What some men say, that a scarcity of money brings down other things, arises from the fact that its excessive rise [in value] makes other things seem lower, just as a short man standing beside a very tall one looks shorter than when he is beside a man of his own height.[64]

According to Azpilcueta, it is licit to pay a larger sum in a country where the purchasing-power of money is small in exchange for a smaller sum payable in another country where the purchasing-power of money is greater. Or, to put the matter in the language of the Bullion Report of 1810:

In the event of the prices of commodities being raised in one country by an augmentation of its circulating medium, while no similar augmentation in the circulating medium of the neighbouring countries has led to a similar rise in prices, the currencies of the two countries will no longer continue to bear the same relative value to each other as before. The exchange will be computed between these two countries to the disadvantage of the former.

Tomás de Mercado, like Soto, bases 'modern exchange transactions' on 'the diversity in the estimation of money', brought about by the forces of supply and demand.[65] Mercado's chief concern was to distinguish between *estimación* and the value or tale of the money in question:

> The third reason that is regarded as the foundation of the exchanges is the diversity that exists in the estimation of money. And in order to understand it (for it is a very weighty reason) we must realise that the value and price of money are not the same thing as its estimation. A clear proof of this is that in the Indies money is worth the same as here; that is to say, a *real* is worth 34 *maravedis*. A *peso* is worth 13 *reales*, and its price is the same in Spain, but although the value and price are the same the estimation is very different in the two places. For money is esteemed much less in the Indies than in Spain. The quality and disposition of the country engender in the hearts of all who enter it so generous a temper that they esteem a dozen *reales* of no greater value than a dozen *maravedis* here.[66]

Our early purchasing-power theory was stated unequivocally by other Spanish Doctors. Thus, in 1594, Domingo de Bañez concluded that:

> in places where money is scarce, saleable goods will be cheaper than in those where the whole mass of money is bigger, and therefore it is lawful to exchange a smaller sum in one country for a larger sum in another. The conclusion is clear. Since the primary end for which money was ordained is the purchase of goods, it follows that wherever money is more highly esteemed for this purpose it may be exchanged for a larger sum than where it is less so. . . .[67]

Molina, who frequently cites Mercado, says that there are two ways in which money may be worth more in one place than in another. The first is when law or custom attributes different values to the money. The second is when money is more abundant in one place than in another. All else being equal, wherever money is more abundant, there will it be worth less in comparison with other things. Just as an abundance of goods causes their price to fall when the quantity of money in the market does not vary, so does abundance of money cause money to fall in value. Molina adds that this is the reason for the rise in prices in Spain, which, he says, at the time when he wrote were three times as high as they had been eighty years before.[68]

Using the term 'extrinsic value' instead of 'estimation', Juan de Lugo in 1642 explained the purchasing-power theory as follows:

It is to be noted with Lessius, Molina, and Salas, that the excess of this unequal value which money has in different places is not derived only from the higher intrinsic value of money, proceeding from its superior metal content of higher legal tale, but may also be caused by diversity in its extrinsic value. Thus, in the place to which the money is sent there may be a general scarcity of money, or more people may require it, or there may be better opportunities for doing business with it and making a profit. And, since money will there be more useful for satisfying human needs, more goods will be bought than elsewhere with the same sum of money, and therefore money will rightly be regarded as more valuable in that place.[69]

The Quantity Theory of Money

Let us revert to the passage we have quoted above, in which Azpilcueta Navarro, writing in 1556, first traced a necessary connection between the price level and the quantity of gold and silver in circulation.

The foundations of the quantity theory had been laid by medieval writers. But Azpilcueta brought the theory to life, observing at first hand how prices and wages had risen in Spain as a result of the imports of American gold and silver. Thus, the influence of American treasure on the European price level was first noted, as might be expected, in Spain, where it was first felt. The effect of American treasure on prices was again observed by Jean Bodin in 1568, and by the editor of John Hales in 1581.[70] By that time our primitive form of quantity theory had become a commonplace. Richard Carewe, writing towards the end of the sixteenth century (his *Survey* was finished in 1602 but had been long in hand), remarks that the increase of prices in his day was largely due to the influx of precious metals from America.[71]

Were Azpilcueta and later authors right in holding that the Spanish inflation of the sixteenth century was caused by the import of precious metals from the New World?

In 1934 Professor Earl J. Hamilton collected much information on American treasure and Spanish prices, and concluded that 'the extremely close correlation between the increase in the volume of treasure imports and the advance of commodity prices throughout the sixteenth century, particularly from 1535 on, demonstrates beyond question that the "abundant mines of America" were the principal cause of the Price Revolution in Spain'.[72]

Hamilton's results were generally accepted at the time, but in more recent years various objections have been made to his thesis. It has been shown that Spanish prices in fact increased more sharply in the first half of the sixteenth century, whereas silver imports reached their peak between 1580 and 1630: and there are other gaps in Hamilton's price figures. On the treasure side of the equation, although we know the quantity of precious metal that arrived at Seville, we cannot tell how much of it entered the Spanish economy and how much passed immediately to other countries.

These arguments are not, I think, sufficiently conclusive to disprove Hamilton's views, or those of Azpilcueta, Bodin, the editor of Hales, Carewe, and other contemporary witnesses whose evidence supports Hamilton. It is probable that the influx of American treasure was the principal but not the sole cause of the price-revolution in Spain. 'Real' factors must also have played their part. These additional forces were clearly described by the Spanish political economists, whose views on the inflation of the sixteenth century and the economic decay of the seventeenth we shall examine in our final chapter.

THE SURVIVAL OF THE SCHOLASTIC DOCTRINE OF VALUE

One of the notable features of the work of our Spanish Doctors was the adoption and development of a theory of value inherited from earlier writers and based on the concepts of utility and scarcity. We have already seen something of this subjective theory of value, and I should like to conclude this chapter by showing how it was transmitted from writer to writer during the later seventeenth and eighteenth centuries.

Italy

In Italy, as in Spain, scholasticism continued to flourish until well on into the eighteenth century. Among the numerous treatises of moral theology that appeared at this later period we may mention those of Pietro Catalano,[73] Martino Bonacina,[74] Antonino Diana,[75] Giambattista de Luca[76] and Clemente Piselli.[77] In these and other works we find frequent references to the Spanish Doctors, whose teaching is passed on with little modification.

Non-scholastic works on political and economic subjects had begun to be written at the beginning of the sixteenth century, and as time went on they appeared in increasing numbers. The authors of such books had received a scholastic education, and the ideas they imbibed at the universities were reflected in their work. But they had also learned how to present traditional doctrine in a new and attractive form. It was no longer the fashion to arrange one's treatise in the form of a long chain of scholastic disputations, probably written in highly technical Latin and rendered still more abstruse by the employment of an elaborate code of references and abbreviations that could be understood only by experts. On the contrary, there was a vogue for freely composed works, meant to entertain as well as instruct, in which the scholastic form and apparatus were discarded while the doctrines themselves suffered no sudden modification.

A good example of such a composition is Davanzati's *Lezione delle Monete* (1588). Davanzati simply presents, yet again, the Platonic and Aristotelian account of the origin and functions of money, develops the scholastic theory of value based on utility and scarcity, and condemns debasement of the currency. Yet he does so in so delightful and winning a manner, and with such a wealth of adornment and illustration, that these well-worn ideas strike us as charming novelties.[78]

We have seen that the famous 'paradox of value' – the observation that many useful commodities such as water have a low exchange-value, or none, whereas others less useful such as diamonds have a high one – had been glimpsed by Aristotle and stated in many scholastic treatises, from the time of St Antonino onwards. Davanzati allots the 'paradox' some paragraphs of his *Lezione*, and resolves it in the traditional way by appealing to the concept of scarcity.

It was left, however, to a philosopher of the Enlightenment, the Abbé Galiani (1728-87), to carry the utility theory of value to the highest point of development that it reached before the time of Jevons and Menger. After remarking that 'it is evident that air and water, which are elements most useful for human life, have no value whatsoever, because they are not scarce; and that a bag of sand from the shores of Japan may well be rare, but, since it is of no particular use, it would have no value,'[79] Galiani goes on to define the term 'scarcity' as 'the proportion that exists between the quantity of a thing and the use that is made of it'. He thus treats utility and scarcity as the two faces of a single coin.

In pointing out the interrelation between utility and scarcity Galiani was, so far as I know, original. But in some respects he owed much to his scholastic predecessors and contemporaries. Galiani often refers to Aristotle, 'the Aristotelians', 'the corpus of moralists and juriconsults', 'the scholastics' and 'many theologians', but names only Covarrubias, passing on immediately to such non-scholastic authors as

Davanzati, Locke and Petty. This does not mean that he was less well read in scholastic literature than he claims to be. On usury and the exchanges he closely follows scholastic doctrine, employing the accepted technical terms (*mutuum, cambium minutum, cambium per litteras, cambium siccun*, and so on). It is probable, if not certain, that he drew his basic theory of value from the same source. This supposition is in no way weakened by the fact that Galiani, after expounding a subjective theory of value based on utility and scarcity, suddenly declares that *fatica* (labour) is the element that gives value to things. We have already noted that in the writings of the scholastics it is by no means unusual to find a psychological theory of value running side by side with some form of labour theory.

Many such glimpses of scholastic doctrine may be gleaned from the work of the numerous other Italian writers who so brilliantly advanced the progress of economic theory in the seventeenth and eighteenth centuries. An outstanding example is Cesare Bonesana, Marchese de Beccaria, who adopts a markedly subjective theory of value that centres on utility and scarcity.[80]

France

The reign of scholasticism came to an end rather sooner in France than in Italy. As early as 1546 Charles du Moulin had impugned the prohibition of usury, advocating the toleration of a moderate rate of interest and poking fun at the jargon and oversubtle distinctions of the Doctors. But his boldness was premature, and shocking to both Catholics and Calvinists.

By the second half of the seventeenth century the climate of opinion was changing. Few writers now cared to put up a vigorous defence of the Church's traditional usury doctrine, though one or two paid it lip-service.[81] Among the handbooks for confessors popular in France was that of the Spanish Jesuit, Antonio de Escobar, based on the teaching of the School of Salamanca.[82] Escobar's laxness on the subject of usury and dubious contracts, especially the *mohatra*, was severely castigated by Pascal in the eighth of his *Provincial Letters*. The scholastic theory of value is faithfully reproduced by Escobar, according to whom the natural price of a thing depends on the estimation of men, taking into account the scarcity or plenty of goods, buyers, sellers and money, the utility of the article in question, the manner of sale, and the labour and expenses of merchants.

As the eighteenth century wore on, the ecclesiastical doctrine of usury fell more and more into disrepute. The subjective theory of value that had been forged in the medieval discussions of the Just Price survived, however, in France as in Italy. True, the *philosophes* refer to the

Doctors with contempt, but their own *Encyclopédie* frequently echoes scholastic doctrine: as, for example, in its distinction between the legal price (*prix légitime*, set by ordinance) and the market price or *prix courant*, set by common estimation, and also in its treatment of monopoly and dry exchange.

The value-theory of Condillac and Turgot is strongly reminiscent of the teaching of the School of Salamanca and other late scholastics. The two French writers agree in minimising the effects of cost-of-production on price, and hold that value is determined primarily by the need felt for the article in question, and by its utility and rarity. The medieval concept of 'common estimation' is reflected in Turgot's doctrine that price is the expression of '*valeur appréciative*', which is the *valeur estimative moyenne* arrived at by comparing the subjective value of the article in the minds of the various individuals who make up the market. Goods and money are treated from the same subjective standpoint, the foreign exchanges being held to reflect the relative utility of money in the various countries.[83]

Yet another link between the late scholastics and the economics of *laissez-faire* is formed by the value-theory of François Quesnay, leader of the physiocratic school of economists that flourished between 1750 and 1770. Quesnay's theory of value is not easy to track down and is sometimes contradictory. The clearest statement of a utility theory of value that I have found in his work is contained in the article 'Hommes' which he wrote for the *Encyclopédie* in 1757 but which was not published until 1908.[84] In this article we find the scholastic distinction between value-in-use (which Quesnay calls *valeur usuelle*) and value-in-exchange (*valeur vénale*), the 'paradox of value' (Quesnay follows tradition by using diamonds as his example, but, by way of novelty, contrasts their value with that of food instead of water), and the traditional insistence upon rarity as the chief determinant of price, all concepts that were to reappear in the work of Quesnay's friend and admirer, Adam Smith.

The value-theory of Condillac, Turgot and other French authors led up to the more sophisticated utility-theory of Jean-Baptiste Say (1767-1832). Say regarded himself as a faithful disciple of Adam Smith and as his interpreter in France. Yet, so far as the pivotal concept of value was concerned, Say turned away from Smith's labour-theory (the work of Ricardo, the continuator of the labour-theory of value, had not been published when Say's *Traité d'Economie politique* appeared in 1803) and, starting from Condillac's principle that value depended on utility and scarcity, established a subjective theory of value that was retained by all the important French economists of the nineteenth century, and that awaited only the more systematic treatment of the concept of diminishing utility to culminate in the marginal-utility analysis of modern economics.

Belgium and Holland

The leading exponent of 'Salamancan' economic doctrine in Belgium was the Jesuit theologian Leonard Lessius (1554–1623). Lessius completed his studies in Rome, where Suárez was among his teachers, and taught for many years at the University of Louvain. He was especially celebrated for his expert knowledge of commercial practice and was often consulted by the merchants of Antwerp on problems of business morality, just as their forefathers had appealed to Vitoria and the Doctors of Paris some eighty years before.

Lessius was the author of a treatise *De justitia et jure* which appeared in 1605 and ran through nearly forty editions published in Antwerp, Louvain, Lyons, Paris and Venice.[85] In Book 2 of this work, Lessius closely follows, and frequently quotes, Domingo de Soto, Diego de Covarrubias, Martín de Azpilcueta, Luís de Molina and other Spanish Doctors, as well as earlier authors such as Sylvester, Cajetan and St Antonino.

Lessius has recently found a warm admirer in Professor B. Gordon, who regards him as 'a master of scholastic economic analysis' and 'certainly the foremost continuator of the Spanish school of economic thought', adding that Lessius used the conclusions of his Spanish predecessors 'as points of departure for further extensions of their work and for new directions of his own'.[86]

The scholastic theory of value emerges clearly in the thought of Lessius. Particularly penetrating is his discussion of exchange-business on the Antwerp bourse, a feature of commercial life with which he was thoroughly familiar. On questions of commercial morality Lessius inclines to leniency and gives us the impression that he wishes to remove such doctrinal obstacles as continued to hamper trade. Like other leading Catholic theologians of his day, Lessius defended the basic principles of the usury doctrine while making concessions to current practice.

From the beginning of the seventeenth century onwards we find the scholastic theory of value appearing in the work of Protestant as well as Catholic authors. The Spanish writers on the Law of Nations had included a chapter on commercial contracts in their treatises, because of the universal nature of international trade. In their discussion of price they had reproduced the accepted view that value rests on utility and scarcity, a doctrine that was taken over without question by their Protestant successors and that forms, perhaps, the most important and lasting of the scholastic contributions to economic history.

The Dutch jurist Hugo Grotius (1583–1645) includes a section on commercial contracts in his principal work on the law of nations which owes much to the Spanish theologians and jurists.[87] Grotius quotes Aristotle's dictum that the natural measure of a thing's value is the need felt for it. Yet, he adds, utility is not the only measure of value, for sometimes the most necessary things are worth little owing to their abundance. The common estimation in which a thing is held, the labour and expenses of merchants, and the abundance or scarcity of buyers, all affect prices. The value of money similarly varies according to its abundance or scarcity.[88]

Germany and Scandinavia
Our subjective theory of value, which Grotius had briefly touched upon, was more firmly established in Protestant economic thought by Grotius's most distinguished follower, the German jurist Samuel von Pufendorf (1632–94).

Pufendorf was the son of a Lutheran pastor. He was sent to study theology at Leipzig but turned instead to law. On completing his education he became a tutor in the family of the King of Sweden's envoy at Copenhagen. He went on to occupy the chair of international law at Heidelberg and afterwards at Lund, and served first the King of Sweden and later the Elector of Brandenburg as official historian. Pufendorf wrote many learned works, including several on the law of nations in which he discusses the subject of price and value.[89] During the last years of his life Pufendorf returned to the study of theology with which he had begun his career as a scholar.

Pufendorf was always emphatic in his profession of Lutheranism and seldom appealed to the views of Catholic authors. He occasionally quotes Suárez, and once at least Covarrubias, and he shows some knowledge of the Spanish historians of the Indies. When we consider Pufendorf's aloof attitude towards Roman Catholic authors, and more especially the theologians, we must remember that not only was he a convinced Lutheran himself but that he also depended on the favour of Protestant princes. The late scholastics still flourished in Catholic countries during Pufendorf's lifetime, and found little sympathy in Protestant circles.

Pufendorf conceives price as the expression of the value of the thing to which the contract refers. Proceeding on Aristotelian lines he quotes Grotius to the effect that 'the most natural measure of the value of each thing is the need for it'. Things are valuable in so far as they help to preserve human life or to render it more pleasurable. Yet want is not the sole foundation of price. A thing cannot have a price unless it is rare as well as useful. No price can be set upon some things –

the warm light of the sun, for instance, pure and wholesome air, or wind and shade – which are nevertheless of great use to mankind.

According to Pufendorf, a thing is commonly estimated at whatever price it will fetch, and this price may justifiably fluctuate within reasonable limits, unless it is fixed by law. In determining the 'common' or uncontrolled price of a thing, we should also consider the labour and expenditure of the merchant, the cost of transport, the mode of sale (whether wholesale, retail or by auction) and the abundance or scarcity of purchasers, money and goods.

For Pufendorf the value of money is governed by the same laws as that of goods. Money derives its value from its metal content and from its tale, but

> that increase or decrease which other things undergo because of scarcity or abundance, money itself does not entirely escape, as a coin made of the same material and with the same weight is worth now more and now less, although that variation is not as sudden or as frequent as the variations of value among other things.

Thus, in the work of Pufendorf the subjective or utility theory of value inherited from the scholastics was preserved intact, greatly though he may have differed from the Catholic Doctors in other respects. Pufendorf's writings were translated into the principal European languages soon after their publication and remained for long the standard textbooks on the law of nations. They constitute an important link between the scholastic theory of value and the utility-theory of a later day.

England

In England the survival of the utility theory of value seems to have taken a fitful course. The most influential economist of the seventeenth century, Sir William Petty (1623–87), regards labour as the chief source and measure of value, a proposition he elaborates in several notable passages.

The value-theory of John Locke (1632–1704) is less easy to define. In one of his works, in the course of a discussion on the origin of private property, Locke follows Petty in regarding labour as the main source of value. Men, he says, justly acquired property, in the first place, by mingling their labour with the gifts of nature.[90] But in another of his writings Locke takes over the scholastic theory of value inherited from Aristotle, the scholastics and Grotius:

> The Intrinsick Natural worth of any Thing consists in this, that it is

apt to be serviceable to the Necessities or Conveniences of human life, and it is naturally more worth, as the Necessity or Conveniency it supplies is greater[91]

although

the Being of any good and useful quality in any thing, neither increases its Price, nor indeed makes it have any Price at all, buy only as it lessens its quantity or increases its vent, each of these in proportion to one another.[92]

What more useful things, continues Locke, are there than air and water? Yet these generally have no price at all. As soon as water becomes scarce, however, it does have a price, and is sometimes sold dearer than wine.

John Law (1671–1729) was recognised by L. Mises as a forerunner of the Austrian school on account of his subjective theory of value, which he applied to money as well as goods.[93] Law brings forward yet again, our old paradox of value:

Goods have a value from the Uses they are apply'd to; and their Value is Greater or Lesser, not so much from their more or less valuable, or necessary Uses; as from the greater or lesser Quantity of them in proportion to the Demand for them. *Example.* Water is of great use, yet of little value; because the Quantity of Water is much greater than the demand for it. Diamonds are of little use, yet of great Value, because the Demand for Diamonds is much greater than the Quantity of them.[94]

Francis Hutcheson (1694–1746) – the 'never-to-be-forgotten Dr Hutcheson', as his pupil, Adam Smith called him – is unlikely to need any introduction to readers of this book. As professor of moral philosophy at Glasgow, Hutcheson lectured on natural theology, natural ethics, natural jurisprudence and civil policy. The course roughly covered the social sciences as they had been bequeathed by the scholastic Doctors and the philosophers of natural law, standing in contrast to natural philosophy, which covered the physical sciences and mathematics.

Hutcheson's *Introduction to Moral Philosophy* (first published in 1747) preserves to a large extent the contents and arrangement of the old treatises *de justitia et jure*. In the customary chapter on value, Hutcheson duly reproduces the doctrine of the scholastics and the philosophers of natural law: 'The ground of all price must be some *fitness* in the things to yield some use or pleasure in life; without this, they can be of no value. But this being presupposed, the prices of things will be in a compound proportion of the *demand* for them, and the *difficulty* in acquiring them.'

This 'difficulty', according to Hutcheson, may be occasioned in many ways: if the things are rare, if much labour is required in their production or 'a more elegant genius in the artist', or if those employed in their manufacture are 'men in high account', accustomed to live 'in a more splendid manner, for the expense of this must be defrayed by the higher profits of their labours'. Some things of the highest utility, such as air and light, yet have no price, or only a very small one. This is because nature has provided them in plenty, and we may have them almost without labour.[95]

Discussing the 'standard' or measure of value. Hutcheson notes that money is not perfectly satisfactory for the purpose, since its own value may vary from time to time. Salaries, he thinks, might more justly be fixed in 'so many days' labour of men' or in some common product of labour, such as a certain quantity of grain.[96]

We have here an anticipatory glimpse of Adam Smith's doctrine that labour 'is the only universal, as well as the only accurate measure of value, or the only standard by which we can compare the values of different commodities at all times and at all places'.[97] And labour is not only the best possible measure of value. Wages, or the amount of labour that a thing has cost to produce, together with rent and profit, are the factors that make up the 'natural price' of that thing. The natural price, however, does not necessarily coincide with the market price, which is regulated by supply and demand.

In thus diverging from the old utility theory of value, Hutcheson and Smith indicated the path that was to be more firmly trodden by Ricardo and Marx. Yet Smith did not altogether discard the concept of utility, and, in making his famous distinction between value-in-use and value-in-exchange, took care to hand on the ancient 'paradox of value', using the time-honoured examples of water and diamonds.

The predominantly subjective or utility theory of value held by the Doctors was thus preserved and transmitted through many channels. It is not too much to say that from the rediscovery of Aristotle until modern times utility-theory has developed continuously, even the prestige of the English classical economists, and of Marx, being insufficient to submerge it completely. From the middle of the sixteenth century to the end of the seventeenth, the Spanish late scholastics played a leading part in this work of transmission and development.

NOTES

1 There are several lists of scholastic writers, including Spanish authors, whose work offers a more or less developed body of economic thought. For our purpose the two most helpful are R. de Roover, *L'Évolution de la lettre de change* (Paris, 1953), pp. 170-219; and D. Iparraguirre, 'Las fuentes del pensamiento económico en España en los siglos XIII al XVI', *Estudios de Deusto*, 2ª epoca, Vol. 2, No. 3, 1954 (Bilbao).

De Roover lists authors of all nationalities who are notable for their discussions of exchange-business. Since many of them also wrote on other economic problems, de Roover's bibliography is of wider interest than appears at first sight. Iparraguirre lists Spanish authors only, but includes writers who covered a considerable range of subjects. The two bibliographies therefore supplement one another usefully. From them may be gleaned about fifty names of Spanish scholastic writers who are, or who may be expected to be, of interest to the historian of economic doctrine. Most belong to the sixteenth or seventeenth centuries, and many expounded and developed the teaching of the School of Salamanca.

A valuable supplementary list of Spanish moralists of the sixteenth century who discussed economic problems is given by B. Alonso Rodríguez, *Monografias de moralistas españoles sobre temas ecónomicos (s. XVI)*, in *Repertorio de Historia de las Ciencias Eclesiásticas en España*, published by the Instituto de Historia de la Teología española (Salamanca, 1971), pp. 147-81.

The economic thought of the Spanish scholastics is discussed by B. W. Dempsey, *Interest and Usury* (London, 1928); J. Larraz, *La época del mercantilismo en Castilla, 1500-1700* (Madrid, 1943); Marjorie Grice-Hutchinson, *The School of Salamanca* (Oxford, 1952); R. de Roover, 'Scholastic economics; survival and lasting influence from the sixteenth century to Adam Smith', *Quarterly Journal of Economics*, Vol. 69, May 1955, pp. 161-90; D. Iparraguirre, *Francisco de Vitoria: una teoria social del valor económico* (Bilbao, 1957); W. Weber, *Wirtschaftsethik am Vorabend des Liberalismus* (Münster, 1959) and *Geld und Zins in der spanischen Spätscholastik* (Münster, 1962); Ichiro Iizuka, *Studies in the History of Monetary Theory* (Tokyo, 1969) (in Japanese); B. Gordon, *Economic Analysis Before Adam Smith* (London, 1975), pp. 212-17 and 236-43; R. Sierra Bravo, *El pensamiento social y económico de la escolástica* (Madrid, 1975).

2 *Politics*, 1256a.
3 ibid., 1257a-1258b.
4 ibid., 1254a.
5 ibid., 1323b.
6 K. S. Cahn, 'The Roman and Frankish roots of the Just Price of medieval canon law', *Studies in Medieval and Renaissance History* (Lincoln, Nebraska), Vol. 6, pp. 12-36.
7 St Albert, *Commentarii in Sententiarum Petri Lombardi*, in *Opera omnia* (Paris, 1890-9), Vol. 29, p. 638, dist. 16, art. 45.
8 St Albert, *In X libros Ethicorum*, edn cit., Vol. 7, Lib. 5, tract. 2, cap. 7.
9 St Thomas, *Summa theologia*, in *Opera omnia* (Paris, 1871-80), Vol. 3, 2, 2, qu. 77, art. 1.
10 St Thomas, *In X libros Ethicorum*, edn cit., Vol. 25, ch. 5, lect. 9.
11 ibid., lects 7 and 8.
12 Duns Scotus, *In IV librum sententiarum*, dist. 15, q. 2, no. 22.
13 Langenstein's treatise on contracts was published as an appendix to Vol. 4

of John Gerson's *Opera omnia* (Cologne, 1483), but has not been included in later editions. An account of his doctrine is given by E. Schreiber, *Die volkswirtschaftlichen Anschaungen der Scholastik seit Thomas von Aquin* (Jena, 1913).

14 For the names of some of the more prominent supporters of this thesis consult R. de Roover, 'The concept of the Just Price: theory and economic policy', *Journal of Economic History*, 18, December 1958.

15 St Bernardino of Siena, *De Evangelio aeterno*, sermons 32–45, in *Opera omnia*, (Florence, 1950–63), Vol. 4. St Antonino, *Summa theologica* (Verona, 1740–1). St Antonino's theory of value is developed in pt 2, tit. 1 (De Avritia).

On the economic thought of these two writers we have R. de Roover's study, *San Bernardino of Siena and Sant' Antonino of Florence: The Two Great Economic Thinkers of the Middle Ages*, Publication No. 19 of the Kress Library of Business and Economics (Cambridge, Mass., 1967). A full bibliography is given.

16 St Bernardino, op. cit., serm. 35, art. 1, ch. 1. St Antonino, op. cit., pt 2, tit. 1, ch. 16, p. 2.

17 St Bernardino, op. cit., serm, 35, art. 2, chs 2 and 3. St Antonino, op. cit., pt 3, tit. 8, ch. 2.

18 John Buridan, *Quaestiones super VIII libros politicorum Aristoteles* (Paris, 1513), Bk 1, Q. 11, art. 2. See J. T. Noonan, *The Scholastic Analysis of Usury* (Cambridge, Mass., 1957), pp. 67–8.

19 A short list of works describing the mechanics of the 'exchanges' is given in note 98 to Chapter 1. Some of them also consider doctrine. W. Endemann, *Studien in der romanischkanonistischen Wirtschaftslehre* (Berlin, 1874–88), Vol. 1, pp. 168 *et seq.*, remains indispensable, and R. de Roover, in his *L'Evolution de la lettre de change*, provides a full bibliography of the subject, as well as valuable summaries of the teaching of many medieval and modern authors. In addition to the titles mentioned in note 98, the following studies deal chiefly with the history of doctrine: Luciano dalle Molle, *Il contratto de cambio nei moralisti del secolo XIII all metà del secolo XVII* (Rome, 1954); Noonan, op. cit., pp. 175–92.

20 Hostiensis, *Summa aurea*, written about the middle of the thirteenth century (1st edn Rome, 1470), numerous later editions. Hostiensis devotes part of Lib. 5 to the exchanges. His doctrine is summarised by de Roover, *L'Evolution de la lettre de change*, p. 187, and dalle Molle, op. cit., pp. 37–8.

21 Giles of Lessines, *De usuris*, in St Thomas Aquinas, *Opera omnia*, Vol. 17 (Parma, 1864). See Schreiber, op. cit., p. 164; and Noonan, op. cit., pp. 182–3.

22 Alexander Lombard, *Tractatus de usuris* (Vatican Library, MS Cod. Lat. 1237), fols 154–74. Written about 1237. A short summary is given by de Roover, *L'Evolution de la lettre de change*, pp. 172–3. Alexander's views on exchange-banking are also discussed by Noonan, op. cit., pp. 183–4.

23 Lorenzo Rodulfis, *Tractatus de usuris et materiae montis*, (Pavia, 1490), 1st edn; reprinted in *Tractatus universi juris*, Vol. 7.

24 St Bernardino, op. cit., serm. 39, art. 3, cap. 2.

25 St Antonino, op. cit., pt 3, tit. 8, cap. 3.

26 Tommaso de Vio, Cardinal Cajetan, *Commentarium in summam theologicam S. Thomae Aquinatis*, in St Thomas Aquinas, *Summa theologica* (Rome, 1882); *De cambiis* (Milan, 1499), 1st edn; reprinted in *Tractatus universi juris*, Vol. 6, and re-edited, together with Cajetan's two other economic treatises,

by P. Zammit, under the title *Scripta philosophica opuscula oeconomico-socialia* (Rome, 1934).

27 Sylvester of Prierio, *Summa summarum quae Silvestrina dicitur* (Bologna, 1514); numerous re-editions. The work is arranged in alphabetical order. The exchanges are discussed under the heading of '*Usura* IV' ('Quo ad cambio').

28 Notably Angelo of Chivasso, *Summa angelica* (Venice, 1511), title '*Usura*'. Angelo's doctrine is discussed by dalle Molle, op. cit., pp. 50–4, and Noonan, op. cit., p. 318 (note).

29 The value of the Spanish contribution to the science of natural law and to the law of nations was recognised as early as 1730 by H. Conring, *Opera* (Brunswick, 1730), Vol. 4, p. 78. Among the many modern studies of the subject, the following may be recommended: E. Nys, *Le Droit des gens et les anciens jurisconsultes espagnols* (Brussels, 1914); J. B. Brown Scott, *The Spanish Origin of International Law and of Sanctions* (Washington, 1934); and Luciano Pereña Vicente, *La Universidad de Salamanca, forja del pensamiento político español en el siglo XVI* (Salamanca, 1954).

30 The merchants' Report of 1532, and the Doctors' Reply, are printed by J. A. Goris, *Études sur les colonies marchandes méridionales à Anvers de 1488 à 1567* (Louvain, 1935), 2nd edn, pp. 510–45. An extract, translated into English, is included in Grice-Hutchinson, op. cit., Appendix 1.

31 From the point of view of economic doctrine, Francisco de Vitoria's most important work is his commentary on the *Secunda secundae* of St Thomas, included in the Biblioteca de Teólogos españoles, ed. V. Beltrán de Heredia, Vols 4–6 (Salamanca, 1934). The same three volumes appear under the title of *De Justitia* in the series published by the Asociación Francisco de Vitoria. The principal passages relating to value-theory are reprinted by D. Iparraguirre, in his *Francisco de Vitoria: una teoría social del valor económico*.

32 Domingo de Soto, *Libri decem de justitia et jure* (Salamanca, 1553); numerous re-editions.

33 Martín de Azpilcueta Navarrus, *Manual de Confesores y penitentes* (Coimbra, 1553). Three years later, in 1556, an edition was published at Salamanca which includes the commentaries on usury and the exchanges that interest us. Thereafter, the commentaries were included in most of the numerous re-editions of the Manual (or *Enchiridion*, as it is called in some editions), and in the Latin and Italian translations and abridgements, that continued to be published in many places throughout the sixteenth century and earlier decades of the seventeenth.

A critical edition of the Commentary on the Exchanges is *Martín de Azpilcueta: Comentario resolutorio de cambios*, ed. A. Ullastres, J. M. Pérez Prendes and Luciano Pereña, Vol. 4 of *Corpus Hispanorum de Pace*, published by the Consejo Superior de Investigaciones Científicas (Madrid, 1965). English translation of short extract in Grice-Hutchinson, op. cit., pp. 89–96.

34 Juan de Medina, OFM, *De poenitentiae, restitutione et contractibus tractatus ... de usura, de cambiis* (Salamanca, 1550).

35 Cristóbal de Villalón, *Provechoso tratado de cambios y contrataciones de mercaderes y reprobación de usura* (Seville, 1542), another edition at Valladolid in the same year, and a third in Cordova, 1546. Reprinted in facsimile at Valladolid, 1945.

36 Luís de Alcalá, OFM, *Tractado de los préstamos que passan entre mercaderes y*

tractantes, y por consiguiente de los logros, cambios, compras adelantadas, y ventas al fiado (Toledo, 1543; 2nd edn, 1546).

37 Luís Saravia de la Calle Veroñense, *Instrucción de mercaderes muy provechosa ... cambios licitos y reprobados* (Medina del Campo, 1544); Italian translation, *Institutione de' mercanti che tratta del comprare et vendere ... con un trattato de' cambi*, by Alfonso de Ulloa (Venice, 1561).

38 A. M. Venusti, *Compendio utilissimo di quelle cose, le quali a nobili e christiani mercanti appartengono* (Milan, 1561). Contains five tracts, of which the last two appear to be translations of Saravia's treatise.

39 Diego de Covarrubias y Leyva, *Variarum resolutionum ex jure pontificio, regio, et caesareo Libri IV* (1552–70). In Book 3 the author treats the subject of usury. Covarrubias's best-known work, *Veterum numismatum collatio* (1550), is mainly numismatic in character but contains interesting remarks on the debasement of the coinage and the alteration in the value of money that had occurred in Spain.

40 Domingo de Bañez, *Commentarium in 2.2. De Justitia et Jure* (Salamanca, 1594).

41 Tomás de Mercado, *Tratos y contratos de mercaderes* (Salamanca, 1569).

42 Francisco García, OP, *Tratado utilisimo de todos los contratos, quantos en los negocios humanos se pueden ofrecer*, 2 vols (Valencia, 1583). English translation of extracts in Grice-Hutchinson, op. cit., pp. 103–8.

43 Luís de Molina, SJ, *De justitia et jure'* (Cuenca), 6 vols. The first two volumes and the first half of the third were published in 1593, 1597 and 1600 respectively, the second part of the third volume in 1609 and the last three volumes at a later date. Numerous re-editions. English translation of extract in Grice-Hutchinson, op. cit. The best general study of Molina's economic doctrine is Weber, *Wirtschaftsethik am Vorabend des Liberalismus*. Molina's doctrine of usury, together with that of Lessius and Lugo, is studied by Dempsey, op. cit. (Washington, 1943). Dempsey's book was praised by J. A. Schumpeter (*History of Economic Analysis*, pp. 94–5) but criticised by Noonan (op. cit., pp. 403–6), and the discussion was continued by F. Belda, 'Etica de la creación de créditos según la doctrina de Molina, Lesio y Lugo' and 'Valoración de la doctrina de Molina Lesio y Lugo sobre la creación de créditos', *Pensamiento*, Vol. 19, 1963, pp. 53–92, 185–214.

44 Miguel Salón, *De Justitia in 2.2, S. Thomae tomi duo* (Valencia, 1581).

45 Juan de Salas, *Commentarii in secundum secundae D. Thomas* (Lyons, 1617).

46 Francisco Suárez, *Disputationes Metaphysicae*, in *Opera omnia* (Paris, 1856–78), 25 vols.

47 Juan de Lugo, *De justitia et jure* (Lyons, 1642), 2 vols.

48 See Chapter 1, note 4.

49 I have said 'value or price' because the Latin words *valor* and *pretium* were used more or less indifferently by scholastic writers, and I do not think we need try to draw any rigorous distinction between them.

50 See note 31.

51 Iparraguirre, *Francisco de Vitoria*, pp. 49–70.

52 Juan de Medina, *Codex de Restitutione*, cited by Sierra Bravo, op. cit., p. 177.

53 Luís Saravia de la Calle Veroñense, op. cit., p. 27, rev. An English version of short extracts is included in Grice-Hutchinson, op. cit., pp. 79–82.

54 Diego de Covarrubias y Legra, *Variarum ex pontificio regio, et caesareo jure resolutionum libri IV* (1554), Lib. 2, ch. 3.

55 Domingo de Soto, op. cit. English translation of short extracts in Grice-Hutchinson, op. cit., pp. 83–8.
56 Francisco García, op. cit. English translation of short extracts in Grice-Hutchinson, op. cit., pp. 103–8.
57 Bartolomé de Albornoz, *Arte de los contratos* (Valencia, 1573), p. 64.
58 Juan de Salas, op. cit., pp. 9, 11, 32–4, 357, 573b.
59 Juan de Lugo, op. cit., disp. 26, sec. 4, paras 41–4.
60 Pedro de Valencia, *Discurso sobre el precio del trigo* (1605), in *Pedro de Valencia, Escritos Sociales*, ed. C. Viñas Mey (Madrid, 1945).
61 Martín de Azpilcueta Navarrus, Comentario, resolutono de usuras, p. 58.
62 Domingo de Soto, op. cit., Lib. 7, Q. 5, art. 2.
63 ibid., Lib. 6, Q. 11, art. 1.
64 Martín de Azpilcueta Navarrus, op. cit., p. 84, English translation in Grice-Hutchinson, op. cit., pp. 80–96.
65 Tomás de Mercado, op. cit., p. 94. See Grice-Hutchinson, op. cit., pp. 96–103 for English version of passages that contain the gist of Mercado's doctrine.
66 Tomás de Mercado, op. cit., pp. 92–3.
67 Domingo de Bañez, *De justitia et jure* (Salamanca, 1594), Q. 78; *De cambiis*, art. 4.
68 Luís de Molina, op. cit., Vol. 2, dist. 406, notes 1–2.
69 Juan de Lugo, op. cit., dist. 26, sec. 4, paras 41–4.
70 Jean Bodin, *Réponse à M. de Malestroit*, ed. H. Hauser (Paris, 1932), pp. 9–10. John Hales, *A Compendious or Briefe Examination of Certayne Ordinary Complaints of Divers of our Countrymen* (1581), 2nd edn. The first edition, that of 1565, does not include the passage in question. A critical edition, edited by E. Lamond, was published in 1893 under the title of *A Discourse of the Common Weal of this Realm of England*.
71 Richard Carewe, *Survey of Cornwall* (London, 1603), p. 37 verso.
72 Earl J. Hamilton, *American Treasure and the Price Revolution in Spain* (Cambridge, Mass., 1934), p. 301.
73 Pietro Catalano, SJ (1658–1732) *Universi juris theologico-moralis corpus* (Venice, 1728).
74 Martino Bonacina (*c.* 1585–1631), *Opera omnia* (Lyons, 1646).
75 Antonino Diana (1585–1663), *Summa diana* (Venice, 1646).
76 Cardinal Giambattista de Luca (1613–83), *Theatrum veritatis et justitiae* (Rome, 1669–81), *Il dottor volgare* (Rome, 1673).
77 Clemente Piselli (1650–1715). *Theologiae moralis summa* (Rome, 1710).
78 Barnardo Davanzati (1529–1606) *Lezione delle Monete* (lecture read by the author before the Florentine Academy in May 1588, but not published until 1638), *Notizia de' cambi* (1588). Both pamphlets are given in *Custodi, Scrittori Classici italiani di economia politica* (Milan, 1804), parte antica, Vol. 2.
79 Ferdinando Galiani (1728–87), *Della Moneta* (Naples, 1750), p. 28. See Schumpeter, op. cit., pp. 300–2.
80 Cesare Bonesana, Marchese de Beccaria (1735–94), *Elementi di economia politica*, in *Scrittori Classici italiani di economia politica* (Milan, 1804), parte moderna, Vol. 12.
81 Among the more conservative authors we may include J. L. Le Semelier (1660–1725), *Conférences ecclésiastiques sur l'usure et la restitution* (Paris, 1724), 4 vols; and Antoine Godeau, *Morale chrétienne pour l'instruction des curés du diocèse de Vence* (Lyons, 1710).

82 See Chapter 1, note 4.
83 E. B. de Condillac, *Le Commerce et Le Gouvernement* (Amsterdam, 1776) pp. 9–30; A. R. J. Turgot, 'Valeurs et monnaies', in *Oeuvres* (1808), Vol. 3, pp. 256–93.
84 F. Quesnay, article 'Hommes', not included in the *Encyclopedie*, but published by E. Bauer in *Revue d'histoire des doctrines économiques et sociales*, No. 1, pp. 3–88, and reprinted in *Francois Quesnay et la Physiocratie*, ed. Robert Debré (Paris, 1958), Vol. 2, pp. 511–73.
85 L. Lessius, *De justitia et jure* (Louvain, 1605).
86 Gordon, op. cit., pp. 244–71.
87 Hugo Grotius, *De jure belli et pacis* (1625) (English translation, Oxford, 1925). Grotius's debt to the Spanish jurists is discussed in the Introduction to the English translation, pp. 13–14.
88 Grotius, op. cit., Bk 2, ch. 12, para. 17.
89 Samuel von Pufendorf, *Elementorum jurisprudentiae universalis libri 2* (The Hague, 1660) (English translation, Oxford, 1931), Bk 2, def. 10; *De jure naturae et gentium* (Lund, 1672) (English translation, Oxford, 1934), Bk 5, ch. 1; *De officio hominis et civis juxta legem naturalem* (Lund, 1673) (English translation, Oxford, 1927), ch. 14.
90 J. Locke, *Two Treatises Concerning Government* (London, 1690), Bk 2, ch. 5, passim.
91 J. Locke, *Some Considerations of the Consequences of the Lowering of Interest and Raising the Value of Money* (London, 1692), p. 65.
92 J. Locke, *Some Considerations . . .*, p. 62.
93 L. Mises, 'Die Stellung des Geldes im Kreise der Wirtschaftlichen Güter', *Wirtschaftstheorie der Gegenwart*, Vol. 2, 1932, p. 310.
94 J. Law, *Money and Trade Consider'd* (1705), ch. 1.
95 F. Hutcheson, *Introduction to Moral Philosophy* (Glasgow, 1747), pp. 209–10.
96 F. Hutcheson, *System of Moral Philosophy*, Vol. 2 (1755), p. 63.
97 A. Smith, *Wealth of Nations*, 1st edn (1776). I have used the edition of Edwin Cannan (1904), numerous reprints, Vol. 1, ch. 5.

4

The Political Economists

In the Middle Ages 'economy' had simply meant the government of the household. But, if the term 'political economy' was not coined until 1615 (by Antoine de Montchrétien), the subject itself was ancient. The oriental mirror-books in which the prince was offered counsel, and the Christian treatises for which St Thomas in his *De regimine principum* set a pattern that was followed by many later writers, often discussed matters pertaining to national husbandry. By the middle of the sixteenth century the art of government had come to form a branch of what was loosely called 'moral philosophy' to distinguish it from the natural sciences that also belonged to 'philosophy'. The study of moral philosophy was at this period, and for long afterwards, regarded as essential for a prince and his advisers.[1]

The branch of moral philosophy that dealt with the material wealth of a kingdom may, in anticipation of Montchrétien and for the sake of convenience, be called 'political economy' from about 1550 onwards. Some scholars seek to draw a clear-cut distinction between the earlier Spanish political economists and the late scholastics who were their contemporaries. This, it seems to me, is labour spent in vain. The political economists of the sixteenth, seventeenth and even early eighteenth centuries were mostly educated at the universities where the late scholastics taught, and some of them taught there themselves. Sancho de Moncada, for instance, was professor of Scripture at Toledo, having applied unsuccessfully for the chair of moral philosophy. He was a scholastic by training and career. Yet no one would think of denying him an important place among the Spanish political economists.

While in Spain there was no ideological rift between the late scholastics and the political economists, since all were Catholics as well as patriots, the two groups of writers had different objects in view. The main purpose of the scholastic Doctors was to ensure the salvation of each man's soul and to establish the reign of justice upon earth. That of the political economists was to save Spain from the ruin that threatened her. These aims were not incompatible.

In general, we may perhaps say that the scholastics point the way to psychological subjectivism and equilibrium-theory, and the political economists to the theory of international trade and of the balance of payments. The scholastics were primarily theorists, though they never lost sight of facts. The political economists were, above all, fact-finders, though they took account of theory. Men of both groups were the founders of economic science in Spain, and they were no more at variance than the right hand is from the left.

In the writings of the late scholastics we often find passages relating to problems of economic policy. Such discussions, removed from their moral or legal framework, belong to the literature of economics. When Mariana, for example, in his treatise on the debasement of the coinage, objects to debasement on the ground that such a measure is illegal, being not only against Spanish law but also against reason and natural law, he is writing as a scholastic philosopher. When he passes on to consider that all commodities will become dearer in proportion to the fall in the value of money, that price-control will be useless because goods will no longer come on to the market, and that, if debasement is persisted in, Spanish commerce will fall into decay and the Crown itself be impoverished, he is writing as a political economist.[2]

Again, in their discussions on taxation the Doctors' chief concern was with justice in the widest sense of the term. They were absorbed in such problems as the right of the prince to impose taxation either on his own subjects or on his conquered enemies, the purpose and extent of his powers and the duty of the people to obey him. In the course of the argument the question sometimes arose as to which taxes were beneficial and which harmful to Spain, and here too we enter the field of economic policy and theory.[3] It is unnecessary to multiply examples. If in the course of this chapter I sometimes mention a late scholastic author it should be understood that I am here considering him in his role as a political economist.

The converse is also true. We shall expect to find the political economists echoing scholastic teaching, and we shall not be disappointed. In our last chapter we noted the survival of scholastic ideas on value in later economic literature. Here we need only say that these and other scholastic doctrines are continually to be found reproduced in the writings of the seventeenth- and eighteenth-century economists.[4]

THE YEARS OF OPTIMISM (1500–60)

The first half of the sixteenth century was a time of expansion and enterprise. The heedless use of the new-found colonial resources, both of labour and of the accumulated treasure of the Incas, enabled gold to be sent to Spain in return for goods that fetched a high price in the colonies. The first settlers were dependent on supplies from home. As time went on European crops were introduced, but they were slow to develop and their cultivation in the New World was not encouraged by the Spanish Government. The shipping of merchandise from Seville to America yielded immense profits, and merchants of all nations outbid one another for goods that would find a ready sale in the colonies.

The effect of American demand on Spanish prices was noted by Tomás de Mercado in 1569 (the text is late but Mercado's remarks apply also to the period we are now considering). The Indian trade, he says, raised prices for two reasons: it created a heavy demand for goods, and it was based on credit that eventually had to be paid for. He describes in concrete terms the mechanism of the rise in prices:

I saw velvets in Granada that were priced at 28 and 29 *reales*. A fool arrived from the steps, and began to treat and bargain so indiscreetly for the lading of a caravel that within a fortnight he had put up prices to 35 and 36. And the velvet-merchants and weavers went on in this way, and afterwards charged the same prices to their fellow-countrymen. So, in Seville, is the daily trend of prices, as much in the mercery that comes from Flanders as in the cloths from Segovia and Toledo, and the wine and oil produced in the Axarafe.[5]

The products most in demand for export to the colonies were those that were essential to life at home: among them, in addition to the textiles, wine and oil mentioned by Mercado, were wheat and other foodstuffs, soap, glass, leather and arms. Between 1511 and 1549 the price of wheat rose from 89 to 187 maravedises, that of wine from 20 to 151, and that of oil from 80 to 238.

Under the stimulus of American demand, of a widened European market, and of a growth in the population of Spain, Castilian industry and, in the south at least, agriculture, expanded promisingly. The Guadalquivir valley was planted with cereals, vines and olives, and the looms of Segovia, Toledo, Cordova, Cuenca and Granada were seldom idle.

The merchants of this period amassed large fortunes. The boom was sustained not by gold and silver imports alone but also, as Mercado observed, by a great expansion of credit. Only the consumers were unhappy. Their anxiety was voiced by the Cortes on several occasions. Excessive exports were seen as the main cause of the alarming increase in the cost of living. In 1548 the Cortes suggested that textiles might well be manufactured in the Indies instead of imported from Spain. But this advice was not followed. The Crown, it would seem, was unwilling to renounce the economic benefits that Castile's commerce with the Indies was assumed, as a matter of course, to bring.

By the middle of the century the Spanish price-level had drawn away from that of the rest of Europe. At about this time, protests began to be made against the import of foreign manufactures, which, attracted by the high level of Spanish prices, were competing successfully with home products. The balance of trade was turning against Castile, and the hard-won American treasure beginning to melt away. People complained that Spain was 'the Indies of the foreigner'. And it was true enough. The colonies had paid high prices for Spanish goods, and sent large quantities of the precious metals in return for them. Now, in response to the rise in Spanish prices, foreigners were flooding the Spanish market with relatively cheap merchandise, and draining gold and silver from Spain. They were also capturing an increasingly important share of the Indian trade.

From 1550 to 1562 there was a marked recession, and, in 1557, a severe financial crisis, the first of many to come. The finances of the Crown were in confusion, a state of affairs that was to prevail under the rule of the remaining Habsburg kings. The reluctance or inability of Charles V to cut his coat according to his cloth must surely be seen as in itself a sufficient cause for the economic ruin of Spain. The political economists, at any rate, recognised the lack of coherent financial planning as the root of their country's ills. We shall not be able to appreciate their work unless we briefly glance at some of the financial problems that arose under Charles V and were to bedevil Spain for the next century and a half.

The Emperor's Finances

Charles the First of Spain and Fifth of the Holy Roman Empire was essentially a warrior. His imperial destiny claimed all his thoughts and energies, and he 'shared the traits that one day were to be embodied in another pathetic knight, the sublime image of Spanish idealism'.[6]

Frugal, even parsimonious in his personal expenditure, the emperor spent recklessly on his military enterprises. The struggle against France, against the Turk, and against Protestantism and revolt in Germany left him permanently short of funds. At first it was the Netherlands and Italy that bore the heaviest burdens. Later the emperor fell back more and more on Spain. Since the contribution of the Crown of Aragon remained relatively small throughout his reign, this meant in practice Castile.

Perhaps I should here point out that by 'Castile' is meant in this chapter not only the modern territory that we know under that name but the whole Crown of Castile, which at this period covered about two-thirds of the total area of the Iberian Peninsula and included Galicia, Asturias, Leon, Extremadura, Old and New Castile, Murcia and Andalusia. These regions formed a single state with common frontiers, Cortes and legislation, currency and fiscal system. The Crown of Aragon comprised Navarre, the modern Aragon, Catalonia and Valencia, which were autonomous in these respects.

The Castilian resources were considerable for that day. The revenues payable by the Spanish Church to the Crown were an important item. The secular taxes included a bewildering array of customs duties, taxes on the transit of cattle and a tax on the Granada silk industry. The *alcabala*, a tax paid on nearly everything that was bought and sold, had been collected throughout the fifteenth century and was a rich source of revenue to the Crown. Now, however, it was converted into a fixed quota that was paid by each town or village, and as prices rose it declined in value.

These and other revenues were insufficient to meet the cost of empire. Charles was often obliged to ask the Cortes for a *servicio*, traditionally a temporary subsidy but which after 1523 became a regular tax amounting to some 400,000 ducats a year. The royal share of the American treasure that arrived from the Indies came to about the same sum.

The clergy and the *hidalgos* (noblemen and gentlemen who enjoyed the ancient privileges of their rank as a reward for the services rendered by their ancestors to the Crown) were exempt from payment of the *servicio*, which fell as an additional burden on the shoulders of the *pechero*, or person liable to pay this and other direct taxes. The proportion of *hidalgos* to *pecheros* is difficult to determine and varied greatly from place to place. In Leon, for instance, there were as many *hidalgos* as *pecheros*, while in the south there were relatively few *hidalgos*. Grants of *hidalguía* were readily sold by the Crown, and were bought by everyone who could afford to do so.

Even with the aid of the *servicios*, sales of patents of *hidalguía*, and other expedients, the emperor was unable to meet his commitments. In 1534, for instance, the Crown's net income amounted to some 110,000 ducats, whereas its anticipated outgoings came to 420,000. In order to close the gap between income and expenditure Charles resorted to methods that were bound to prove ruinous. On nine occasions he seized the remittances of American treasure destined to private persons, compensating the latter by issuing them with *juros* or government bonds that yielded a high rate of interest and were assigned in turn to the various sources of revenue. The *juros* multiplied like weeds and ended by devouring more than half the royal revenues, which went to meet the interest payments. Any suggestion by the Crown that it might attempt gradually to redeem the *juros* evoked an outcry from the holders, who formed a rapidly growing class of rentiers.

Another and even more pernicious method of deficit financing was to borrow from German, Genoese, Flemish and Spanish bankers against payment from the next treasure-fleet or against future tax revenues. In short, the emperor's lack of a prudent financial policy ensured that the resources of Castile were mortgaged for years ahead. As J. H. Elliott points out, the reign of Charles V saw three dangerous developments that were to be of incalculable importance for sixteenth- and seventeenth-century Spain. In the first place, it established the dominance of foreign bankers over the country's sources of wealth. Second, it determined that Castile would bear the main weight of the fiscal burden within Spain. In the third place, it ensured that within Castile the brunt of the burden was borne by those classes which were least capable of bearing it.[7]

Luis Ortiz. The economic plight of Castile was clearly perceived by the first of the Spanish political economists and one of the earliest mercantilists to appear in any country: Luis Ortiz, comptroller of the royal finances, in a memorial which he addressed to Philip II in 1558, two years after the latter's accession to the throne.[8] The work has little literary merit, but its doctrine, particularly with respect to the balance of payments, is well formulated for the period at which it was written. The opening passages set the tone not only of this memorial but of countless other books and pamphlets that were to appear at a later date. After duly invoking the Holy Trinity, the Virgin Mary, 'the Lord Saint James, light and sword of the Spains, the nine choirs of angels, and all the saints of the heavenly court', our author comes down to earth as follows:

It is well known that out of an *arroba* of wool, which to foreigners costs 15 *reales*, they manufacture outside Spain tapestries, cloth, and other things, and send them back again worth 15 ducats. And from raw silk worth two ducats, which costs them a pound, they manufacture Florentine satins and Genoese velvets, cloth of Milan and other cloths, on which they make a profit of over 20 ducats.

The same thing happens in the case of steel and iron sent abroad.

Out of what costs them a ducat, foreigners manufacture brakes, tongs, hammers, guns, swords, daggers and other arms, and things of little value, on which they make over 20 ducats and sometimes over 100.

Spain, continues Ortiz, is a laughing-stock among nations, who indeed 'treat us much worse than Indians, because in return for their gold and silver we do at least bring the Indians some more or less useful things', whereas foreigners take money out of Spain in exchange for worthless rubbish, and without even the trouble of having to mine it. The remedy for this state of affairs is to forbid the export of raw materials and the import of foreign manufactures. Ortiz shows himself to be an excellent keeper of the national accounts, reckoning not only the excess of imports over exports but also the invisible items that added to the deficit: the interest paid to the king's foreign creditors, payments made to foreigners who held monopolies in Spain, sums remitted to Rome in payment of benefices and indulgences and, above all, the remittances sent back to their countries of origin by the many foreign workers who flocked into Spain to take advantage of the high level of wages that prevailed there.

It would be wrong to conclude from Ortiz's preoccupation with the need to secure a favourable balance of trade that he regarded 'treasure' as an end in itself. Like al-Turtushi – indeed, like men of sense in every age – he saw that unless the royal coffers were kept well filled the king could neither defend the country nor promote the welfare of his subjects. After pointing out the advantages of improved irrigation of the land, Ortiz adds:

> but let us leave this for its own time, since it cannot be done at present owing to the poverty of the kingdom. When the outflow of money is stopped and there be money in Spain, this and other things of good policy, such as sumptuous and necessary buildings, and roads, may be afforded smoothly.[9]

Again

> when kings are rich, and their patrimonies neither sold nor alientated, many good things come to their subjects. The chief benefit is that the rulers do not try to take away from the Church and from sacred things what is theirs by right, nor lay impositions on their kingdoms. They pay their servants punctually, and boundless prosperity comes to everyone in general. . . . When kings are in need, there not only follow the contrary and other evils, but also the breakdown and derogation of good laws. Necessity knows no law, and less where princes are concerned.[10]

There is no trace of quantity theory in the work of Ortiz, and thus no logical conflict between his anxiety to keep large quantities of treasure in Spain and his recognition of the need to bring prices down. Ortiz attributes the high level of prices in Spain to the following causes:

(1) the excessive exports to the Indies, more especially of manufactured goods brought in from other countries for re-export;

(2) the fact that the public authorities of the various cities had a personal interest in keeping prices high;

(3) the bad organisation of Spanish commerce. From Andalusia, Toledo, Granada and Murcia, says our author, goods were sent to the fairs of Medina del Campo, Rioseco and Villalón, and afterwards travelled back again, either to supply their places of origin or to be used in the colonial trade. To the original price of the merchandise, therefore, was added the cost of transport and the taxes payable on the journey and at the fairs. Ortiz advocates the abolition of the 'dry ports' that impeded trade at the frontiers of the diverse ancient kingdoms that made up Spain under the personal union of their crowns. Had Ortiz's advice been taken, Spain would have moved more quickly towards a customs union that, as things were, was not fully achieved until the nineteenth century.

Ortiz was a staunch Catholic, one of his main concerns being to preserve Spain from any taint of heresy. Yet some of his most cherished tenets are those which, when held in Protestant countries, are supposed to have made up the 'Puritan ethic'. Ortiz admires the frugality that characterised the Spaniards of ancient times, and, above all, the virtues of industry and diligence. Dress, he held, should be plain and luxury eschewed. Since labour, when applied to raw materials, was capable of increasing their value 'by ten or even a hundredfold', then the whole nation must be set to work. Everyone, even the sons of gentlemen and grandees, must learn a trade and follow it, on pain of being deprived of their citizenship. Only the country labourers and the carriers should be exempt from this duty.

Ortiz was not against foreigners as such. He holds that foreign artisans should be encouraged to settle in Spain, bringing their skills with them and marrying poor young women, 'of whom there is a multitude going to perdition for lack of husbands'. All this will do away with 'the idleness and ruin of Spain, which nowadays is such that no one, of whatever condition or state he may be, knows any trade or business but to go to Salamanca, or to the war in Italy, or to the Indies, or to be a Scrivenor or a Procurator, and all to the prejudice of the republic'.[11]

Other measures recommended by Ortiz include the reform of the navy, currency and taxation, the creation of a war-chest, reafforestation, the improvement of the waterways and the control of banking practice, with severe punishment meted out to those who 'invent strange ways of making a profit, never before seen or heard of, by which they not only sin themselves but cause others to do so'.[12]

Similar common-sense views, characteristic of early mercantilist doctrine, had been a good deal more ably expressed by our own John Hales, probably in 1549, while one or two other authors had treated various branches of theory and policy in a way more or less in harmony with the basic principles of mercantilism.[13] However, if only because of the date of its compilation, Ortiz's *Memorial* is of considerable interest, serving as a point of comparison not only for the history of economic thought in Spain but for that of mercantilist literature in general.

Agriculture

The decay, or perhaps I should rather say the stagnation, of Castilian agriculture in the sixteenth century has received less attention from historians than other branches of the economy. Yet the sorrows of the *campo* – the word means more, perhaps, to the Spanish farmer than our own word 'land' to his English counterpart – played a decisive part in the larger tragedy of the economic decadence of Spain.[14]

At the beginning of the sixteenth century agriculture was far from flourishing. The Catholic kings had made some attempt to improve matters, but with only moderate success. They tended, also, to favour sheep-farming, on which the profitable wool-trade depended, at the expense of tillage.

The earlier decades of the sixteenth century brought a certain prosperity to the countryside. American demand stimulated production, especially in the south. On the other hand, the inclusion of Castile in the Habsburg Empire may have prejudiced agriculture, since in bad years it was always possible to import grain from other parts of the imperial domain.

As the American colonies became self-sufficient, the demand for Spanish products began to fall away. At some point not as yet fully defined the inflation outpaced the rise in the prices of farm-products, and the market price no longer covered costs. Nor was the farmer, in theory at least, allowed to receive even this market price. He was hampered by the *tasa* or fixed price imposed on grain and other products, and by a multitude of regulations that were intended to ensure a cheap and plentiful supply of foodstuffs, but which in fact achieved little except to encourage fraud and the growth of a black market.

Carande attributes the miserable condition of the greater part of the Castilian countryside to the social structure, the distribution of the land, the system of cultivation, the abuses of the larger landowners and other causes.[15] To these adverse factors we may add the recurrent series of epidemics, droughts and famines that were the scourge of town and countryside alike.

The greatest of all the Spanish writers on agriculture has left us a wonderful picture of the daily life of the farm in the early sixteenth century. Gabriel Alonso de Herrera based his book of husbandry on his long experience of farming in Talavera and Granada and on his travels in Spain, France and Italy.[16] The popularity of Herrera's book only increased with time, and he continued to be consulted, abroad as well as in Spain, until well into the nineteenth century. But, though Schumpeter includes the book in the literature that 'contributed considerably to the formation of some of the habits of thought that are most characteristic of modern economics',[17] to consider it more fully would be beyond the scope of this study.

Transport

The subject of transport had received attention long before it came to trouble Ortiz. The first of various schemes to make the River Guadalquivir navigable was read to the town council of Cordova in 1524. The author, Fernán Pérez de Oliva, was a native of that city who had studied philosophy at Salamanca and Alcalá, and later taught in Paris and Rome. On his return to Spain Pérez de Oliva became rector of the University of Salamanca, where he held the chair of theology. He seems to have known a good deal about a wide range of subjects, including grammar, rhetoric, geometry, architecture and (so it was rumoured) astrology. His chief merit as an economist is that of distinguishing what was, in fact, one of the fundamental causes of the dearness of Spanish goods: the antiquated transport system, which made it difficult to carry merchandise from places where there was a glut to those where there was a dearth.[18] Pérez de Oliva shows in lucid style how the high cost of transport helped to keep up prices.

The Poor Law Controversy

Sixteenth-century Spain was an unsettled place to live in. The texts of the period leave us with the impression of a people always on the move, fleeing from disaster or allured by the promise of riches. Soldiers on their way to the wars, emigrants to the Indies, Castilians and Galicians to the more prosperous south, hangers-on drifting after the court, French immigrants attracted by the promise of high wages, all were to be found on the Spanish roads. The problem of destitution or, as we should say, unemployment, grew more and more acute. Five times between 1523 and 1534 the Cortes complained of the host of beggars and vagrants who were over-running Castile. Several books and pamphlets offered solutions. These works belong rather to the literature of sociology than to that of economics, but, as they are usually mentioned by the few scholars who have discussed the history of economic thought in Spain, we will glance at them briefly here.

A figure of especial interest to us in England is that of Juan Luis Vives (1492–1540). A Valencian of New Christian origin (his father was burned at the stake, and his mother's remains were dug up from the grave and burned likewise), he understandably spent most of his life outside Spain, and became the tutor and trusted counsellor of the future Queen of England, the Princess Mary.[19] Vives's treatise on poor relief was published in 1520 and translated immediately into Dutch and other languages. Vives writes as a philosopher of natural law. Society he felt, was not organised as God and nature had intended:

> We in our wickedness have appropriated what a generous Nature gave to us in common. The things she openly laid forth we have enclosed and hidden away by means of doors, walls, locks, iron, arms, and finally laws. Thus our greed has brought want and hunger into the abundance of Nature, and poverty into the riches of God.[20]

And Vives goes on to draw up a plan of poor relief, designed to help the sick, blind, mad and other destitute persons, placing the duty of caring for the helpless squarely on the shoulders of the civil power, and, at the same time, insisting that the able-bodied should be set to work and not permitted to beg.

Juan de Medina (not to be confused with the better-known theologian of that name whose work on commercial morality I referred to in my previous chapter) was a Benedictine monk, and abbot of the monastery of St Vincent at Salamanca. His tract on poor relief was published in 1545. Medina wished to see established in Salamanca a system that had already been set up in Zamora and included the control of vagrants, the clearing of beggars from the streets and their reclusion in workhouses, and the general organisation of charitable relief.[21]

Medina was strenuously opposed by Domingo de Soto, who argued that so rigid a plan would deprive the poor man of his rightful liberty. For Soto there are no 'good' or 'bad' poor, and he was against any form of means test, discrimination on religious grounds or herding into workhouses.[22]

There is little economic theory in any of these tracts. If Soto's contribution points the way to liberalism it does so on philosophic and religious grounds. But even at this early period of the long-drawn-out controversy over poor relief we may discern the beginnings of an important tendency. In the Middle Ages it had been the exclusive duty of the Church and the rich to relieve poverty in the name of Christian charity.

Now, at the beginning of the sixteenth century, men like Vives and Juan de Medina were starting to invoke the responsibility of the state, and to bring into the sphere of civil legislation a matter that had formerly been left to conscience. This movement towards centralisation was sometimes opposed in the interests of liberty. But in the end it won the day, and was to become an essential characteristic of mercantilism.

DISILLUSION (1560–1600)

The middle of the sixteenth century saw the development of new mining techniques, which were applied in Mexico from 1559 onwards and in Peru after 1570. Broadly speaking, gold production remained stationary while that of silver greatly increased. Shipments of silver to Seville reached their peak in the periods 1580–5 and 1590–1600 (2,707,626 kilos in 1591–1600, as against 86,193 in 1531–40).

After the recession of 1550–60 prices resumed their upward course and credit again expanded. But there was no solid basis for prosperity. Decay was concealed for a time, but by 1580 it was generally apparent. There were many reasons for this stagnation. Some had been suggested by Luis Ortiz in 1558, and some continue to be put forward, occasionally in sophisticated form, by modern scholars. Among them were uncompetitive prices as a result of the influx of American gold and silver, a rise in wages that made manufacture unprofitable, crushing taxation, the increasing power and rigidity of the guilds, the growth of a rentier class whose members shunned the risks of productive enterprise and preferred to live on the interest from the *juros* that the Crown was continually forced to issue, an increase in the numbers of ecclesiastics and other inactive persons accompanied by a fall in the population as a whole, and other adverse circumstances, none of which was in itself decisive but which combined to ruin industry as well as agriculture. In 1594 we find the Cortes complaining that

> the Kingdom is wasted and destroyed, for there is hardly a man in it that enjoys any fortune or credit. And, if he does, he chooses not to lay it out for profit but retires into the narrowest and most modest way of life he can find, hoping only to keep what he has in a poor way, and to live on it as long as it lasts.

Nevertheless, Spain was still a great power and the mistress of a vast empire. Her Indian trade, though falling ever more into foreign hands, was enjoying a second period of expansion. The death of Philip II in 1598 left the country in a sombre mood, but the day of final reckoning was yet to come.

The political economists of this period include several important writers who suggested lines of thought that were often followed by their successors of the seventeenth century. Nor were the king and the Cortes deaf to their advice, and their suggestions were, in some cases, reflected in the legislation of their day.

Taxation and Finance

The load of debt inherited by Philip II became increasingly heavy in the course of his reign and forced him to make ever more imperious calls upon the purses of his subjects. And it was not only the Crown that found itself in debt. The revenues of the noble families also failed to keep up with prices. As early as 1563 the Cortes of Castile recorded the popular belief that 'the great seigneurs and principal people of this realm are wasted and destroyed by debt', and in 1604 an anonymous pamphleteer estimated that a nobleman spent half his income in paying interest on the *censos* based on his estates.[23] So it went on down the social scale, until we come to the small farmer or shopkeeper, living a hand-to-mouth existence, held fast in the meshes of the local money-lender.

The worsening economic position of Spain evoked a certain amount of discussion concerning problems of finance and taxation. The best work was still scholastic. We will pass over the Doctors' teaching on such general principles as the right of a prince to tax his subjects, the justice of taxation and kindred philosophical and juridical questions. Nor need we concern ourselves with the fairly numerous descriptions and classifications of the sources of revenue that appeared during this period, the best of which is probably that of Molina.[24]

Turning to the more specifically economic aspects of fiscal policy, the indirect taxes of the period, the *alcabala*, and the *millones* (a duty on meat, wine, oil, vinegar and other essential foodstuffs, introduced in 1590, that was to bulk large in the later fiscal history of Castile) may be regarded as characteristically Spanish. At first sight these taxes appear more equitable than the *servicios* from which the clergy and *hidalgos* were exempt. But in practice it was the poor who suffered most from them, since the duties occupied a totally disproportionate place in their modest household budgets.

In 1595 Philip II called a Council of Ministers in order to examine the parlous condition of the royal finances. Several plans were discussed, and that of Gaspar de Pons, a Catalan civil servant was adopted.[25] Such was the state of the Castilian treasury, however, that Pons could only recommend the sale of such royal revenues and property as re- remained, the strict observance of sumptuary laws and the general restoration of order in the public administration.

Gaspar de Pons was a man of experience and of some importance. He was a member of the currency committee that sat in 1587, and, after being appointed to the Council of Finance, was prominent among the advisers of Philip III. Between 1587 and 1600 he presented various memorials to the Crown, and may be regarded as a forerunner of the *arbitristas* or 'projectors' who, called up by the plight of their country, were to proliferate throughout the seventeenth century and roughly correspond to Schumpeter's 'consultant administrators and pamphleteers'.[26]

The work of Gaspar de Pons illustrates my contention that there was no intellectual rift between the Doctors of the universities and the laical economists and projectors. All drew many of their ideas, and a considerable part of their method and style, from the same traditional sources. Pons observes that

there is a science of preserving Empires, and it has many certain principles derived from natural law. Many of these principles are specified in the Old Testament, the canon and common laws, and the laws of these kingdoms and of others under Your Majesty's rule, and many have been noted by Plato, Aristotle, Cicero, St Gregory and St Thomas, and other authors in their various treatises.[27]

Typical of the 'projector' but borrowed from the schools was the symmetrical arrangement of Pons's arguments. The plan of the 'Ten Points' of 1599, for example, is to list ten 'ills' that afflict Spain, each 'ill' being followed by a 'remedy', and finally a 'benefit', the whole being accompanied by summaries and preceded by a lengthy prologue. Pons, too, like any schoolman, thinks it quite natural, where questions of usury are concerned, to consult the theological commissions that met from time to time in order to consider the problems of commercial morality.

The last years of the sixteenth century were to see the beginning of a long and in the end fruitless movement in favour of the establishment of credit-banks in Castile. Its initiator was Peter van Oudegherst, a citizen of Lille, who, after much study and extensive travels, developed a detailed plan for the foundation of credit-banks and pawnshops which he presented to the Spanish ambassador in Austria. The scheme was remitted to the Council of Flanders and was receiving favourable consideration when Oudegherst died. A friend of his, Luís Valle de la Cerda, who had met Oudegherst while in Flanders on the king's business, took up the dead man's ideas and presented them in a memorial addressed to the Cortes in 1576. The plan was still under discussion in 1598, when Valle de la Cerda joined forces with Pedro de Miranda

Salon, a member of a New Christian family of Burgos and the representative of that city in the Cortes of 1598–1601. The proposed programme included the abolition of all private banks, so that the new credit-banks would have a monopoly of deposits and credit, and was envisaged as an instrument to be placed in the hands of the Cortes for the purpose of controlling the royal expenditure on political and military enterprises.

Valle de la Cerda was a strong Aristotelian, and his work provides us with yet another example of the application of Greek and scholastic doctrine to the practical affairs of life. When money was first invented to serve as a medium of exchange, he says, it could not itself be bought and sold. But, given the ruinous condition of the Spanish economy and the abuse of credit that prevailed, all interest could not be abolished immediately. It would be necessary to return gradually to the proper use of money. The suggested credit-banks would lend to the Crown and to private persons at 6 per cent and borrow at 5 per cent. This would help to hold inflation in check and money would revert to its original function 'and measure the value of goods according to their abundance and scarcity, instead of the abundance of money ruling the value of all things, as at present'.[28]

Valle de la Cerda's project was well received by the Cortes; so much so, in fact, that they attempted to make the granting of the *servicio* dependent upon its introduction. But in spite of receiving wide support the plan was shelved 'for the time being', as is all too often the fate of plans in Spain.

Poor Relief

The swarm of vagrants that had infested the roads of Spain in the time of the emperor seems, if anything, to have grown even bigger and more menacing in that of Philip II.[29] Driven from place to place, continually set back on the roads to resume their wanderings, the vagrants were a threat to town and countryside alike. The authorities were impotent against this constant invasion, and the convents where soup was distributed found their doors perpetually besieged. Respectable citizens, aghast at the misery around them, angrily accused the beggars of being impostors. And, certainly, the ragged figures who sat all day gaming in the public squares seemed anything but anxious to be offered honest work. Yet the numerous writers who continued the discussion begun half a century before by Vives, Soto and Medina adopt a tolerant attitude towards the beggars.

Among those who, towards the end of the sixteenth century, occupied themselves with the problem of poor relief was a resident of Lisbon, the canon Miguel de Giginta, author of various pamphlets published between 1579 and 1587 in which he proposes a mild and liberal policy.[30] Giginta established in Lisbon a system of hostels in which the inmates were allowed to follow their normal pursuit of begging (a profession that many of them had brought to a fine art) as well as doing the work provided for them. The Cortes of 1575 and of 1586-8 proposed the foundation of hostels in Spain to be run on similar lines.

Cristóbal Pérez de Herrera, physician to the galleys, was the author of numerous memorials that appeared between 1595 and 1617.[31] Like Martínez de Mata some years later, he seems to have been inspired to write by the scenes of despair that he had witnessed during his visits to the galleys. Pérez de Herrera wrote on many topics but is best known for his work on poor relief. He was much concerned with the perennial difficulty that besets the charitable: how to distinguish between the genuine poor and the impostors and idlers. He urges the foundation of hostels for the destitute, for children, for old soldiers returned from the wars, and for women taken off the streets, without requiring any regime of compulsory labour, or in fact any kind of discipline. He merely seeks to distinguish between the true and the false poor, and to ensure that licences to beg should be given only to those in need.

Transport

Fernan Pérez de Oliva's project, formulated in 1524, for opening up the Guadalquivir to traffic between Seville and Cordova had come to nothing. It was put forward again in 1585, a time when several attempts were made to improve the Spanish waterways, but was not carried out. More fortunate was a scheme evolved by Juan Bautista Antonelli, the great Italian engineer, who came to Spain in 1559. Antonelli drew up a plan for making the River Tagus navigable up to Toledo. Philip II ordered Antonelli to carry out the work, and, for some years at least, river traffic was actually possible between Lisbon and Madrid. In 1581 Antonelli presented a plan for improving other Spanish rivers and linking them by a system of canals.[32] Antonelli's technical arguments do not concern us here. Like Pérez de Oliva, he earns a place among political economists by showing, with a judicious use of figures, how the cost of transport was added on to the price of goods throughout the Spanish provinces.

RECESSION AND DECLINE (1600–1700)

At the time of Philip II's death Spain was still politically great and powerful, even though economically weakened. With the turn of the century there began her decline to the rank of a second-class power. Spanish hegemony could not be maintained on inadequate foundations.

The adverse tendencies that we have noted in the Castilian economy of the sixteenth century became even stronger in the seventeenth. We need not insist on them further. Instead we will take into account such features of the economy as were peculiar to the seventeenth century.

Silver production in the New World was at its height in the decade between 1591 and 1600. Silver remained plentiful until 1630; after that date its production declined, at first gradually and later more abruptly. Over the years between 1503 and 1660 the quantity of silver that arrived at Seville had been sufficient to triple the existing European supplies, while gold stocks had been increased by a fifth. We cannot, surely, doubt that this increase in the stock of gold and silver did contribute towards the rise in prices that took place during roughly the same period. Precisely how, and in what measure, remains a matter for dispute.

Faced with the exhaustion of the royal exchequer, Philip II had resorted to various expedients, including the bankruptcies of 1557, 1575 and 1598. But, except for making a few minor adjustments, he had always refused to debase the currency.[33] His successor, Philip III, opened the gates to the copper inflation that characterised the seventeenth century and led up to the monetary chaos of the 1670s.

Gold and silver coins were not used for the small transactions of daily life. For these there existed a coinage of copper and silver alloy, known as *vellón*. Between 1599 and 1606 large quantities of *vellón* coins were minted, while at the same time their silver content was abolished and their weight reduced by half. The Cortes of 1607 protested against the excessive minting of copper, but the Crown made a considerable profit out of debasing the coinage, and minting was resumed in 1617.

By 1628 the country was flooded with debased copper money. Prices, together with the premium on silver, rose alarmingly, and the government was forced to reduce the sale of the copper coins by half. But the effects of this measure were short-lived. The next half-century saw an overall continuance of *vellón* inflation, broken by spasmodic and unsuccessful efforts to deflate the coinage. The continual fluctuations in the ratio between *vellón* and silver sowed general mistrust and confusion. Everyone hastened to get rid of their copper money by exchanging it for gold, silver or goods of lasting value.

The top of the *vellón* inflation came at an unfortunate moment for Castile. The days of her political greatness were over, and her golden age of art and literature had faded into the past. All was disillusion, inertia and ruin. The government made a last despairing attempt at deflation. On 10 February 1680, the nominal value of the *vellón* minted since 1660 was reduced by half. The immediate consequences were appalling. Prices plummeted, industry was shaken, bankruptcies abounded and, worst of tragedies, the royal family had to forgo their annual visit to Aranjuez. Yet, once the first shock had been absorbed, it was seen that Spain had not, after all, been dealt her death-blow. On the contrary, she began at last to show some semblance of life. By the end of the 1680s the monetary situation was stabilised and no more *vellón* was minted after 1693: the great copper inflation was over. There was no spectacular recovery, but decay was arrested. Spain lifted her head again, and slowly, painfully, began the long pull back to a state of relative prosperity.

The problems that troubled Spain throughout the seventeenth century were not all of a political and economic character. Together with the awareness of poverty and decay came a sense of spiritual loss. Members of great empires are apt to see themselves as especially favoured by God, and when those empires fade away are disconcerted at being deserted by the Almighty. So it was with Spain in the time of her decadence. 'O judgement of God, by what ways does Our Lord choose to punish our wretched Spain!' exclaims Sancho de Moncada, for the fatalism inherent in Spanish society was shared even by economists. The bewilderment was general, and it was harder to bear even than poverty.

Economists and Projectors

It has been customary among historians of economic thought in Spain to distinguish between the political economists proper and the *arbitristas* or (to accept the term preferred by English translators) 'projectors'. The first group receives general approval; the second remains under a cloud.

The figure of the projector has recently been made the subject of a delightful study.[34] The author traces the complex history of the word *arbitrio*, which, by the end of the sixteenth century, had come to combine the various meanings of 'advice' or 'opinion', and 'measure' or 'expedient', more especially a fiscal measure. The first notable use of the word *arbitrista*, 'one who proffers advice to the Crown', occurs in Cervantes's short story, *The Dogs' Colloquy*, which appeared in 1613. 'I, sirs,' says a pauper lying in the hospital at Valladolid,

> am a projector, and I have presented to His Majesty at different times many and various projects, all for his good and harmless to the Kingdom. And now I have written a memorial in which I request him to appoint a person to whom I may communicate a new project I have, which ensures the complete redemption of his debts; but, judging by what has befallen me in the case of other memorials, I expect this one, too, to end up in the charnel-house.

The project turns out to suggest, with much solemn calculation, that all Spaniards between the ages of 14 and 60 should be obliged to observe a monthly fast-day and to pay the money thus saved to the king, 'without defrauding him of a single farthing'. The listeners 'all laughed at the project and the projector, and he, too, laughed at his own nonsense; and I wondered at what I had heard and at seeing that, for the most part, men of this humour end by dying in the workhouse'.

This passage sets the tone for later satire. As the seventeenth century wore on and projects multiplied, so did the popular mistrust of projectors – dare I call them 'planners'? – turn to a lively detestation. Novelists and dramatists portray the projector as an elderly, dowdy, pretentious bore and busybody, at once a failure and a menace. Above all, he is that stock figure of fun, an intellectual, so deeply absorbed in his frantic scribblings that he is capable of putting out his own eye with a goose-quill, almost without noticing the fact.

And yet, were all the projects that were put forward so very foolish? González de Cellorigo, for instance, was undoubtedly a projector, yet he is universally admired as an excellent economist. And there were others. Here, at least, no distinction will be made between 'political economists' and such 'projectors' as dealt with economic problems. All, wise and simple alike, shall here be dignified with the name of political economist.

A certain number of writers set out to create systems or models that covered several aspects of economic life, diagnosing many of the ills that afflicted Spain and proposing remedies for them. Among the better-known authors of such quasi-systems are Sancho de Moncada, Pedro Fernández de Navarrete, Francisco Martínez de la Mata and Alvarez Osorio. Following upon their heels came the army of projectors who dealt with single topics, or with one or two topics only.

Space does not permit me to summarise the views of each writer separately. In this section, therefore, I shall continue to follow the plan, adopted earlier in this chapter, of grouping under various headings the ideas of some of the leading seventeenth-century economists.

But first let us get to know a few of the writers themselves.

Martín González de Cellorigo was a Valladolid lawyer whose *Memorial* was probably addressed to Philip III early in 1600.[35] The population of Valladolid had been declining for some years previously, and the process was hastened by an outbreak of plague in 1599. González de Cellorigo already speaks of the need to 'restore' Spain and to 'redeem the kingdom from debt'. If there was any one aim that united the seventeenth-century economists, it was that of throwing off the burden of debt that was crushing the whole country. González de Cellorigo was among the first to use the term *desempeño* (*empeño*, pledge, *desempeño*, the redemption of a pledge) that was to be the key-word of later economic literature.

Sancho de Moncada was Professor of Scripture at the university of Toledo. He came of a Toledan merchant family of New Christian origin, many of whose members were churchmen. The ruin of Toledo, a once thriving industrial town, touched him closely. Moncada's *Discourses* were probably presented to Philip III in 1618 and were printed in the following year.[36] The moment was one of crisis and confusion, and there was a sense of danger in the air. 'We see', says Moncada

> the general hatred that all nations feel for the Spanish, and how in Spain at every moment the means of defence are lacking – people, money, arms, horses (for now they are all carriage-horses) – and the people all spoilt and effeminate. So, as we know, have other Kingdoms been ruined, and so will Spain be lost.

Furthermore, 'the remedy calls for speed, for the threat to a man bleeding to death increases with each hour that passes'.

Sancho de Moncada's book is succinct and his style laconic. In presenting his arguments he employs the dialectical method of the schools. A rich apparatus of citations, which includes the names of Covarrubias, Vitoria, Soto and Azpilcueta Navarro, accompanies the text. Moncada was also strongly influenced by the Italian writer Giovanni Botero (1544–1617).

Moncada follows scholastic doctrine in attributing the rise in Spanish prices to the influx of gold and silver from America – 'the abundance of silver and gold has caused a fall in their value . . . and consequently a rise in the things that are bought with them' – but thinks that the main reason for the poverty of Spain lies in the fact that her commerce has fallen into the hands of foreigners. In his *Discourses* Moncada outlines a strongly protectionist policy designed to deliver Spain from their machinations.

Sancho de Moncada held that there was a science (*ciencia*) of government whose laws should be learned by every administrator. He suggests that a chair of 'politics' should be founded in all universities, and that an entire university devoted to the arts of government should be established in Madrid.

In his preface to Moncada's book, Tomás Tamayo de Vargas approves the idea of training future administrators to be 'scientifically (*científicamente*) capable' of doing their work. Spanish talent, he adds, is not inferior in 'invention, profundity, and enlightenment (*lucimiento*)' to that of foreign nations. In their plea for the creation of a professional bureaucracy Moncada and Tamayo spoke in the accents of a later age.

Another celebrated political economist was Pedro Fernández de Navarrete, a canon of Santiago de Compostela. He held the post of chaplain and secretary to Philip III, and was a counsellor of the Inquisition. His *Political Discourses* are written in the form of a commentary on the Report on the condition of Spain that was drawn up by the Council of Castile in 1620.[37]

A picturesque figure of the next generation is that of Francisco Martínez de la Mata, whose 'Memorials' were published in 1656. Little is known of his life, except that he calls himself a 'native of Motril, brother of the Third Order of Penitence, and servant of the afflicted poor', and was probably, at some time, procurator to the galleys. The Royal Academy of History possesses the report of a trial that took place in Seville in 1660, in which Mata is accused of 'going through the city dressed in the robes of a tertiary of the Franciscan Order, preaching his doctrines, converting the ignorant to his praises and credit, and exhorting the guilds and councils to contribute towards his expenses'. Declaiming his views 'in a calm voice but with lively gestures' and surrounded by a little company of disciples who distributed circulars, plastered the walls with posters, and used all the arts of propaganda to attract new recruits to the cause, he strove to awaken the people to his own burning sense of their grievances.[38]

Count Campomanes, who re-edited Mata's writings, together with those of Alvarez Osorio, in 1775, compares him with Sir Josias Child and Sir William Petty, who, he says, 'though less profound, had the good fortune to be well received by their nation'.[39] The comparison with Petty, whose first treatise appeared in 1662, is particularly apt. Like Petty, Mata bases many of his theories on statistics. Some of his data he appears to have collected himself, but he more often relies on the material assembled by an earlier writer, Damián de Olivares, whose report on the Toledan silk industry, presented to Philip III in 1620, is often quoted by the political economists of the seventeenth and eighteenth centuries.

We shall touch upon the lives and careers of other Spanish political economists in the remaining pages of this chapter. It is time for us now to turn more specifically to their writings. Much of their energy went into the presentation of facts: Spanish economic history has been largely built up on their findings. We shall leave aside this aspect of their work, and turn to what they saw as 'theory'. By this they meant, in general, economic policy. However, in the course of assembling data and suggesting policy they did sometimes formulate pieces of analysis that were something beyond the mere commonplaces of the popular mind.

The Role of the Precious Metals

The basic aims of the Spanish mercantilists were those of mercantilism everywhere, and did not greatly depart from the lines that had been laid down by Ortiz in 1558. The argument ran as follows. It is desirable to keep as much gold and silver as possible circulating in Spain. Legislation alone cannot staunch the outflow of the precious metals. An excess of exports over imports is the only thing that can reverse the flow. To achieve an export surplus it is necessary to discourage the export of raw materials and the import of manufactures, and to spare no effort in order to encourage Spanish agriculture and industry.

This programme, if such it can be called, was put forward by countless Spanish writers, gaining in elaboration with the passage of time, until the appearance in 1740 of the last great mercantilist treatise, that of Bernardo de Ulloa. Among the many authors who held this doctrine of the export surplus, fundamental to the whole mercantilist position, we may mention Sancho de Moncada, Mateo Lisón, Francisco Martínez de la Mata, Juan Cano and Miguel Alvarez Osorio.[40] I shall not devote space to the quotation from their works of passages urging that the balance of trade should be turned, by hook or by crook, in favour of Spain – such utterances are common to the mercantilist literature of all countries – but shall rather dwell on the more characteristically Spanish features of mercantilism in Spain.

On the whole, the Spanish political economists subscribed to the idea that money was 'the sinews of war', the 'life-blood of commerce' and 'the soul that vivifies all the members of the Republic', and they naturally wished to see their country well supplied with a commodity that was essential to her very life. But money was not esteemed only as a store of value. The emphasis was rather placed on its use as a medium of exchange. The concept of 'treasure' as the life-blood of commerce implied that the precious metals should not be hoarded but made to circulate and to fertilise the economy. This idea was common to mercantilists in all countries, but a lively circulation of money seemed especially desirable in Spain, owing to the important part played by the *alcabala* (purchase tax) and other indirect taxes in the fiscal system. The greater the volume of commerce, the more revenue would accrue to the Crown. The life of the Republic, says Martínez de la Mata, consists in every man's spending what he has earned there, and its death is the contrary:

These two functions are necessary for the preservation of the State, for they are the motive-power of the soul that gives life to the mystical body of the Republic. By them alone each member shares in the virtue of all the others. When some spend in order that others may take the money they need, why, this is only providing the means by which it may be earned again, with no loss of what has been spent. So that, if some people feel no need to spend, others will not find the means of earning money in order to spend it again.[41]

And Mata proceeds to reckon how a ducat, as it passes through the hands of a hundred families 'in a week, a month, a year, or perhaps even a single day', besides 'benefiting all in general' by providing them with the corresponding amount of goods, also brings ten ducats into the royal treasury by way of *alcabala* and other duties.

Not all Spanish writers of the 'age of mercantilism' desire to keep a large stock of the precious metals within the country. González de Cellorigo, writing in 1600, mistrusts the inflationary effect of a big circulation:

It is likewise an error to suppose that in good politics the wealth of a Kingdom is increased or diminished because the quantity of money in circulation is larger or smaller. Since money is only the instrument of exchange, a small circulation has as good an effect as a large one, or even better, for instead of clogging the wheels of trade and commerce, it makes them run more easily and lightly.[42]

The cause of the ruin of Spain, continues Cellorigo:

is that wealth has been and still is riding upon the wind in the form of papers and contracts, *censos* and bills of exchange, money and silver and gold, instead of in goods that fructify and attract to themselves riches from abroad, thus sustaining our people at home. We see, then, that the reason why there is no money, gold or silver in Spain is because there is too much, and Spain is poor because she is rich. The two things are really contradictory, but although they cannot fittingly be put into a single proposition, yet we must hold them both true in our single kingdom of Spain.[43]

Pedro de Valencia calls a large stock of 'silver and money' 'the poison that destroys Republics. It is thought that money sustains them, and it is not so. Well cultivated estates, stock-farming and fisheries are the things that support life.'[44] Similar views were expressed by Fernández de Navarrete and Caja de Leruela.[45] Yet we cannot help noticing that even those writers who, in one part of their treatise, deny that treasure is synonymous with wealth, often appear to set great store by it in another. Adam Smith observed the same habit among English economists. His remarks put the matter in a nutshell and apply equally well to the economic literature of Spain:

Some of the best English writers upon commerce set out with observing, that the wealth of a country consists, not in its gold and silver only, but in its lands, houses, and consumable goods of all different kinds. In the course of their reasonings, however, the lands, houses and consumable goods seem to slip out of their memory, and the strain of their argument frequently supposes that all wealth consists in gold and silver, and that to multiply those metals is the great object of national industry and commerce.[46]

The Balance of Trade

Just as there were some authors who did not subscribe – or at least not wholeheartedly – to the general desire to check the outflow of the precious metals from Spain, so there were one or two who did not hold the mercantilist doctrine of the export surplus. The most notable of these was Alberto Struzzi, a gentleman of Italian origin who was in the service of the Infanta Isabella, wife of the Archduke Albert and co-sovereign of the Netherlands.

Struzzi was an indefatigable projector.[47] In a pamphlet on Castilian commerce he argues in favour of free trade between Castile and other countries, on the ground that such freedom is ordained by the law of nations; that the clandestine entry of merchandise cannot be stopped; that to try to prevent foreigners from taking part in the colonial trade would greatly diminish the volume of commerce, with the result that 'there would not be returned so much as half the silver that arrives every year from the Indies'; and that 'since the greater part of the mines at present in production are in the Indies, it is clear that their yield must be distributed over other parts, or the whole world would be in an uproar'. Struzzi develops these precepts at length, anticipating by some seventy years Davenant's remark that: 'Trade is in its nature free, finds its own Channel, and best directeth its own Course.'[48]

Some historians are unable to credit Struzzi's sincerity in rejecting protectionism. Larraz suggests that he may have wished to further the interests of the states that were subject or allied to the Crown of Castile rather than those of Spain herself. Jean Vilar roundly accuses him of wanting only to protect Flemish industry.[49]

Yet the idea that the course of economic life could not be altered by means of legislation was common among mercantilists of every country. Liberty of internal commerce was universally held to be desirable, and it was only taking the argument a step further to recognise the advantages of freedom in international trade. In fact, *laissez-faire* ideas do occur here and there in the literature of the later seventeenth century. However, it is certainly unusual to find such uncompromising support for free trade in 1624, the year when Struzzi's pamphlet appeared.

Public Finance

The woes of Castile did not shake the faith of the people in the institution of kingship, or loosen the personal bond that had existed between the monarch and his subjects since the Middle Ages. Public finance was not the dry, abstract affair that it is today. Our seventeenth-century economists still spoke of the 'service of His Majesty and the welfare of these Kingdoms', the 'redemption of the Royal Revenues', the 'manner and form that must be observed in order to redeem the debts and succour the needs of the King, the Kingdom, and the nobles' and the 'means of redeeming the Royal Treasury and the fortunes of the vassals'.

True, the political economists often addressed their kings in grave and haughty tones: 'Most powerful, most high, and most excellent Sir: Monarchs are but journeymen. You merit according to your works', admonishes Quevedo. And Alvarez Osorio asks: 'Of what did it avail Alexander to be lord of the world, if at the age of thirty-three he died and was damned for ever? . . . Your Majesty is powerful and can bestow greatness, but you cannot take or give a single hour of life, and this I need in order to attain a place in Heaven.'

Yet despite their readiness to remind the king that he, like themselves, was subject to the decrees of a higher power, the loyalty and sympathy felt by Spaniards for their monarch remained, through all vicissitudes, unshaken.

The concept of the king as a 'journeyman' implied that he was to 'look for the general good'. Above all, his was the task of defending the Catholic faith and the kingdom from the attacks of their enemies. and no one doubted that it was the duty of the 'vassals' to help him by providing him with funds sufficient for the purpose. The only matter for argument was how this aim could be achieved.

The position of the royal exchequer – or, as we should say, the public finances – was desperate. In 1610 the royal revenues are thought to have amounted to 15,648,000 ducats, of which 8,508,500 were already mortgaged and 4 million owed to Genoese bankers. The debts left by Charles V and Philip II amounted to another 3 million. Thus, if these figures are correct, the credit balance was nil. The position had not improved by 1650. In that year we find the President of the Council of Castile, after enumerating the twenty or so taxes that made up the Castilian revenues, affirming that: 'Your Majesty has not a *real* free in any of them, for [on your accession to the throne] you found them all sold and pledged, except for the ordinary and extraordinary *servicios*, and those have been sold and pledged in Your Majesty's reign'.[50]

Still heavier taxation, fresh borrowing when this was possible and repeated debasement of the currency, all were powerless to avert

146

bankruptcy. The people were as poor as their kings. The Cortes continually lamented the wretched state of the provinces and the depopulation and decay of whole districts that had once included the richest lands in Spain.

A great part of the Spanish economic literature of the seventeenth century is devoted to the subject of taxation. The unjust distribution, geographical and personal, of the fiscal burden; the discrepancy that was apparent between the high rate of taxation and the low yield to the exchequer, caused chiefly by the heavy expenses of tax collection and by fraud; and the pernicious effect on the economy of certain specific taxes, were the principal problems that confronted the economists.

Of particular interest is a group of writers who (to quote Schumpeter again) 'looked upon a single tax as the wand by which to conjure up the benign spirits of fiscal order'.[51] The doctrine of the single tax has been propounded in several countries and at different periods. In France, in 1707, Vauban was to put forward his famous project for a general income tax, the *dixme royale*. Quesnay, in 1760, wished to rationalise the French fiscal system by basing it upon a tax on the net rent of land. And the same idea was taken up in America by Henry George in 1879. It is not to be expected that among the very numerous Spanish economists of the seventeenth century none should seek to cure their country's ills by the same rather obvious panacea. Schemes for a rough approximation to a personal income tax were developed by Jacinto de Alcázar Arrizia in 1646[52] and Bautista Dávila in 1651.[53] Quesnay and George were preceded in their advocacy of a single tax on land or on agricultural produce by Sancho de Moncada (1619), who thought it right to 'tax Nature, who is never weary, and not human industry', and who therefore proposed to remove all taxes on industry and commerce and to tax grain instead, raising its minimum fixed price proportionately; Alvarez Osorio (1686), in whose work the tax takes the form of the *mediodiezmo* on grain, wine and meat; and Francisco Centani (1665), who proposed to tax the land itself.

Of these variations on the theme of the single tax, Centani's is the most remarkable.[54] His is the first clear exposition of the doctrine that land is the only true source of wealth, and the first rationally constructed programme for replacing the existing plethora of indirect taxes by 'a small charge or tribute to fall equally on those who hold the lands that produce the native fruits by which these Kingdoms are sustained and which constitute their physical and true wealth'. An advantage of Centani's plan was that it circumvented the exemption from taxation enjoyed by the Church and the nobility, since it took account only of the productiveness of the land without regard to the condition of the landowner.

Centani advises that a survey should be made of each district over the whole of Spain, covering 'commons, roads, rivers, and all else that pertains to the district, distinguishing the quality and quantity of arable land productive of annual fruits, vineyards, olive-groves, orchards and pastures, and waste-land'. A quota based on the information supplied would then be fixed for the district, whose authorities would be held responsible for its collection. All this is well ahead of its time, the chief stumbling-block to the plan being the difficulty of making the preliminary survey at a period when surveying methods were not yet sufficiently advanced.

In Centani, as in many of the best political economists of his age, there is a vision of the economy as a whole made up of interrelated parts – Mata speaks of a 'general harmony' – which is absent in the work of the scholastics. Thus Centani, in urging the claims of his single tax, points out that besides being certain, just, and easy to collect, the tax may be expected to bring down prices by freeing commodities from the sales tax, and that this lowering of prices will, in turn, enable the people to live better and work more efficiently, and will encourage home production and discourage imports. But all these benefits, adds our author, can only be reaped if the Crown proceeds to a reform of the currency and abandons debasement (which raises prices and ultimately brings ruin) as a method of solving its financial problems.

The Currency

In his condemnation of debasement Centani was faithful to a tradition that went back to medieval times. The adulteration of the *vellón* currency was attacked by many economists throughout the seventeenth century. Between September 1605 and January 1606 twenty provinces reported on a plan for the contraction of the *vellón* circulation.[55] In 1606 the city of Burgos petitioned the king to end the minting of debased *vellón*. They advanced two main reasons for the request: First,

> although the law may determine and name the value and price of money and require it to be received and used at that price, it cannot give money a value that it does not itself possess, since the estimation of men will not value money at more than its intrinsic and essential worth is known to be.

And second,

> all the silver and gold there is will surely leave these kingdoms and be very soon consumed at the hands of merchants who will collect and export it, however many safeguards and harsh penalties may be

imposed to prevent them from doing so. As *vellón* money is worth nothing outside the Kingdom (being, in particular, so reduced in value, tiresome to count, costly to transport, and hindering to trade that all the merchants and everyone else use in their dealings silver and gold money which is valuable in all parts) it is certain that in a few years' time the only money left in Castile will be *vellón*, for the reasons just stated and because the little silver that remains will be hidden away.[56]

These hoary but true ideas were expounded by numerous writers of the period, of whom the ablest and best known, inside and outside Spain, was Juan de Mariana. An unusual feature of Mariana's life is that nothing of his vast literary output appeared until he was in his fifties and that he continued to write works of the first importance into extreme old age, consistently expressing boldly radical views.[57]

Born in 1536, Mariana entered the Jesuit Order in 1554, going on to teach in the Jesuit colleges of Rome and Sicily and at the University of Paris, where his expositions of the writings of Aquinas attracted large audiences. He returned to Spain in 1574 and settled down at Toledo to a life of study. His history of Spain, which appeared between 1592 and 1605, is still read with pleasure by all who love good Spanish. In his treatise on kingship and the institution of monarchy (1598) Mariana expounds a theory of social contract, going so far as to allow the right of tyrannicide.

On the subject of the currency Mariana sketches out the principles that he was to develop more fully later on. Recapitulating the scholastic doctrine that money has two values, its intrinsic or natural value, which corresponds to the value of its metallic content, and its extrinsic or legal value, which is fixed by the king, he adds that

Only a fool would try to separate these values in such a way that the legal price should differ from the natural. Foolish, nay, wicked the ruler who orders that a thing the common people value, let us say, at five should be sold for ten. Men are guided in this matter by common estimation founded on considerations of the quality of things, and of their abundance or scarcity. It would be vain for a Prince to seek to undermine these principles of commerce. 'Tis best to leave them intact instead of assailing them by force to the public detriment. What is done in the case of other commodities should also be done with money. The Prince should pass a law fixing its value, taking into account the just price of the metal and its weight, without exceeding this in any way, except that the expense and cost of minting may be added.[58]

In his treatise on the *vellón* currency, published at Cologne in 1609, Mariana complains that the debasement of the copper coinage violates these principles. Proceeding to develop this thesis on scholastic lines, he first considers the advantages of debasement (a saving in silver, a reduction in the weight of the *vellón* coins, the discouragement of the export of *vellón*, a reduction in imports and consequent retention of silver in Spain, and the temporary relief of the royal finances), next demolishes certain arguments commonly advanced against debasement, and finally brings forward his own more solid reasons for not adulterating the *vellón* coinage. These are:

(1) that the coinage of large quantities of *vellon* is illegal;
(2) that debasement is contrary to natural law;
(3) that prices are bound to rise as money is debased.

> There is no doubt but that in this [debased] money are united the two circumstances that have made goods dearer: firstly, its being, as it will be, in great profusion and without count or number, a thing that cheapens any commodity whatsoever and raises the price of anything exchanged for it; secondly, its being bad and base money that every man will want to throw out of his house, so that owners of goods will refuse to sell except for a larger sum.

Debasement, continues Mariana, is invariably followed by a shortage of goods. As the price of copper rises, the legal value of the money has to be raised, or no profit could be made. The price of copper is driven still higher, and the tale of the coinage must be raised yet again. Attempts to check this process by fixing the price of copper are generally useless. The discount on silver rises to 15, 20 or 30 per cent and the prices of other commodities rise in proportion. Seeing the continuous drop in the value of money, sellers hold back their wares and a general scarcity ensues.

(4) The dearth of goods clogs the wheels of trade and the whole kingdom is impoverished. The king is at last forced to adopt deflationary measures, and holders of *vellón* are ruined.
(5) The royal revenues will be greatly reduced, since they are bound, in the long run, to suffer from the general impoverishment of the country.

Mariana advances similar arguments against the debasement of the gold and silver currencies. He particularly stresses the desirability of maintaining a sound silver coinage, since this, he says, helps to check the evils of *vellón* inflation. In the case of gold the results of debasement would be less grave, since gold plays a smaller part in the transactions of the market.

Mariana ends his treatise by showing how the needs of the royal treasury could be met without resorting to debasement of the currency. His language in this part of his book is bold in the extreme, and he castigates the disorders and excesses of the monarchy with such vehemence that he was arrested for treason and confined for some months to a convent.

In its general framework Mariana's treatise follows traditional lines. Among its more interesting passages is one where he expounds an argument that was, so he tells us, commonly advanced in favour of debasement, but which we do not readily associate with the early seventeenth century. It runs as follows: Debased *vellón* will not leave the country and will circulate plentifully within it. Holders of *vellón* will be ready to make loans to any who wish to pay their debts, undertake all kinds of labour, raise cattle and produce silk. Thus there will be abundant production of fruits and manufactures, and prices will, in the short run, fall, whereas before debasement no one could borrow except at a high rate of interest. Mariana accepts this thesis as true. He later shows, however, that the prosperity that attends the earlier stages of inflation will be short-lived. In the long term, debasement must lead to a *rise* in prices and to general impoverishment.

Mariana was a quantity theorist in the sense that he regarded the increase in the circulating medium that resulted from debasement as an important cause of the rise in Spanish prices. Whereas earlier writers had ascribed the inflation of the sixteenth century to (among other causes) the influx of American treasure, Mariana, standing at the threshold of the *vellón* inflation that continued to drive up prices, correctly predicted the shape of things to come.

Mariana's advice was echoed by many writers. Among them was one of the most tireless and earnest of all the Spanish economists, the Sevillian sea-captain, Tomás de Cardona, who in a long series of memorials written throughout the reign of Philip III and in the early years of that of Philip IV, expounds detailed plans for curing the ailing currency of Castile.[59]

The reckless coining of debased *vellón*, which, as well as being minted in Spain, also entered the country in large quantities from abroad, caused a grave shortage of goods and a general economic crisis. Projects continued to be presented with unabated zeal by would-be reformers. Among the better-known of these projectors were the Milanese, Gerardo Basso, whose proposal to call in and restamp the *vellón* coins anticipated by a few months the government's deflationary measures of 1628,[60] and Mateo Lisón, procurator for Granada in the Cortes. Lisón urged that, if deflation was held to be inevitable, care should be taken not to reveal the government's intentions in advance, since the fear and confusion engendered in the public mind by the crying down of the copper coinage would be even more harmful than the excessive quantity of *vellón* in circulation.[61]

The government finally found itself forced to deflate. In 1628 the nominal value of *vellón* was reduced by half and a period of recession ensued. One of the more able economists who wrote during the years of deflation was Alfonso de Carranza, an admirer and follower of Cardona's. Carranza was mainly concerned to adjust the constantly shifting ratio between the gold, silver and copper coinages, and, like many of his contemporaries, advocates an increase in the price of gold and silver in order to check the flight of the precious metals from Spain.[62]

Similar views were propounded, also in 1628, by Captain Guillén Barbón y Castañeda, together with suggestions for other measures designed to check the depopulation and ruin of Spain.[63]

The deflationary policy was short-lived. In 1634 the *vellón* coinage was called in and restamped at double its value, and the years that followed saw further debasement of *vellón*. The result was a prodigious rise in the price of goods calculated in *vellón*, and in the premium on silver, a condition of affairs that caused the government to deflate once again in 1642. In was doubtless in support of this measure that Antonio de Alarcón, arguing on oldfashioned lines, urged that the value of money depends not on the whims of princes but on common estimation, and that the schemes put forward by Cardona, Carranza and Basso to tamper with the currency were 'unworthy of men'.[64]

For a decade, between 1642 and 1652, the tide of inflation was held in control, but thereafter it surged forward with renewed strength, and, except for occasional checks, reached its height between 1671 and 1680. By that time 95 per cent of the Castilian currency consisted of *vellón*, and trading, when not carried on by barter, had become a form of weight-lifting. P. Vilar points out that the purchase of 45 kilos of cheese entailed the transport of no less than 184 kilos of copper money.[65] During the same period the premium on silver rose to 275 per cent.

In the last phase of the inflation, when all was misery and ruin, even the projectors faltered in their task, protesting that they had spent their lives and health in vain.[66] Yet there were still some who took up their pens in the king's service. Bautista Dávila, whose doctrine of the single tax we have noted, also tackled the problem of the *vellón* currency,[67] while yet another soldier-economist, Captain Juan Somoza y Quiroga, poured forth in 1679 and 1680 as many as twenty-two memorials, mostly on subjects connected with the currency.[68]

In the almost complete absence of monographs on the Spanish non-scholastic monetary-theorists of the seventeenth century, it is not easy to sum up their achievements. I feel inclined to assess them as follows. They accepted traditional doctrine, as it had been laid down by Aristotle and the scholastics. Thus, they refer continually to the 'intrinsic' and 'extrinsic' value of money, nor do they overlook the part played by supply and demand in the formation of the 'common estimation', and hence of the value, of money. They fully accept, also, the classic doctrine of the functions of money as a medium of exchange and a measure and store of value. But they did not merely transmit the old ideas. They opened up paths that made new progress possible, even if they did not advance very far along them. They abandoned, to begin with, the scholastic habit of asking a series of often loosely connected questions, and coming up with answers that were sometimes contradictory. Instead, they began to see the economy as a whole. They broadened the scope of monetary theory and applied its principles to the problems of their day, even more systematically than the late scholastics had done. Altogether, I would say that by about the middle of the seventeenth century scholastic monetary theory, in Spain as elsewhere, had been outpaced, and that further scientific progress, apart from the discussion of moral issues, would henceforth depend on the efforts of non-scholastic writers.

Agriculture

At the beginning of the seventeenth century Spanish agriculture, already languishing, suffered various disasters that combined to bring about its complete prostration. A series of bad harvests had been followed by the plague of 1599–1600 with its heavy mortality, an acute labour shortage and a rise in prices and wages. The struggle to raise some wheat and barley, or to gather a small crop of olives or grapes, on the dry land; to grow fruit and vegetables on the small area of watered land (estimated at less than 1 per cent of the whole); and to keep animals, migrant or settled, on the scanty pasture available, had become a losing battle. The drift to the towns increased and the villages were left deserted. The final blow was dealt by the expulsion of the Moriscos in 1609–14.

The Moriscos were former Moslems who were forced to accept baptism, in 1502 in Castile, and in 1525 in Aragon. They were the élite of the farming community, skilled in the intricate technique of working the irrigated land that lay along the eastern and southern seaboards. A writer speaks of 'the solicitude and care with which, all perseverance and industry, they broke the hillsides, ploughing and cultivating the land until at last they gathered its fruits, without need of begging'.[69] A few Moriscos were allowed to remain behind in order to maintain the houses, sugar-factories, ricefields and watered areas, and to instruct the untrained colonists who were brought to replace those who had been expelled.

There may, perhaps, have been some justification for the expulsion on religious and political grounds, but its economic effects were bound to be prejudicial. Probably some 3 per cent of the whole population of Spain were expelled, the numbers varying greatly from region to region. Valencia was the area most badly hit: no less than 23 per cent of the inhabitants were expelled. The consequent decay of the Valencian countryside made it impossible for the owners of farms to repay the loans in which much urban capital was invested, and the whole economy suffered from this remarkably ill-timed measure.

The political economists differ as to the merits of the expulsion. Few of them condemn it entirely. Thus, Sancho de Moncada, though he fully shares the mercantilist fear of depopulation,[70] declares that the Moriscos, as enemies of Spain, 'were the cause of many deaths', and that their expulsion therefore actually helped to increase the Spanish population.[71]

Martínez de la Mata also dissents from the view that the expulsion was a mistake, and thinks that any harm that may have been done could be countermanded by forbidding the import of foreign merchandise.[72] Caja de Leruela is more sympathetically disposed towards the Moriscos and seems to regret their departure.[73] Fernández de Navarrete goes further. In one of the four *Discourses* that he devotes to the subject of depopulation he writes:

> I hold it as certain that if in the first instance some means had been found of not marking the Moriscos with a note of infamy they would all have been reconciled to the Catholic faith. If they conceived a hatred and horror for that religion, it was because as Catholics, they were downtrodden and despised, and had no hope of being able, in course of time, to blot out the shame of their low birth.[74]

Besides suffering from a shortage of labour the seventeenth-century farmer, like his medieval forebears and his modern successors, was vexed by the continuance of the *tasa de trigo*, or fixed maximum price on corn, imposed to protect the interests of the consumer without regard to those of the producer. The doctrine that the prince had the right and duty of controlling prices had been questioned by few, if any, scholastic authors, and was not seriously to be attacked until about the middle of the eighteenth century. But many of the seventeenth-century political economists recognised the hardship that the *tasa* imposed on farmers, and the difficulty of trying to fix prices for the long term in a world of constantly changing values. Lope de Deza brings out this point well. If, he says,

> fruits and the other things we use were to observe regularity and keep to the same unvarying course, it would be easy to govern and to impose upon them a perpetual *tasa* suited to their nature. . . . But as . . . everything is subject to such great and continuous changes, and fertility is followed by barrenness, and barrenness by an average crop, . . . and sometimes people will give their jewels for a loaf, and their most precious possessions for a jug of water, and at other times they will pay only a very low price for many loaves, and water is spilled and despised, it cannot be just to fix a stable and perpetual price on things that are subject to change and to such great alteration.[75]

In other words, the *tasa* should be frequently revised and averaged in such a way that farmers may set off the bad years against the good.

A more fundamental problem that occupied many of the Spanish economists was that of the distribution and administration of the land itself. González de Cellorigo (1600) believes that no one ought to hold land if he cannot cultivate it personally. The rich, he says, do not choose to farm their estates, and the poor cannot do so properly for lack of capital. González wishes to see a more equal distribution of wealth without, perhaps, being very clear as to how this is to be achieved.[76]

The distinguished Cordovan humanist, Pedro de Valencia, writing in 1605, expresses profound disquiet at the decline of Spanish agriculture. He urges that all cultivable land should be brought under the plough, allocated to a particular use, and divided into medium-sized lots that could be leased at a moderate rent to the local peasants. The land would be redistributed each year, reserving sufficient pasturage to maintain the flocks.[77]

Miguel Caja de Leruela, himself an official of the Mesta or association of cattle-owners, ascribes the ruin of Spain to the decline of stock-farming, especially among the smaller farmers. He recommends the conservation and extension of pasturage and wishes to see each peasant supplied with the animals necessary for his support.[78]

Several other authors drew up schemes on what would now be regarded as socialistic lines. Costa tentatively speaks of a Spanish school of collectivist economics,[79] and certainly this preoccupation with land reform, and with agriculture in general, is a notable feature of Spanish mercantilist literature.

A Programme for Development: Miguel Alvarez Osorio y Redín
The method chiefly followed in this chapter, that of grouping the ideas
of the Spanish economists according to themes, while it has some
advantages fails to do justice to the work of certain writers. This applies
especially to the authors of ambitious systems or plans for development,
such as Moncada, Fernández de Navarrete, Martínez de la Mata and
Alvarez Osorio. We may usefully conclude this brief account of the
thought of the seventeenth-century economists by glancing at the
Discourses of the last-named writer, whose merits primarily consist in
his vision of the economy as a whole.

Osorio was the author of seven memorials presented to Charles II
between 1686 and 1691.[80] Unlike Mata, whose colourful style helps to
explain his following among the people of Seville, Osorio's talents as
a writer are minimal. Even Costa, whose literary digestion was of the
strongest, admits to having found difficulty in assimilating the thought
of this author. Nevertheless, Osorio's thorough knowledge of Spanish
affairs (he had travelled to every part of the kingdom and voyaged at
his own expense with the Armada in order to acquaint himself with the
economic system and government of his country), his passionate earnest-
ness, the painstaking detail in which he worked out his scheme for the
regeneration of Spain, and the modernity of much of his teaching,
enlists the reader's sympathy and curbs his impatience at the strenuous
effort he is called upon to make.

Osorio was first and foremost a statistician. By way of gaining some
idea of his mode of procedure, let us take his treatment of the colonial
trade. He begins by giving us about thirty pages of tables reducing to
tons the weight and volume of many different kinds of merchandise –
textiles, clothes, ironmongery, foodstuffs, drugs, etc. For instance, he
lists some twenty varieties of linen, and calculates the length and weight
of the cloth that goes to each bale and the number of bales that go to
the ton. He next proceeds to load, arm, provision and man an imaginary
ship, accounting for every cubic foot of space; multiplies his ship into
a phantom navy; estimates how many ships would be needed to clothe
the entire population of the West Indies (allowing three shirts and three
pairs of drawers for each man and four voluminous white petticoats for
each woman); calculates the monetary value of the cargoes; assesses
the duties payable to the Royal Treasury; and so on.[81] By similar
methods, applied in minute detail to every branch of economic policy,
Osorio slowly builds up a vast system embracing agriculture, industry,
finance and foreign and colonial trade.

Now, this is not the sort of economic writing that is likely to attract
disciples. Osorio's discourses, indeed, are unutterably wearisome and
clumsy. But his method has one important advantage: it is founded on

fact. No doubt his figures are open to question. But he does at least present his arguments carefully and logically, step by step, and any reader wishing to refute them, and familiar with the material, could put his finger on the exact point where Osorio goes astray. In this respect Osorio's work is thoroughly scientific.

Stripped of its elaborate statistical data and long chains of arithmetical reasoning, the broad outline of Osorio's scheme emerges as follows. Spain must at all costs be made self-supporting. The chief cause of her depopulation and ruin is the import of foreign manufactures, arising from the fact that Spanish manufactures are twice as dear as those bought abroad. The dearness of home manufactures is owing to excessive taxation and more particularly to the system of indirect taxation that oppresses all sections of the population. Osorio paints a melancholy picture of the cruelties committed by the army of tax-collectors (he estimates their number at 100,000) who

> enter the homes of the poor labourers and deprive them of the little money they possess; and if they have none they take away their clothes and even the poor beds on which they lie; and they delay as long as possible in selling them; and even then the proceeds barely suffice to pay their own salaries. When all accounts are balanced, scarce ten per cent falls to Your Majesty. Oh merciful Sir, what a piteous and uncharitable thing it is, that Your Majesty should receive for your sustenance a tenth part of the life-blood of your loyal subjects![82]

To remedy this state of affairs, Osorio proposes to abolish the existing indirect taxes except in Madrid and certain other large towns, and to replace them by the *medio-diezmo*, a tax of 5 per cent to be paid in kind by all farmers, wine-growers and cattle-owners. This tax, he says, would not suffice to maintain the population unless a further 2 million *fanegas* of wheat, barley and oats were brought under cultivation by the Crown. The land would be taken over compulsorily if necessary, but the owners would receive compensation. The seed would be obtained partly by a forced loan to be made by the richer farmers to their poor neighbours, and partly by a levy to be paid by all classes of the population on a progressive scale. The farmers would be chosen for their skill and honesty, and overseers, appointed from among the more God-fearing and public-spirited of the community, would be empowered to eject any who failed to use his land to full advantage. At harvest-time one half of the crops would go to the Crown and the other half to the farmers and their families. The proposed system was not unlike that of the old Russian *mir* or the modern collective farm, and, indeed, Osorio seems to have known something of Russian institutions, and alludes to them in terms of praise.

Turning to manufacture, Osorio proposes that the Crown should set up throughout the kingdom some 300,000 looms for the weaving of linen, wool and silk. Only the manufacturers themselves (Osorio was, of course, envisaging domestic industry, and by 'manufacturers' he meant the actual weavers) would be allowed to sell their wares to the public, and middlemen would thus be deprived of their unjust gains and forced to seek more useful work. The old medieval mistrust of middlemen was strong in Osorio, and to frustrate their machinations in the corn, wool and fruit trades he works out a detailed plan which he chooses to call 'simple' and which mainly depends for its success on the 'disinterestedness of all who take part in it'. According to this plan, every farmer with grain to sell would enter his stocks in a public register not later than December, and the price of grain could thus be fairly determined in accordance with the size of the harvests, only the actual producers being allowed to take part in the sale.

Osorio pictures the agricultural and industrial systems as complementary and of equal importance to the state; and he intended the Crown to devote its half-share in the produce of the newly cultivated land to providing food for the new manufacturing class. 'The whole population will be increased by aiding both farmers and manufacturers, who are like soul and body. If manufacturers languish farmers perish, for their are none to consume their crops.'[83]

Osorio's zeal for planning was by no means confined to the reform of agriculture and industry. The army, the navy, the Church, justice, poor relief, irrigation, education – hardly a branch of public administration escapes his net. In particular, he longs to reform the colonial trade and suggests establishing a single Spanish company to wrest it from foreign interlopers. In one of his discourses he extends the functions of his company to embrace the whole of Spanish industry. All Spaniards would be obliged to take shares in it, and every able-bodied man and boy could earn his living in its employ.[84]

There can be no doubt of Osorio's 'collectivist' ideals or that they went beyond the kind of state interventionism that we generally associate with mercantilism. His discourses display that mixture of sound common sense and exuberant fancy that Cervantes so clearly perceived in the character of his countrymen. His work, like that of many Spanish mercantilists, is deeply religious in tone and for him religion and patriotism were closely linked:

Now is the time to answer in the words of Christ, 'Get thee behind me, Satan', to all who defend private interests against the common good. Loyal men must seek with all their hearts the preservation of the whole state, and they must do so in the service of God.[85]

SIGNS OF RECOVERY (1700–40)

The reader who has followed me thus far may perhaps see no great mystery in the economic decline of Spain, the causes of which were well enough defined by the contemporary economists. More puzzling are the signs of recovery that began to show themselves, it would seem, even before the death of Charles II in 1700 and the establishment of the Bourbon dynasty on the Spanish throne.

The first hesitant indications of revival appeared not in Castile but in the peripheral regions of the Mediterranean. The Catalans had always declined to join Madrid on the see-saw of inflation and deflation, and in the second half of the seventeenth century had kept the issue of new coins under careful control.

Catalonia, under the Treaty of the Pyrenees (1659), was forced to adopt a measure of free trade which actually favoured the growth of the textile industry. Stimulated by foreign competition, the Catalan had no choice but to set to work at a time when Castile was sunk in inertia. By the end of the century traffic in the port of Barcelona was double what it had been in 1605, whereas in that of Seville it fell to a tenth part of its volume during the same period.[86] Valencia, also, which enjoyed monetary autonomy, seems to have escaped the worst consequences of the inflation.

The Bourbons unified Spain for the first time, and centralised the administration. The autonomous régimes of Valencia, Catalonia and Aragon were abolished, though the Basque provinces and Navarre kept some of their ancient privileges. Above all, the new dynasty brought a general will for reform, a readiness to learn from other nations, and a belief in the good effects of education and culture, more especially in the fields of science and economics.

These changes did not come all at once. The full effects of the Enlightenment were not felt in Spain until the second half of the eighteenth century. The long reign of Philip V, the first Bourbon king, is regarded as a mere prolongation of the 'decadence' by some historians, for whom the transition from stagnation to progress did not take place until the middle years of the century. But even in its earlier decades important reforms were introduced, many of which had been repeatedly urged upon the Habsburg monarchs by the old Spanish economists.

For instance, in 1558 Ortiz had pleaded that

in the first Cortes to be held in Castile or in Aragon there be joined some deputies from both kingdoms, and that they arrange for the duties at the 'dry ports' and for others that are payable between the said kingdoms to be removed and the guard passed to the frontiers of France and Portugal, and that merchants and travellers should move freely between the said kingdoms, since all belong to His Majesty.[87]

Now, in 1714 and 1717, a beginning was made towards unifying the customs and removing the 'dry ports' to the frontiers and sea-ports.

Pérez de Oliva in 1524 and Antonelli in 1581 had seen the need for reforming the Spanish transport system and had pointed out that a free circulation of goods was impossible without an adequate network of communications. An ordinance of 1718 purports to regulate the waterways and promote the building of roads, bridges and ports.

Many of the seventeenth-century political economists had pleaded for the reform of the *vellón* currency and urged, more especially, that the nominal value of *vellón* should correspond to the commodity value of its metal content. In 1718 this was achieved. New coins of pure copper were minted, the 'intrinsic' and 'extrinsic' value of which were made to coincide.

Alvarez Osorio had planned the creation of a chain of great trading companies. In 1714 the Honduras company was formed, followed by others as the century progressed.

The old economists had clamoured for agrarian reform. Such reform was a conspicuous feature of the Enlightenment in Spain, though not, it is true, until the second half of the eighteenth century.

Thus many of the projects of the old Spanish political economists, which had often seemed chimerical in their day, came to be realised by later generations. Their writings, too, were reprinted long after their death and studied with respect by the great statesmen of the eighteenth century.

Jerónimo de Uztáriz

So far as economic literature is concerned, there is no well-defined boundary dividing mercantilism from physiocracy or economic liberalism. In the second half of the eighteenth century many writers still held mercantilist views on certain aspects of the economy, while they repudiated them on others. However, for the practical purposes of this study we may tentatively regard the age of mercantilism as having closed, in Spain, around 1740, the year of publication of Bernardo de Ulloa's treatise.[88] The most important writer of this earlier period of Bourbon rule was Jerónimo de Uztáriz.

Uztáriz was born in 1670 and came of an ancient Navarrese family. At the age of 16 he went to Flanders, and, after receiving his military training at the Royal Academy in Brussels, served with distinction in several campaigns. In 1698 he was attached to the service of the Marquis of Bedmar, who appointed him as First Secretary to the military government of Flanders, and in 1705 when Bedmar became Viceroy of Sicily, Uztáriz accompanied him to Palermo as Secretary of State and of War.

While still a young man Uztáriz travelled extensively in Holland, France, England, Germany and Italy, acquiring the first-hand knowledge of the commerce of the principal countries of Europe which established his reputation as an expert in economic affairs.

Uztáriz received various marks of favour from Philip V and in 1707 returned to Spain, a warm supporter of the new dynasty, to occupy posts in the Ministries of War and of Marine, and on the Council of Finance. In 1730 he was appointed Minister of the Board of Trade and the Mint, in which capacity he carried out important reforms. He was also secretary to the Council and Chamber of the Indies, a member of the king's Privy Council, and a knight of the Order of Santiago. He died in Madrid in 1732.

Uztáriz's first contribution to economic literature was his 'Approbation' of the Spanish translation of a work on Dutch commerce by Huet.[89] Uztáriz shows how Louis XIV, guided by Colbert, had succeeded in reviving French industry, shipping and commerce, and suggests that Spain might profitably adopt the same policy.

Uztáriz's best-known work, *The Theory and Practice of Commerce*, was first published in 1724 and seems to have circulated privately.[90] During the last years of his life Uztáriz improved and corrected his treatise. He intended to add an extensive supplement which was to include an account of 'the grand policy of the English in allowing and encouraging the export of grain', a measure, he thought, that would 'raise great astonishment almost everywhere for the novelty of the thing, and its contradiction to what seems prudent at first sight'. Unfortunately he died before he was able to complete his work.

In 1740 Bernardo de Ulloa summarised Uztáriz's ideas in his own treatise, frankly acknowledging his debt to Uztáriz and enlarging on certain points that the latter had not fully treated. At last, in 1742, Uztáriz's son published a second edition of his father's treatise. This, unlike the first, was widely read. The book was translated into English in 1751, and supplied Adam Smith with some of the material on Spain that he uses in the *Wealth of Nations*. A French translation by Forbonnais appeared in 1753, and an Italian in 1793. A third Spanish edition was published in 1757.

The Theory and Practice of Commerce was the most accurate and solidly-documented handbook of its day. Until quite recently Uztáriz's estimate of the population and revenues of Spain, and of the quantity of precious metals shipped from the New World, were accepted without question and reproduced by writers in many countries. The merit of the work resides chiefly in the vast mass of factual information it presents rather than in its doctrinal content, which is sound but in no way original.

Of all the Spanish political economists of the age of mercantilism, Uztáriz most closely resembled the stock figure of a 'mercantilist'. Early in his treatise he quotes Huet's dictum that

> Commerce is the only thing which can draw gold and silver, the main springs of action, into any state. And it is so glaring a truth that Spain, in whose dominions these are found in plenty, is in great want of both, from their having slighted traffick and manufactures, and all the mines of America are scarce sufficient to pay for the merchandise and commodities which other nations carry to Spain.[91]

Uztáriz proceeds to develop systematically the theory of the balance of trade that had been sketched by Ortiz nearly two centuries before and adopted by Moncada, Navarrete, Lisón, Mata, Osorio and other seventeenth-century political economists.

Uztáriz divides commerce into two classes, the 'profitable' and the 'injurious' (he also uses the terms 'active' and 'passive') according to whether it produces a favourable or unfavourable balance of payments and consequent inflow or outflow of gold and silver. A favourable balance was for Uztáriz the key to national prosperity:

> ... we ought to labour with great zeal and address in all those measures that can avail towards selling more commodities and fruits to foreigners than we buy of them, for here lies all the secret, good conduct, and advantage of trade; or at least, that we be on a par in the barter of commodities, which might even be sufficient for the constitution of this kingdom.[92]

An unfavourable balance will bring about disaster,

> for it is an infallible maxim, that the more our importation of foreign merchandise shall exceed the exportation of our own, so much more unavoidable will be our misery and ruin at last, and the damages such a traffick usually brings upon a whole kingdom are even greater than the most devouring locusts.

National prosperity, then, was bound up with the accumulation of gold and silver, to the attainment of which object the greater part of

Uztáriz's treatise is devoted. Our author shows in detail how the methods of Colbert – the freeing of internal commerce from the multifarious tolls and taxes by which it was hampered, the encouragement of home manufactures and their protection from foreign competition, the import of raw materials duty-free the prohibition of the export of raw materials used in the national factories, and other protectionist measures – might be adapted to Spanish conditions.

As always when we are considering mercantilist literature, we are constrained to wonder whether treasure was thought of as an end in itself or as a means to national prosperity. Did Uztáriz want production in order to attract treasure or treasure in order to develop production? Light is thrown on this problem in several passages, of which the following is a fair sample:

> . . . the more our manufactories are enlarged and flourish, so much easier and happier will be the circumstances even of the peasants, and the nation in general; for as more money will circulate in the kingdom, merchandise and fruits bear a higher value, and will be more consumed; both of them will come to a ready and constant market, our lands will be better cultivated, and yield more; payments be duly and regularly made; in short, the whole political body in this full health and vigour will impart to every member constant supplies of life and spirits. . . .[93]

This insistence upon the beneficial effects of a plentiful circulation of wealth, characteristic of mercantilism in general, was especially strong among the Spanish economists. The fact that the royal revenues were largely drawn from indirect taxes, of which the most obvious and inescapable was the *alcabala* payable on almost all goods sold or bartered, early drew their attention to the need for maintaining a fluent stream of trade. As an example of their often quite elaborate attempts to examine the mechanism of the circulation of money, we have already considered the work of Martínez de la Mata.

Uztáriz shared the mercantilist desire for a large population, and cites the care shown for the welfare of the common people by Vauban, whose *Dixme Royale* he praises warmly. In some passages he describes the hardships of the poor in the cool, matter-of-fact tone of the true mercantilist.

> One of the principal steps towards the increase and preservation of commerce is having the kingdom well supplied with working hands, both for the manufactures of silk and wool, and other trades, and for the cultivation of land, which administer plenty, and this has a great influence upon the price of goods.[94]

In others he is more sympathetic, citing Vauban's dictum that 'The grandeur of a prince is in proportion to the number of his subjects', and that 'he should never agree to have the common people slighted or oppressed, since it is their labour, commerce, and tribute that enriches a king and his kingdom'.[95] And on one occasion he surprises and endears himself to us by painting an almost Dickensian picture of a starving family living on bread and water, without shelter, bedding or medical aid, whose mother, struggling against constant fatigue and depression, sees her children dying before her eyes.[96]

But such sentimental flights are rare. Towards religion Uztáriz was business-like. Anxious to deprive the English of the profits derived from their cod-fisheries, he hopes that, in place of the numerous fast-days customary in Spain, the Holy Father will allow

> another species of abstinence and restraint, that equally administers to the mortification of our souls, and does not turn out so much to the advantage of the rivals of the crown, and the catholick church, as these fast-days do, by opening a way for the importation and consumption of English salt fish, which is a main branch of their commerce and the foundation of their riches and strength.[97]

Here, indeed, we have travelled far from Ortiz's invocation of saints and angels, and from the religious fervour of Osorio.

Uztáriz, like other mercantilists, wished to free internal commerce from the legislative restraints that hindered its expansion. He also tentatively suggests that in years of good harvests the export of grain might be allowed in order to prevent its price from falling so low that farmers would be discouraged from sowing grain for the next year. He was, too, in sympathy with the spirit of later theory in his mistrust of all laws that ran counter to the natural course of trade:

> It is evident that penal laws and statutes cannot prevent the extraction of gold and silver, though they be severe as in this kingdom, and extend to forfeiture of life and effects. With so great rigour is the prohibition enforced here, and yet it neither is nor can be observed in Spain, or in any other kingdom under the same circumstances, as the experience of whole ages manifests.[98]

And again:

> If in seven or eight ages we have not been able to enforce the execution by such severe laws often repeated and revived, we ought not to expect to see it done in our times, except it be by substituting other,

more natural, effectual and secure measures, such as have been proposed by a good regulation of commerce, in order to sell foreigners
more than we buy of them; and not by penal laws, prohibitions,
and guards at the ports and other places.[99]

Such practical considerations were among the elements in mercantilist
thought that, in Spain as elsewhere, paved the way for liberal economics.

It is clear that as late as 1753 Uztáriz's brand of mercantilism appeared
topical and acceptable to his French translator, Forbonnais, who
recommends a 'noble emulation' of Uztáriz's precepts, adding that 'we
have so few books on commerce in our language that I have regarded
the details given in this one as most useful for the instruction of those
who wish to study this great subject'. The long-continued interest
evoked by Uztáriz's treatise may serve to remind us that mercantilism,
of which Forbonnais was at that time the leading French exponent,
flourished in France for some years side by side with physiocracy, and
that the older ideas, though partly discarded, did not completely fade
away until the end of the eighteenth century.

It was, perhaps, Uztáriz's cosmopolitan training, and the ample
space he devotes to considering the economic policies of England,
France and Holland, that made his work especially acceptable to his
foreign contemporaries. Together with Ulloa, he is better known
abroad than any other Spanish economist, with the possible exception
of Mariana. He was not an analytical economist. As he himself tells us,
he was a practical man, uninterested in 'speculative questions'. But he
was a diligent collector of facts, a great systematiser, and a lucid stylist.
It would be ungracious to complain that what we miss in his work is the
peculiarly Spanish blend of other-worldliness and robust common
sense that gives its special flavour to earlier economic literature.

Bernardo de Ulloa
Ulloa was born in Seville and represented that city in the Cortes.
His admiration for Uztáriz, whose treatise was known to few readers
until the publication of the second edition in 1742, led him to expound
many of the views of the Navarrese economist in his own book, which
appeared in 1740.[100]

In the first part of this work Ulloa discusses the reasons for the decay
of Spanish industry and puts forward suggestions for its revival. Like
Uztáriz, he advocates the reform of the tax system, more especially
of the indirect taxes that weighed upon manufactured articles. He also
follows Uztáriz in wishing to open up the home market by abolishing
the multitude of tolls and taxes that impeded commerce between the
different regions of Spain, and to improve the roads and waterways

whose bad condition caused prices to vary greatly from place to place. In the second part of this treatise Ulloa turns to foreign trade. He stresses the need for a strong navy and a large population, advocates the protection of Spanish industry by suitable reform of the customs and excise duties and wishes to see a more general use made of Spanish shipping in the conduct of foreign trade. He devotes great attention to the decline of commerce between Spain and America, and deplores the Treaty of Utrecht (1713), by which England secured a monopoly of the slave trade and the right to send each year a ship of 500 tons laden with merchandise to the Indies. Ulloa hesitates to recommend a more liberal policy towards the establishment of industries in the colonies on the ground that home manufactures might suffer thereby, but suggests measures for improving the colonial agriculture.

In short, Ulloa's main preoccupations were to turn the balance of trade in favour of Spain by means of a protectionist policy, and to direct the American economy in a way that would best promote the interests of the metropolis.

Miguel de Zavala

In 1732, the year of Uztáriz's death, there appeared a work that may be said to have opened a transitional period of preparation for the acceptance of physiocracy and *laissez-faire*.[101] Miguel de Zavala addressed to the king a memorial that is divided into three parts. In the first of these the author condemns the *alcabala* and other indirect taxes on lines that were by now traditional, and suggests their replacement by a 'royal contribution' of the kind proposed by Vauban.

In the second part of the memorial Zavala attacks the *tasa* or fixed price of grain, on the ground that if prices were allowed to rise freely farmers would grow more grain and merchants bring it from places where prices were lower. Shortages would thus be automatically corrected. On the other hand, if the *tasa* is lower than the price of grain would be on a free market, farmers will cut down production and holders of grain hoard it away, with the result that grain will not be cheaper but even scarcer than it would be if the *tasa* were abolished. In this part of his work Zavala anticipates some of the physiocratic ideas that were to prevail in France between 1757 and 1776.

The third part of the memorial is devoted to commerce, a topic the author treats on the usual mercantilist lines.

The Inflation Through Spanish Eyes

Every generation distinguishes, from among the chorus of voices that echoes down from the past, such utterances as have meaning for its day. For us, surely, the Spanish economic literature of the mercantilist period holds a special message: it provides us with a running commentary on one of the worst and longest inflations on record. Thanks to the wide range of problems discussed by the Spanish political economists, and the very diversity of their views, their work illuminates the whole course of that inflation as it passed through its successive phases.

The effect of the influx of American treasure on the Spanish price level was observed, as we have seen, by the scholastic writers of the day. They were not, however, content to believe that the mere expansion of the circulating medium in itself caused prices to rise. Tomás de Mercado, for example, went further than to propound a primitive form of quantity theory: he took pains to show by concrete examples the mechanism by which the demand for goods destined to supply the colonial market caused an increase in prices at home.

The second phase of the inflation was recognised, and its consequences foreseen, by Mariana, who attributed the renewed rise in prices to the continuance of monetary expansion, in this case caused by the excessive issue of debased *vellón*.

The first hundred years of the inflation were analysed by Diego de Saavedra Fajardo, writing in 1640. He notes the following sequence of events:

(1) Discovery of the American mines and exaggeration in the public mind of the wealth to be drawn from them.

The people on the banks of the Guadalquivir marvelled at those precious products of the earth that had been brought to light by the labours of the Indians and carried hither by our daring and industry. But the possession and abundance of so much wealth changed everything.

Agriculture straightway laid aside her plough, and, dressed in silk, took to caring for her hands calloused by toil. Commerce, in a humour for nobility, exchanged the counter for the saddle, and rode forth to parade through the streets. The arts disdained mechanical tools. The silver and gold coins scorned the low parentage of the alloy, and, declining to admit that of other metals, kept themselves pure and noble, so that the nations desired and sought them by various means. Goods grew proud, and, silver and gold being held in little esteem, raised their prices.

(2) Overexpenditure by the Crown in anticipation of the arrival of American treasure, involving a wave of buying, a rise in wages and eventual resort to borrowing.

And, as men are wont to believe that their incomes go further than they really do, so did the royal luxury and pomp increase, together with the wages, salaries, and other expenses of the Crown, in expectation of those newly-acquired riches which, ill administered and ill preserved, were not sufficient to cover all payments and gave rise to borrowing, and this to exchange-dealing and usury.

(3) The Crown attempts to remedy this state of affairs by debasing the *vellón* coinage.

Necessity grew, and called for costly remedies. The most harmful was the debasement of the coinage, regardless of the fact that this should be kept as pure as religion itself. . . . Deaf to all advice, Philip III doubled the value of the *vellón* money, which had hitherto been proportionate to the requirements of petty commerce and to the value of the larger coins.

(4) Foreigners, quick to recognise the overvaluation of *vellón*, bring copper to Spain and export precious metal and goods.

Foreign nations saw the estimation that the die had given to the base metal, and treated money as merchandise, bringing copper already minted to the coasts of Spain and taking out gold, silver and other goods, by which procedure they did us more harm than if they had poured into Spain all the snakes and noxious animals of Africa.

(5) Commerce was hampered by the weight and baseness of that metal. Prices rose and goods were withdrawn as in the time of Alphonso the Learned . . . buying and selling ceased, and in their absence the royal revenues diminished, and new measures and impositions had to be devised. Thus was the substance of Castile consumed, for there was no longer any trade or commerce.[102]

Taken as a thumbnail sketch of a century of inflation there seems to be nothing much wrong with this analysis. The economic decline of Spain was explained in similar terms by many of the political economists of the later seventeenth and eighteenth centuries. We may doubt whether the resources of modern scholarship have seriously shaken their conclusions.

NOTES

1 John Hales, in *A Compendious or Briefe Examination of Certayne Ordinary Complaints of Divers of our Countrymen in these our Days* (London, 1581) (written about 1549), puts the following remarks into the mouth of his Doctor:

> What parts of the common Weale is neglected by Philosophy morall? doth it not teach first how every man should govern himself honestly? Secondly, how hee should guyde his Family wisely and profitably? And thyrdly, it sheweth how a City or a Realme, or any other common weale should bee well ordered and governed, both in tyme of peace, and also warre. What Common weale can be without either a Governor or Counsaylors that shoulde bee experte in thys kynde of learning? (fol. 9)

2 Juan de Mariana, *De mutatione monetae*, in *Tractatus septem* (Cologne, 1609). Spanish translation, *Tratado y discurso sobre la moneda de vellón*, in *Biblioteca de autores españoles* (Madrid, 1854), Vol. 31 (numerous reprints), ch. 10.

3 Scholastic ideas on taxation are studied by John Laures, *The Political Economy of Juan de Mariana* (New York, 1928). An excellent recent study is by Javier Gorosquieta Reyes, 'El sistema de ideas tributarias en los teólogos y moralistas principales de la escuela de Salamanca (siglos XVI y XVII)', thesis presented to the Universidad Complutense (Madrid, 1971).

4 For the bibliography of the scholastic writers see Chapter 3, note 1. The work of the Spanish political economists has received more attention from historians than has been accorded to the scholastics until quite recent years.

The doyen of the historians of early economic thought in Spain is the Count of Campomanes (1723–1808), illustrious statesman, economist, diplomat, scholar and writer of the Spanish Enlightenment. In the Prologue to his *Discurso sobre la educación popular de los artesanos y su fomento* (Madrid, 1773), Campomanes mentions a number of seventeenth-century economists, and, in the Appendix to the *Discurso* (1775), reprints the treatises of Francisco Martínez de la Mata and Alvarez Osorio, and quotes at length some passages by Sancho de Moncada.

Another fundamental work is the *Biblioteca española económico-política* (Madrid, 1801–21), 4 vols, of Juan Sempere y Guarinos, in which are summarised, or reprinted in part or in their entirety, the books, pamphlets or projects of twenty political economists of the sixteenth and seventeenth centuries.

An important landmark is Manuel Colmeiro's *Biblioteca de los economistas españoles de los siglos XVI, XVII y XVIII*, first published in the *Memorias de la Real Academia de Ciencias Morales y Políticas* (Madrid, 1879), Vol. 1, republished by the same academy in 1954. Colmeiro lists and briefly comments on the writings of some four hundred Spanish political economists, most of whom he knew at first hand. The chief defect of the *Biblioteca* is its inadequate treatment of all but a few minor scholastic works.

Manuel Colmeiro's *Historia de la economía política en España* (Madrid, 1863), republished with an Introduction by Gonzalez Anes (Madrid 1965), 2 vols, is not, as the title asserts, a history of political economy, but an economic history of Spain. Colmeiro, however, drew most of his material from the writings of the political economists, the Acts of the Cortes and legal dispositions. His 'History' provides an abundance of texts and bibliographical information that illuminate the development of economic thought in Spain.

Joaquin Costa, in his *Colectivismo agrario en España* (Madrid, 1898), studies some of the Spanish political economists who have favoured the state ownership of land. According to Costa, numerous writers of the sixteenth and seventeenth centuries belong to what he regards as the 'Spanish collectivist school of economics'. For a summary in English of the relevant section of Costa's book, see G. Brenan, *The Spanish Labyrinth* (Cambridge, 1943), Appendix 2 (Socialist Tendencies in Spain in the Seventeenth Century).

Scattered through the writings of Earl J. Hamilton we find many references to the Spanish political economists. See, for example, *American Treasure and the Price Revolution in Spain, 1501–1650* (Cambridge, Mass., 1934), pp. 289–94; 'Spanish mercantilism before 1700' in *Facts and Factors in Economic History: Articles by Former Students of Edwin Francis Gay* (Harvard, 1932), pp. 214–39; 'The decline of Spain' (1938). The last-mentioned study was published in Spanish in E. J. Hamilton's *El florecimiento del capitalismo* (Madrid, 1948), pp. 131 *et seq.*

Carmelo Viñas y Mey is an economic historian who is also distinguished for his studies of social and economic doctrine. Among other works may be mentioned especially *El problema de la tierra en la España de los siglos XVI y XVII* (Madrid, 1941); *Doctrinas de los tratadistas españoles de los siglos XVI y XVII sobre el comunismo* (Madrid, 1945); and *Pedro de Valencia, Escritos sociales* (Madrid, 1945).

J. Larraz, *La época del mercantilismo en Castilla (1500–1700)* (Madrid, 1943), offers a classification of the Spanish economists, scholastic and non-scholastic, according to whether they agreed or disagreed with the legislation that was in force when they wrote.

Jaime Carrera Pujal, *Historia de la economía española* (Barcelona, 1943–7), 5 vols, includes extensive passages from the works of the Spanish political economists, and adequate summaries of their ideas.

José Luís Sureda Carrión, in *La Hacienda castellana y los economistas del siglo XVII*, published by the Consejo Superior de Investigaciones Científicas, series 6, No. 4 (Madrid, 1949), studies the views of Gonzalez de Cellorigo, Alvarez de Toledo, Sancho de Moncada, Fernández de Navarrete, Alcázar Arriaza, Martínez de la Mata, Centani and Alvarez Osorio on financial problems and taxation.

The economic historian Pierre Vilar has made several important contributions to the history of doctrine. Especially valuable are 'Les primitifs espagnoles de la pensée économique. Quantitavisme et bullionisme', *Mélanges Marcel Bataillon*, special number of the *Bulletin Hispanique*, 1962, pp. 261–84; and 'Le temps du Quichotte', in *Europa*, January 1956. Spanish translation of both articles in Pierre Vilar, *Crecimiento y Desarrollo. Economía e Historia. Reflexiones sobre el caso español* (Barcelona, 1964); Vilar discusses the effect of the price revolution on the thought of the Spanish political economists.

Demetrio Iparraguirre, SJ, 'Los economistas españoles y el desarrollo económico de España', *Boletín de estudios económicos*, Vol. 18, No. 58, January–April 1963, published by the Universidad Comercial de Deusto, Bilbao, broadly follows Larraz while not adhering strictly to his classification of the political economists. Iparraguirre's article 'Historiografía del

pensamiento económico español', *Anales de economía* (Madrid), Nos. 25–6, January–June 1975, is indispensable.
There is a thesis by H. G. Hambleton, 'The economic decline of Spain in the 17th century. Contemporary Spanish views', presented to the London School of Economics in 1964, which is particularly interesting from the bibliographical point of view.
A useful study, which covers considerably more ground than its title leads one to suppose, is Marcelo Bitar Letayf, *Economistas españoles del siglo XVIII. Sus ideas sobre la libertad de comercio con las Indias* (Madrid, 1968).

Lucas Beltrán Flores, in his *Historia de las doctrinas económicas*, 2nd edn (Barcelona, 1970), discusses some of the more important Spanish economists and helps us to place them in the general framework of their time. He provides a short but refreshingly cosmopolitan bibliography.
Jean Vilar Berrogain, *Literatura y economía. La figura satírica del arbitrista en el siglo de oro*, Revista de Occidente (Madrid, 1973), presents the 'projector' in an interesting and novel light.

5 Thomás de Mercado, *Tratos y contratos de mercaderes*, p. 54 verso. The 'steps' were those of Seville Cathedral, the Wall Street of the day.

6 Ramon Carande, 'Gobernantes y gobernados en la hacienda de Castilla (1536–56)', *Arbor*, No. 62, February 1951, pp. 187–209. Reprinted in *Estudios de Historia de España* (Barcelona, 1969), p. 142.

7 J. H. Elliott, *Imperial Spain, 1469–1718* (London, 1963; 2nd edn, 1965), p. 199. See also J. Lynch, *Spain under the Habsburgs*, Vol. 1 (Oxford, 1964), pp. 53–8.

8 Luis Ortiz, *Memorial del Contador Luis Ortiz a Felipe II* (1558), Bib. Nac., MS 6487. Published by Instituto de España (Madrid, 1970), with an Introduction by J. Larraz; my references are to this edition.

9 ibid., p. 43.

10 ibid., p. 95.

11 ibid., p. 37.

12 ibid., p. 134.

13 R. H. Tawney, and E. Power, *Tudor Economic Documents* (London, 1924), 3 vols, Vol. 3.

14 A masterly and well-documented outline of Spanish agriculture in the sixteenth century is given by J. U. Martínez Carreras in his introduction to Gabriel Alonso de Herrera, *Obra de Agricultura*, in *Biblioteca de autores españoles* (Madrid, 1970), Vol. 235.

15 R. Carande, *Carlos V y sus banqueros*, La vida económica en Castilla, 1516–1556 (Madrid, 1965), 2nd edn, p. 117.

16 See note 14. Herrera's book was first published in 1513.

17 Fernán Pérez de Oliva, *Razonamiento que hizo el Mtro ... en el Ayuntamiento de la ciudad de Córdoba sobre la navegación del río Guadalquivir* (Cordova, 1585). The pamphlet is included in Vol. 2 of Pérez de Oliva's works (Madrid, 1787), and is partly reprinted in Sempere y Guarinos, *op. cit.*, Vol. 1.

19 On Vives's neo-Christian origin we may consult Antonio Domínguez Ortiz, *Los judeoconversos en España y América* (Madrid, 1971), pp. 177–8.

20 J. L. Vives, *De subventione pauperum* (Paris, 1530). Spanish translation, *Tratado de socorro de los pobres*, in Nueva biblioteca filosófica, No. 49 (Madrid, 1931).

21 Juan de Medina, *De la orden que en algunos pueblos de España se ha puesto*

en la limosna para el remedio de los verdaderos pobres (Salamanca, 1545). Republished in Valladolid, 1757, under the title of *La caridad discreta practicada con los mendigos, y utilidades que logra la república en su recogimiento.*

22 Domingo de Soto, *Deliberación en la causa de los pobres* (Salamanca, 1545; republished by Instituto de Estudios Políticos, Madrid, 1964).

23 C. Jago, 'The influence of debt on the relations between Crown and aristocracy in seventeenth-century Castile', *Economic History Review*, 2nd series, Vol. 26, No. 2, May 1973, pp. 218–36.

24 Luís de Molina, *De justitia et jure* (Cuenca, 1592), Vol. 3, disp. 661.

25 Gaspar de Pons, *Medios propuestos por . . . del Consejo de Hacienda* (1595), and *Los diez puntos* (1599), Biblioteca Nacional, Madrid, R. Varios 28–26 (not catalogued). On Pons we may consult Colmeiro, *Biblioteca de los economistas españoles de los siglos XVI, XVII, y XVIII*, p. 129; Sempere y Guarinos, op. cit., Vol. 1, p. 43; Canga Arguellos, *Diccionario de Hacienda con aplicación a España* (Madrid, 1833), 2nd edn, Vol. 2, p. 14; and J. Vilar Berrogain, op. cit.

26 J. A. Schumpeter, *History of Economic Analysis* (New York, 1954), ch. 3.

27 Pons, Preamble to *Los diez puntos*, cited by J. Vilar Berrogain, op. cit.

28 Luís Valle de la Cerda, *Desempeño del Patrimonio Real, y de los reynos, sin daños del Rey y vasallos, y con descanso y alivio de todos, por medio de los Erarios públicos, o Montes de Piedad* (Madrid, 1600). Extracts included in Sempere y Guarinos, op. cit., Vol. 1.

On the subject of the credit-banks we may consult E. J. Hamilton, 'Spanish banking schemes before 1700', *Journal of Political Economy*, 57, 1949, pp. 134–56 (see Bibliography); J. Diaz de Diaz Fernández and F. Estapé, 'La creación de erarios públicos en España: el proyecto de Pedro de Oudegherste; notas para la historia de la Banca en España', *Moneda y crédito*, No. 56, March 1956, pp. 41–53; and Felipe Ruíz Martin, 'Los planes frustrados para crear una red de erarios y montes de piedad (1576–1626)', *Cuadernos Hispanoamericanos*, Nos 238–40, October–December 1969, pp. 613 *et seq.*

29 F. Braudel, *The Mediterranean and the Mediterranean World in the Age of Philip II* (Eng. tr., London, 1972), pp. 739–43, gives a brief but vivid account of vagrancy in southern Europe, with special reference to Spain.

30 Miguel de Giginta, *Tratado de remedio de pobres* (Coimbra, 1579), and other works on poor relief. A complete list is given in Colmeiro, *Biblioteca.*

31 In his *Enigmas* (reprinted in Colección Cisneros, Madrid, 1943, p. 97) Pérez de Herrera tells us that he had spent a great deal of money and time in writing some 'forty books that I have in print'. The discourses on poor relief were published in 1595 and 1608. The best-known of these is *Discursos del amparo de los legítimos pobres, y de la reducción de los fingidos* (Madrid, 1958). For a list of the others see Colmeiro, *Biblioteca*, p. 124. Pérez de Herrera's more general doctrine is developed in the *Remedios para el bien de la salud del cuerpo de la república* (1610), the *Memorial a los Caballeros Procuradores de Cortes . . . en razón de muchas cosas tocantes al buen gobierno, estado, riqueza y descanso de estos Reinos* (Madrid, 1617) and the *Discurso al Rey Felipe III sobre el ornato de Madrid* (n.d.).

On Pérez de Herrera we may consult A. Sierra Corella, 'Los forjadores de la grandeza de Madrid. El Doctor Cristóbal Pérez de Herrera', *Revista de la Biblioteca, Archivo y Museo del Ayuntamiento de Madrid*, Vol. 19, Nos 59–60, pp. 231–49, and J. Vilar Berrogain, op. cit., *passim.*

32 Juan Bautista Antonelli, *Propuesta sobre la navegación de los rios de España* (1581), partly reprinted by Sempere y Guarinos, op. cit., Vol. 1, pp. 55–82.

33 Various papers on monetary policy, addressed to Philip II towards the end of his reign, are partially printed in Carera Pujal, op. cit., Vol. 1, pp. 292–301.

34 J. Vilar Berrogain, op. cit.

35 Martín González de Cellorigo, *Memorial de la política necesaria y util restauración a la República de España, y estados de ella, y del desempeno universal de estos Reynos* (Valladolid, 1600).

36 Sancho de Moncada, *Restauración política de España* (Madrid, 1619). Partially reprinted in Sempere y Guarinos, op. cit. (Madrid, 1804), Vol. 2. There is a modern edition with an Introduction by J. Vilar (1974).

37 Pedro Fernández de Navarrete, *Discursos políticos* (Barcelona, 1621). Reprinted under the title of *Conservación de monarquías y discursos políticos* (Madrid, 1626), and summarised in Sempere y Guarinos, op. cit., Vol. 2, pp. 269 *et seq.* Included in the *Biblioteca de autores españoles*, Vol. 25, pp. 457 *et seq.*

38 Francisco Martínez de la Mata, *Memoriales o Discursos*, written between 1650 and 1660. The work was printed several times during Mata's lifetime, but early editions are very rare. An 'Epítome' of the 'Memorials' was reprinted in 1701 and included by Count Campomanes in his *Apéndice a la educación popular* (1775), Vol. 1. The 'Memorials' themselves are reprinted in Vol. 4 of the same work. Sempere y Guarinos published extracts in his *Biblioteca española económico-política* (1804), Vol. 3. There is a modern edition edited by Gonzalo Anes, *Memoriales y Discursos de Francisco Martínez de la Mata* (Madrid, 1971).

39 *Apéndice a la educacion popular*, Vol. 4, p. 49.

40 Larraz, op. cit., pp. 110–19.

41 Francisco Martínez de la Mata, op. cit., Discourse, 7, paras 66–7.

42 Martín González de Cellorigo, op. cit., fol. 22.

43 ibid., fol. 29.

44 Pedro de Valencia, 'Discurso contra la ociosidad', in Carmelo Viñas Mey, *Pedro de Valencia, Escritos sociales*, pp. 36–7.

45 Pedro Fernández de Navarrete, *Conservación de monarquías*, Discourse 21; Miguel Caja de Leruela, *Restauración de la antigua abundancia de España*, quoted by Larraz, op. cit., p. 91.

46 A. Smith, *Wealth of Nations* (edition of Edwin Cannan, 1904), Bk 4, ch. 1.

47 Alberto Struzzi, *Diálogo sobre el comercio de estos reinos de Castilla* (place of publication not stated, 1624). Numerous pamphlets by Struzzi are included in the Biblioteca Nacional, Cat. No. 10, 441.

48 Charles Davenant, *Essay upon the East India Trade* (London, 1696), p. 25.

49 J. Vilar Berrogain, in his Introduction to Sancho de Moncada, *Restauración política de España* (Madrid, 1974), pp. 43, 50.

50 Carrera Pujal, op. cit., Vol. 1, p. 556.

51 Schumpeter, op. cit., p. 203.

52 Jacinto de Alcázar Arriaza, *Medios políticos para el remedio único y universal de España* (Madrid, 1646). Alcázar's work is studied by José L. Sureda Carrión, 'Las doctrinas fiscales de Jacinto de Alcázar y Francisco Centani', *Anales de Economía*, Vol. 6, No. 24; and in the same scholar's *La Hacienda castellana y los economistas del siglo XVII*, pp. 219–21.

53 Bautista Dávila, *Resumen de los medios prácticos para el alivio de la Mon-*

arquía, 1651. Schumpeter, op. cit., regards Dávila's work as a 'milestone on the road to single-tax ideas'.

54 Francisco Centani, *Tierras: medios universales propuestos desde el año 1665 hasta el de 1671 para que con planta, números, peso y medida tenga la Real Hacienda dotación fija para asistir a la causa pública, remedio y alivio general para los pobres, cortando fraudes de que han hecho patrimonio los que los dominan.* (1671). Sureda Carrión, in the article and book mentioned in note 52, discusses Centani's ideas.

55 Earl J. Hamilton, *American Treasure and the Price Revolution in Spain,* p. 92.

56 Carrera Pujal, op. cit., Vol. 1, pp. 388–9.

57 Mariana expounds his economic doctrine in his *De Rege et regis institutione* (Toledo, 1598) and *De mutatione monetae* (Cologne, 1609), included in the *Biblioteca de autores españoles,* Vols 30 and 31, under the titles of *Del rey y de la institución real* and *Tratado y discurso sobre la moneda de vellón.* A good deal has been written on Mariana. Among more recent studies devoted exclusively to him may be mention J. Laures, op. cit.; Moses Bensabat Amzalak, *Las teorías monetarias do P. João de Mariana* (Lisbon, 1944); A. Ullastres Calvo, 'La teoría de la mutación monetaria del P. Juan de Mariana', *Anales de Economía,* 4, 1944, and 5, 1945; and Jaime Lluis y Navas, 'Los estudios del P. Mariana sobre el valor de la moneda a través de los tiempos', *Caesaraugusta,* 17–18, 1961 (Saragossa).
Useful discussions of Mariana's views are included in Carrera Pujal, op. cit., Vol. 1, pp. 350–5 (*De rege*), and 408–11 (*De moneta*); and W. Weber, *Geld und Zins in der spanischen Spätscholastik* (Münster, 1959), pp. 138–51.

58 *De rege,* Bk 3, ch. 8. This chapter on money is omitted in the Spanish translation published in the *Biblioteca de autores españoles,* Vol. 31.

59 Tomás de Cardona's nine memorials may be read in the Biblioteca Nacional, MS 6731, pp. 130 *et seq.* They are summarised in Carrera Pujal, op. cit., pp. 570–4.

60 Gerardo Basso, *Arbitrios y discursos políticos* (Madrid, 1627).

61 Mateo Lisón y Viedma, *Memorial de la ciudad de Granada al Rey sobre el consumo de la moneda de vellón y otros puntos de hacienda* (1627). Summarised in Carrera Pujal, op. cit., pp. 564–7.

62 Alfonso de Carranza, *El ajustamiento y proporción de las monedas de oro, plata y cobre* (Madrid, 1629). Summarised in Carrera Pujal, op. cit., pp. 574–82.

63 Guillen Barbón y Castañeda, *Provechosos arbitrios al consumo de vellón* (Madrid, 1628). An extract of this work is included in Sempere y Guarinos, op. cit., Vol. 3, p. 56. Summary in Carrera Pujal, op. cit., pp. 568–70.

64 Carrera Pujal, op. cit., pp. 584–6.

65 P. Vilar, *Oro y moneda en la historia (1450–1920)* (Barcelona, 1969), p. 330.

66 J. Vilar Berrogain, op. cit., pp. 232–3.

67 B. Dávila, *Indice de los intentos . . . que aplica ahora el P. . . . en orden a la corrección del vellón* (n.d.).

68 For the titles of Somaza's memorials see M. Colmeiro, *Biblioteca de los economistas españoles de los siglos XVI, XVII y XVIII,* pp. 141–2.

69 M. Caja de Leruela, *Restauración de la abundancia de España,* ch. 4, para. 2.

70 E. F. Heckscher, *Mercantilism* (Eng. tr., London, 1935), Vol. 2, 157–63.

71 Sancho de Moncada, *Restauracion politica de España,* Discourse 2, ch. 2.

72 F. Martínez de la Mata, *Memorial en razón de la despoblación y pobreza de España y su remedio,* paras 18, 19.

73 Caja de Leruela, *Restauración política de España*, ch. 4, para. 2.
74 P. Fernández Navarrete, *Conservación de monarquías*, Discourse 7.
75 Lope de Deza, *Gobierno político de agricultura* (Madrid, 1618), p. 54.
76 M. González de Cellorigo, *Memorial de la política necessaria y útil restauración de la república de España*, pt 2, p. 24.
77 Pedro de Valencia, *Discurso sobre el acrecentamiento de la labor de la tierra* (1605). In *Pedro de Valencia, Escritos sociales*, ed. Carmelo Viñas Mey, pp. 29–47.
78 Caja de Leruela, *Restauración política de España, passim.*
79 Joaquin Costa, *Colectivismo agrario en España* (Madrid, 1891), pp. 228–46.
80 Miguel Alvarez Osorio y Redín, *Discurso universal de las causas que ofenden la Monarquía etc.* (1686); *Extension política y económica* . . . (1686); *Zelador general* . . . (1687). These discourses are reprinted in full by Campomanes in Vol. 1 of his *Apéndice a la educación popular* (1775), and are summarised with a commentary by Sempere y Guarinos, op. cit., Vol. 4. The other four discourses are rare. An account of them and of Osorio's work in general is given by Joaquin Costa, op. cit., pp. 588–610. Osorio's contribution to the literature of economic development is discussed by D. Iparraguirre, 'Los antiguos economistas españoles y el desarrollo económico de España', *Boletin de estudios económicos* (Bilbao), 1963.
81 Alvarez Osorio, *Extensión política y económica*. In Compomanes, *Apéndice a la educación popular*, pt 1, pp. 74–134.
82 Alvarez Osorio, 'Discurso universale', in *Apéndice a la educación popular*, pt 1, pp. 345–6.
83 ibid., pp. 43–4.
84 Alvarez Osorio, *Compañía universal de fábricas y comercios*.
85 Alvarez Osorio, 'Discurso universale' in *Apéndice a la educación popular*, pt 1, p. 318.
86 J. Vicens Vives, *Manual de historia económica de España*, pp. 425–6.
87 Luís Ortiz, *Memorial*, fol. 40 verso.
88 Bernardo de Ulloa, *Restablecimiento de las fábricas y comercio español* . . . (Madrid, 1740). A French translation appeared at Amsterdam in 1753.
89 F. Huet, *Mémoires sur le Commerce des Hollandois dans tous les états du monde* (Amsterdam, 1718).
90 Gerónimo de Uztáriz, *Theórica y práctica de comercio y de marina* (Madrid, 1724; 2nd edn, Madrid, 1742; reprinted Madrid, 1968, with an Introduction by Gabriel Franco). English translation, *The Theory and Practice of Commerce and Maritime Affairs*, by John Kippax (London, 1751). My quotations are taken from this edition.
   There is a considerable literature on Uztáriz. The following studies may be recommended: A. Wirminghaus, *Zwei spanische Merkantilisten* (Jena, 1886); A. Mounier, *Les faits et la doctrine économique en Espagne sous Philippe V* (Bordeaux, 1919); A. Castillo, *Spanish Mercantilism, Gerónimo de Uztáriz, Economist* (Columbia, New York, 1930); Earl J. Hamilton, 'The mercantilism of Gerónimo de Uztáriz: a re-examination', *Economics, Sociology and the Modern World* (Cambridge, Mass., 1935); R. E. Planas Koechert, *Gerónimo de Uztáriz und Gaspar Melchior de Jovellanos: Ein Beitrag zur Dogmengeschichte der spanischen Sozialökonomie des 18. Jahrhunderts* (Zurich, 1939).
91 Uztáriz, *The Theory and Practice of Commerce*, Vol. 1, p. 6.
92 ibid., Vol. 1, p. 15.
93 ibid., Vol. 2, p. 292.

94 ibid., Vol. 2, p. 413.
95 ibid., Vol. 1, p. 51.
96 ibid., Vol. 1, pp. 46–7.
97 ibid., Vol. 1, p. 141.
98 ibid., Vol. 1, p. 69.
99 ibid., Vol. 1, p. 71.
100 Bernardo de Ulloa, *Restablecimiento de las fábricas y comercio español* (Madrid, 1740; French translation, Amsterdam, 1753).
101 Miguel de Zavala y Auñón, *Representación al Rey Nuestro Señor D. Felipe V, dirigida al más seguro aumento del Real Erario y conseguir la felicidad, mayor alivio, riqueza, y abundancia de su Monarquía* (Madrid, 1732). See Beltrán, Flores, *Historia de las doctrinas económicas* (Barcelona, 1961), pp. 55–6.
102 Diego de Saavedra Fajardo, *Idea de un Príncipe político* (Münster, 1640), Emblem 69.

Bibliography

Abellán, P. M., 'Una moral para comerciantes en el siglo XVI. Significación de la "Suma" de Fr. Tomás de Mercado en la historia de la teólogía moral', *Miscelanea Comillas*, 15 (1951).

Abu Bakr Muhammad al-Turtushi (Abu-Bequer de Tortosa), *Lámpara de los príncipes*, tr. into Spanish and ed. M. Alarcón, 2 vols (Madrid, 1930).

Abul-Fadl al Dimashqi. See Ritter, H.

Albert the Great, St, *Opera omnia* (Paris, 1890–9).

Albert the Great, St, *Commentarii in sententiarum Petri Lombardi*, edn cit., Vol. 29.

Albert the Great, St, *In X libros ethicorum*, edn cit., Vol. 7.

Albornoz, Bartolomé de, *Arte de los contratos* (Valencia, 1573).

Alcalá, Luís de, *Tractado de los préstamos que passan entre mercaderes y tractantes* (Toledo, 1543).

Alcazar Arriaza, Jacinto de, *Medios políticos para el remedio único y universal de España* (Madrid, 1646).

Alexander Lombard, *Tractatus de usuris* (Bibl. Vat., MS. Cod. Lat. 1237, fols 154–74).

Al-Farabi, *Fusul al-Madani. Aphorisms of the Statesman*, ed. D. M. Dunlop, in University of Cambridge Oriental Publications (Cambridge, 1961).

Al-Ghazali, *Ghazali's Book of Counsel for Kings*, tr. F. R. C. Bagley, in University of Durham Publications (Oxford, 1964).

Ali ibn Bakr, *The Hedaya of Ali ibn Bakr*, tr. C. Hamilton (London, 1791).

Alonso de Herrera, Gabriel, *Obra de Agricultura*, with Introduction by J. U. Martinez Carreras, in *Biblioteca de autores españoles*, Vol. 235 (Madrid, 1970).

Alonso Rodriguez, B., *Monografías de moralistas españoles sobre temas económicos (S. XVI)*, in Repertorio de Historia de las Ciencias Eclesiásticas en España (Instituto de Historia de la Teología Española (Salamanca, 1971).

Alphonso X of Castile, *Las siete Partidas del rey D. Alfonso el Sabio*, in *Los códigos españoles concordados y anotados*, Vols 2, 3 and 4.

Alvarez Osorio y Redín, Miguel, *Discurso universal de las causas que ofenden esta monarquía* (1686).

Alvarez Osorio y Redín, Miguel, *Extensión política y económica* (1686).

Alvarez Osorio y Redín, Miguel, *Compañía universal de fábricas y comercios* (1686).

Alvarez Osorio y Redín, Miguel, *Zelador común general para el bien común de todos* (1687).

Angelo of Chivasso, *Summa angelica* (Venice, 1511).

Antonelli, J. B., *Propuesta sobre la navegación de los ríos de España* (1581).

Antonino of Florence, St, *Summa theologica* (Verona, 1740).

Aristotle, *Nicomachean Ethics*.

Aristotle, *Politics*.

Aristotle, *Rhetoric*.

Aristotle, *Topics*.

Asín, M., 'El averroismo teológico de Sto Tomas de Aquino', in *Homenaje a D. Francisco Codera en su jubilación del profesorado* (Saragossa, 1904).

Averroes, *Commentary on Plato's Republic*. See Rosenthal, E. I. J.

Averroes, *Ethica Aristotelis cum translatione Leonardi Arretini cum Averroi*, 2 vols (Venice, 1489).

Azpilcueta, Martín de, called Navarrus, *Manual de confesores y penitentes* (Coimbra, 1553; 2nd edn, Salamanca, 1556).

Azpilcueta, Martín de, called Navarrus, *Comentario resolutorio de usuras* (Salamanca, 1556).

Azpilcueta, Martín de, called Navarrus, *Comentario resolutorio de cambios* (Salamanca, 1556). Critical edition, *Martín de Azpilcueta, Comentario resolutorio de cambios*, ed. A. Ullastres, J. M. Perez Prendes and L. Pereña (Madrid, 1965).

Babylonian Talmud, The, tr. into English, ed. J. Epstein, 34 vols (London, 1938–52).

Báñez, Domingo de, *Commentarium in 2.2. de Justitia et Jure* (Salamanca, 1594).

Barbón y Castañeda, Guillén, *Provechosos arbitrios al consumo de vellón* (Madrid, 1628).

Baron, S. W., *A Social and Religious History of the Jews*, 10 vols and index (New York, 1952–65).

Barton, G., *Introduction to the History of Science*, 5 vols (Washington-Baltimore, 1929–48).

Basso, Gerardo, *Arbitrios y discursos políticos* (Madrid, 1627).

Baucells Sierra, R., 'La personalidad y obra jurídica de San Raimundi de Peñafort', *Revista Española de Derecho Canónico*, no. 1 (January–April 1946).

Belda, F., 'Etica de la creación de créditos según la doctrina de Molina, Lesio y Lugo', and 'Valorización de la doctrina de Molina, Lesio y Lugo sobre la creación de créditos', *Pensamiento*, Vol. 1 (1963), pp. 53–92 and 185–214.

Beltrán Flores, Lucas, *Historia de las doctrinas económicas* (Barcelona, 1961; 2nd edn, Barcelona, 1970).

Bensabat Amzalek, M., *As teorías monetarias do P. Joao de Mariana* (Lisbon, 1944).

Bernardino of Siena, St, *Opera omnia* (Florence, 1950–63).

Bible, The, Authorised Version.

Bitar Letayf, M., *Economistas españoles del siglo XVIII. Sus ideas sobre la libertad de comercio con las Indias* (Madrid, 1968).

Bodin, Jean, *Réponse a M. de Malestroit*, ed. H. Hauser (Paris, 1932).

Bonacina, Martino, *Opera omnia* (Lyons, 1646).

Bonesana, Cesare, Marchese de Beccaria, *Elementi di economia pùbblica* in Custodi, *Scrittori Classici italiani di economía política*, parte moderna, Vol. 12 (Milan, 1804).

Braudel, Fernand, *La Méditerranée et le Monde Méditerranéen a l'Epoque de Philippe II* (Paris, 1949). Eng. tr. *The Mediterranean and the Mediterranean World in the Age of Philip II* (London, 1972).

Brenan, Gerald, *The Spanish Labyrinth* (Cambridge, 1943).

Buridan, John, *Quaestiones super VIII libros politicorum Aristotelis* (Paris, 1513).

Bussi, E., 'Contractus mohatrae', in *Rivista di storia del diritto italiano*, Vol. 5 (1932).

Cahn, K. S., 'The Roman and Frankish roots of the just price of medieval canon law', in *Studies in Medieval and Renaissance History*, Vol. 6 (1969).

Caja de Leruela, Miguel, *Restauración de la antigua abundancia de España* (Naples, 1631; repr. Madrid, 1732; ed. J. P. Le Flem, Madrid, 1975).

Cajetan, Cardinal Tommaso de Vio, 'Commentarium in summam theologicam S. Thomae Aquinatis', in St Thomas Aquinas, *Summa theologica* (Rome, 1882).

Cajetan, Cardinal Tommaso de Vio, *De cambiis* (Milan, 1499), reprinted in *Tractatus universi juris*, Vol. 6.

Campomanes, Count, *Discurso sobre la educación popular de los artesanos y su fomento* (Madrid, 1773).

Campomanes, Count, *Apéndice a la educación popular*, 4 vols (Madrid, 1775).

Canga Arguellos, J., *Diccionario de Hacienda con aplicación a España*, 2nd edn (Madrid, 1833).

Carande, Ramon, *Carlos V y sus banqueros*, 2 vols (Madrid, 1943–9; complete edn, 3 vols, Madrid, 1965–67).

Carande, Ramon, 'Gobernantes y gobernados en la hacienda de Castilla (1536–56)', in *Arbor*, no. 62 (February 1951), pp. 187–209. Reprinted in *Estudios de Historia de España* (Barcelona, 1969).

Carande, Ramon, *Sevilla, fortaleza y mercado* (Seville, 1972).

Cardona, Tomás de, *Memorial al Rey sobre el ajustamiento de la moneda* (n.d.).

Carewe, Richard, *Survey of Cornwall* (London, 1602).

Carranza, Alfonso de, *El ajustamiento y proporción de las monedas de oro, plata y cobre* (Madrid, 1629).

Carrera Pujal, J., *Historia de la economía española*, 5 vols (Barcelona, 1943–7).

Castillo, A., *Spanish Mercantilism. Gerónimo de Uztariz, Economist* (New York, 1930).

Castro, Américo, *España en su Historia* (Buenos Aires, 1948).

Catalano, Pietri, *Universi juris theologico-moralis corpus* (Venice, 1728).

Centani, Francisco, *Tierras: medios universales propuestos desde el año 1665 hasta el de 1671 para que con planta, números, peso y medida tenga la Real Hacienda dotación fija para asistir a la causa pública* (1671).

Colmeiro, Manuel, *Historia de la economía política en España* (Madrid, 1863); 2nd edn, Madrid, 1965).

Colmeiro, Manuel, *Biblioteca de economistas españoles de los siglos XVI, XVII, y XVIII*, in *Memorias de la Real Academia de Ciencias Morales y Políticas*, Vol. 1 (Madrid, 1879). Reprinted by same Academy in 1954.

Condillac, Étienne Bonnot de, *Le Commerce et le Gouvernement* (Amsterdam, 1776).

Conring, H., *Opera* (Brunswick, 1730).

Coromina, J., *Diccionario crítico etimológico de la lengua castellana* (Madrid, 1954).

Corpus juris canonici, ed. E. Friedberg (Leipzig, 1879–81).

Corpus juris civilis, ed. T. H. Mommsen, W. Kroll, P. Krueger and R. Schoell (Berlin, 1928–9).

Costa, Joaquin, *Colectivismo agrario en España* (Madrid, 1898).

Covarrubias y Leiva, Diego de, *Opera omnia* (Lyons, 1661).

Covarrubias y Leiva, Diego de, *Veterum numismatum collatio* (1550), edn cit.

Covarrubias y Leiva, Diego de, *Variarum resolutionum ex jure pontificio, regio, et caesareo libri IV* (1554), edn cit.

Davanzati, Bernado, *Notizia de' cambi* (1588) and *Lezione delle Monete* (1638), in Custodi, *Scrittori classici italiani di economía política*, parte antica, vol. 2 (Milan, 1804).

Davenant, Charles, *An Essay upon the East India Trade* (London, 1698).

Dávila, Bautista, *Resumen de los medios prácticos para el alivio de la Monarquía* (1651).

Dávila, Bautista, *Indice de los intentos . . . que aplican ahora el P. . . . en orden a la corrección del vellón* (n.d.).

Dempsey, B. W., *Interest and Usury* (London, 1943).

Deuringer, K., *Probleme der Caritas in der Schule von Salamanca* (Freiburg, 1959).

Deza, Lope de, *Goberno político de agricultura* (Madrid, 1618).

Diana, Antonino, *Summa diana* (Venice, 1646).

Diaz de Valdepeñas, Fernando, *Summa de notas copiosas* (Toledo, 1543).

Dictionnaire de droit canonique (Paris, 1950).

Diaz de Diaz Fernandez, J., and Estapé, F., 'La creación de erarios públicos en España: el proyecto de Pedro de Oudegherste; notas para la historia de la Banca en España', in *Moneda y Crédito*, no. 56 (March 1956), pp. 41–53.

Dominguez Ortiz, A., *Los judeoconversos en España y América* (Madrid, 1971).

Duns Scotus, John *Opera omnia* (Paris, 1891–5).

Duns Scotus, John *In IV libros sententiarum, Opus Oxoniensis*, Vol. 18, edn cit.

Elliott, J. H., *Imperial Spain, 1469–1718* (London, 1963).

Emery, R. W., *The Jews of Perpignan in the Thirteenth Century* (New York, 1959).

Encyclopedia of Islam, The (Leyden and Paris, 1908–38).

Endemann, W., *Studien in der romanisch-kanonistischen Wirtschafts – und Rechtslehre bis gegen Ende des siebzehnten Jahrhunderts*, 2 vols (Berlin, 1874–83).

Escobar, Antonio de, *Universae theologiae moralis receptores* (Lyons, 1652).

Faris, M. A., *The Arab Heritage* (Princeton, NJ, 1946).

Fernandez de Navarrete, Pedro, *Discursos políticos* (Barcelona, 1621). Revised edition, *Conservación de monarquías y discursos políticos* (Madrid, 1626).

Galiani, Ferdinando, *Della Moneta* (Naples, 1750).

García, Francisco, *Tratado utilísimo de todos los contratos, quantos en los negocios humanos se pueden ofrecer* (Valencia, 1583).

Giginta, Miguel de, *Tratado de remedio de pobres* (Coimbra, 1579).

Giles of Lessines, *De usuris*, in St Thomas Aquinas, *Opera omnia*, Vol. 17 (Parma, 1864).

Godeau, A., *Morale chrétienne pour l'instruction des curés du diocèse de Vence* (Lyons, 1710).

Goitein, S. D., *A Mediterranean Society: The Jewish Communities of the Arab World as Portrayed in the Documents of the Cairo Geniza*, Vol. 1 (Berkeley, Calif., 1967).

Gonzalez de Cellorigo, Martín, *Memorial de la política necessaria y útil restauración de la república de España* (Valladolid, 1600).

Gordon, Barry, 'Aristotle and the development of value theory', in *Quarterly Journal of Economics*, Vol. 1 (February 1964), pp. 115–28.

Gordon, Barry, *Economic Analysis before Adam Smith* (London, 1975).

Goris, J. A., *Études sur les colonies marchandes méridionales à Anvers de 1488 à 1567*, 2nd edn (Louvain, 1935).

Gorosquieta Reyes, Javier, 'El sistema de ideas tributarias en los teólogos y moralistas principales de la escuela de Salamanca (siglos XVI y XVII)', thesis, Universidad Complutense (Madrid, 1971).

Grice-Hutchinson, Marjorie, *The School of Salamanca. Readings in Spanish Monetary Theory, 1544–1605* (Oxford, 1952).

Grotius, Hugo, *De jure belli et pacis* (1625). English translation (Oxford, 1925).

Grünebaum, G. E. von, *Medieval Islam* (Chicago, 1953).

Hales, John, *A Compendious or Briefe Examination of Certayne Ordinary Complaints of Divers of our Countrymen*, 2nd edn (London, 1581). Reprinted under title of *A Discourse of the Common Weal of this Realm of England*, ed. E. Lamond (Cambridge, 1893).

Hambleton, H. G., 'The economic decline of Spain in the 17th century.

Contemporary Spanish views', thesis, London School of Economics (1964).

Hamilton, Earl J., 'Spanish mercantilism before 1700', in *Facts and Factors in Economic History* (Harvard, 1932).

Hamilton, Earl J., *American Treasure and the Price Revolution in Spain* (Cambridge, Mass., 1934).

Hamilton, Earl J., 'The mercantilism of Gerónimo de Ustáriz: a re-examination', in *Economics, Sociology, and the Modern World* (Cambridge, Mass., 1935).

Hamilton, Earl J., *El florecimiento del capitalismo* (Madrid, 1948).

Hamilton, Earl J., *War and Prices in Spain, 1651–1800* (Harvard, 1947).

Hamilton, Earl J., 'Spanish banking schemes before 1700', in *Journal of Political Economy*, no. 57 (1949), pp. 134–56.

Haskins, C. H., *Studies in the History of Medieval Science* (Cambridge, Mass., 1924).

Hecksher, Eli F., *Der Merkantilismus*, 2 vols (Jena, 1932). English translation by M. Shapiro, *Mercantilism* (London, 1935).

Hostiensis, Henry of Susa, *Summa aurea* (Rome, 1470).

Huet, F., *Mémoires sur le commerce des Hollandois dans tous les états du monde* (Amsterdam, 1718).

Hutcheson, F., *Introduction to Moral Philosophy* (Glasgow, 1747).

Hutcheson, F., *System of Moral Philosophy* (London, 1755).

Ibn Asim, *Traité de Droit Musulman, La Tohfat d'Ebn Acem*, tr. O. Houdas and F. Martel (Algiers, 1882). Another edition, *Al-Acimiya ou Thu'fat*, tr. L. Bercher, was published by Institut d'Études Orientales, University of Algiers (Algiers, 1958).

Iizuka, Ichiro, *Studies in the History of Monetary Theory* (Tokyo, 1969, in Japanese).

Inflation: Causes, Consequences, Cures. A debate between Lord Robbins, Samuel Brittain, A. W. Coats, Milton Friedman, Peter Jay and David Laidler, with Addenda by F. A. Hayek and Peter Jay (Institute of Economic Affairs, London, 1974).

Iparraguire, Demetrio, 'Las fuentes del pensamiento económico en España en los siglos XIII al XVI', in *Estudios de Deusto*, vol. 2, 2a. época, no. 3 (Bilbao, 1954) pp. 79–113.

Iparraguire, Demetrio, *Francisco de Vitoria: una teoría social del valor económico* (Bilbao, 1957).

Iparraguire, Demetrio, 'Los antiguos economistas españoles y el desarrollo económico de España', in *Boletin de estudios económicos*, vol. 18, no. 58 (January–April 1963) pp. 99–118.

Iparraguire, Demetrio, 'Historiografía del pensamiento económico español', in *Anales de economía*, nos 25–26 (January–June 1975), pp. 5–38.

Jago, C., 'The influence of debt on the relations between crown and aristocracy in seventeenth-century Castile', in *Economic History Review*, 2nd series, vol. 26, no. 2 (May 1973), pp. 218–36. *Jewish Encyclopedia, The* (New York and London, 1901–25).

Kauder, E., 'Genesis of the marginal utility theory from Aristotle to the end of the 18th century', in *Economic Journal* vol. 63 (September 1953), pp. 638–50.

Kauder, E., *A History of Marginal Utility Theory* (Princeton, NJ, 1965).

Koran, The, tr. by J. M. Rodwell, in Everyman's Library, no. 380 (London, 1909).

Lacy, Evans O'Leary de, *How Greek Science Passed to the Arabs* (London, 1951).

Langenstein, Henry of, *Tractatus de contractibus*, in Gerson, *Opera omnia* (Cologne, 1483), Vol. 4, pp. 185-224.

Larraz, J., *La época del mercantilismo en Castilla, 1500-1700* (Madrid, 1943).

Laures, John, *The Political Economy of Juan de Mariana* (New York, 1928).

Law, John, *Money and Trade Consider'd* (1705).

Lepeyre, H., *Une famille de Marchands, les Ruiz* (Paris, 1955).

Le Semelier, J. L., *Conférences ecclésiastiques de Paris sur l'usure et la restitution*, 4 vols (Paris, 1724).

Lessius, Leonard, *De Justitia et Jure* (Louvain, 1605).

Lévi-Provençal, E., *Histoire de l'Espagne musulmane* (Paris, 1953).

Lex Romanum Visigothorum, ed. G. Haenel (Leipzig, 1849).

Lisón y Viedma, Mateo, *Memorial de la ciudad de Granada al Rey sobre el consumo de la moneda de vellón y otros puntos de hacienda* (1627) Lluis y Navas, J., 'Los estudios del P. Mariana sobre el valor de la moneda a traves de los tiempos', in *Caesaraugusta*, nos. 17-18 (Saragossa, 1961).

Locke, John, *Two Treatises Concerning Government* (London, 1690).

Locke, John, *Some Considerations of the Consequences of the Lowering of Interest and Raising the Value of Money* (London, 1692).

Lopez, R. S. and Raymond, I. W., *Medieval Trade in the Mediterranean World* (Columbia University Press, 1955).

Los códigos españoles concordados y anotados, 6 vols (Madrid, 1847-51; 2nd edn, Madrid, 1872-73).

Luca, Cardinal Giambattista de, *Theatrum veritatis et justitiae* (Rome, 1669-81).

Luca, Cardinal Giambattista de, *Il dottore volgare* (Rome, 1673).

Lucala, Bartolomé, *Baculus clericalis* (Saragossa, 1592).

Lugo, Juan de, *De Justitia et Jure* (Lyons, 1642).

Lynch, J., *Spain under the Habsburgs*, 2 vols (Oxford, 1964).

Mahmassani, S., *Les Idées Économiques d'Ibn Khaldoun. Essai historique, analytique et critique* (Leyden, 1932).

Maimonides, Moses, *The Code of Maimonides* (Yale, 1941-51); Book 13, *The Book of Civil Laws*, tr. I. J. Rabinowitz (1949).

Mandich, G., *Le pacte de Ricorsa et le marché italien des changes au XVIIe siècle* (Paris, 1953).

Marchesi, C., *L'Etica Nicomachea nella tradizione latina medievale* (Messina, 1904).

Mariana, Juan de, *De regis et regis institutione* (Toledo, 1598). Spanish translation, *Del rey y de la institución real*.

Mariana, Juan de, *De mutatione monetae* (Cologne, 1609). Spanish translation, *Tratado y discurso sobre la moneda de vellón*. Both works in *Biblioteca de autores españoles*, Vols 30 and 31 (Madrid, 1854).

Martinez de la Mata, Francisco, *Memoriales o discursos (c. 1650-60)*. Republished, ed. Gonzalo Anes (Madrid, 1971).

McLaughlin, T. P., 'The teaching of the canonists on usury (XII, XIII, and XIV centuries)', in *Medieval Studies*, I (1939), pp. 81-147, and 2 (1940), pp. 1-22.

Medina, Juan de, O. S. B., *De la orden que en algunos pueblos de España se ha puesto en la limosna* (Salamanca, 1545). Reprinted under title of *La caridad discreta practicada con los mendigos* (Valladolid, 1757).

Medina, Juan de, O. F. M., *De poenitentiae, restitutione et contractibus tractatus* (Salamanca, 1550).

Mercado, Tómas de, *Tratos y contratos de mercaderes* (Salamanca, 1569).

Mercado, Tómas de, *Summa de tratos y contratos* (Seville, 1571; modern edn, ed. R. Sierra Bravo, Madrid, 1975).

Mieli, A., *La Science Arabe et son rôle dans l'évolution scientifique mondiale* (Leyden, 1938).

Migne, J. P., *Patrologiae cursus completus*, Latin series (Paris, 1844–55), 217 vols and index in 4 vols. Greek series, with Latin translations (Paris, 1857–66), 166 vols and index in 3 vols.

Miller, C., *Studien zur Geschichte der Geldlehre* (Stuttgart, 1925).

Mises, L., 'Die Stellung des Geldes in Kreise der wirtschaftslichen Güter', in *Wirtschaftstheorie der Gegenwart*, Vol. 2 (1932), pp. 310 *et seq.*

Molina, Luís de, *De Justitia et Jure*, 6 vols (Cuenca, 1592).

Molle, Luciano dalle, *Il contratto di cambio nei moralisti dal sècolo XIII alla meta del sécolo XVII* (Rome, 1954).

Moncada, Sancho de, *Riqueza firme y estable de España*, and other discourses (Madrid, 1619). Reprinted under title of *Restauración política de España* (Madrid, 1746; ed. Jean Vilar, Madrid, 1974).

Mosse or Moses, Miles, *The Arraignment and Conviction of Usurie* (London, 1595).

Mounier, A., *Les faits et la doctrine économique en Espagne sous Philippe V* (Bordeaux, 1919).

Nelson, Benjamin N., *The Idea of Usury. From Tribal Brotherhood to Universal Otherhood* (Princeton, NJ, 1949).

Neumann, A., *The Jew in Spain. Their Social, Political, and Cultural Life during the Middle Ages*, 2 vols (Philadelphia, 1942).

Neusner, J. T., *A History of the Jew in Babylonia* (Leyden, 1969).

Noonan, J. T., *The Scholastic Analysis of Usury* (Cambridge, Mass., 1957).

Novísima recopilación de las leyes de España, 5 vols (Madrid, 1805–29).

Nys, E., *Le Droit des gens et les anciens jurisconsultes espagnols* (Brussels, 1914).

Ortiz, Luis, *Memorial del Contador Luis Ortiz a Felipe II*, with Introduction by J. Larraz (Madrid, 1970).

Pascal, Blaise, *Les Provinciales* (Paris, 1656).

Pereña Vicente, L., *La Universidad de Salamanca, forja del pensamiento político español en el siglo XVI* (Salamanca, 1954).

Pérez de Herrera, Cristóbal, *Discursos del amparo de los legitimos pobres* (Madrid, 1598).

Pérez de Herrera, Cristóbal, *Remedios para el bien de la salud del cuerpo de la república* (Madrid, 1610).

Pérez de Herrera, Cristóbal, *Memorial a los Caballeros Procuradores de Cortes* (Madrid, 1617).

Pérez de Herrera, Cristóbal, *Discurso al Rey Felipe III sobre el ornato de Madrid* (n.d.).

Pérez de Herrera, Cristóbal, *Enigmas* (Madrid, 1943).

Pérez de Oliva, Fernán, *Obras* (Madrid, 1787).

Pérez de Oliva, Fernán, *Razonamiento que hizo el Maestro . . . en el Ayuntamiento de la ciudad de Córdoba sobre la navegación del rio Guadalquivir* (Cordova, 1585), edn cit., Vol. 2.

Piselli, Clemente, *Theologiae moralis summa* (Rome, 1710).

Pitt-Rivers, J. A., *People of the Sierra* (London, 1954).

Plato, *The Republic*.

Pons, Gaspar de, *Medios propuestos por . . . del Consejo de Hacienda* (1595).

Pons, Gaspar de, *Los diez puntos* (1599).

Pufendorf, Samuel von, *Elementorum juris prudentiae universalis libri 2* (The Hague, 1660; Eng. tr., Oxford, 1931).

Pufendorf, Samuel von, *De jure naturae et gentium* (Lund, 1672; Eng. tr., Oxford, 1934).

Pufendorf, Samuel von, *De officio hominis et civis juxta legem naturalem* (Lund, 1673; Eng. tr., Oxford, 1927).

Quesnay, Francois, 'Hommes', in *Revue d'histoire des doctrines économiques et sociales*, no. 1 (1908), pp. 3–88, and in *Francois Quesnay et la Physiocratie*, ed. R. Debré, Vol. 2, pp. 511–73 (Paris, 1958).

Raymond of Peñafort, St, *Summa de Poenitentia* (1st edn, 1480); reprinted under title of *Summa ad manuscriptorum fidem recognita* (Verona, 1744).

Raymond of Peñafort, St, *Summa pastoralis*, ed. J. G. Ravaisson, *Catalogue général des Mss. des Bibliothèques publiques des Departements*, Vol. 1 (Paris, 1849) pp. 621–3.

Renan, E., *Averroès et l'Averröisme* (Paris, 1852).

Ritter, H., 'Ein arabisches Handbuch der Handelswissenschaft', in *Der Islam*, Vol. 7 (1917). German translation of Abul-Fadl al Dimashqi, *The Book of Knowledge of the Beauties of Commerce and of Cognizance of Good and Bad Merchandise and Falsifications*.

Rodulfis, Lorenzo de, *Tractatis de usuris et materiae montis* (Pavia, 1490), reprinted in *Tractatus universi juris*, Vol. 7.

Roover, Raymond de, *Gresham on Foreign Exchange* (Cambridge, Mass., 1949).

Roover, Raymond de, *L'Évolution de la Lettre de Change* (Paris, 1953).

Roover, Raymond de, 'Scholastic economics: survival and lasting influence from the sixteenth century to Adam Smith', in *Quarterly Journal of Economics*, vol. 69 (May 1955).

Roover, Raymond de, 'The concept of the just price: theory and economic policy', in *Journal of Economic History*, no. 18 (December 1958).

Roover, Raymond de, *San Bernardino of Siena and Sant' Antonino of Florence: The Two Great Economic Thinkers of the Middle Ages* (Cambridge, Mass., 1967).

Roover, Raymond de, *La Pensée economique des Scolastiques. Doctrines et Méthodes* (Paris, 1971).

Rosenthal, E. I. J., 'Some aspects of Islamic political thought', in *Islamic Culture*, vol. 22, no. 1 (January 1948).

Rosenthal, E. I. J., 'The place of politics in the philosophy of ibn Rushd', in *Bulletin of the School of Oriental and African Studies*, vol. 15 (June 1953).

Rosenthal, E. I. J., *Averröes' Commentary on Plato's Republic*, with introduction, translation and notes (Cambridge, 1965).

Rosthenal, F., *A History of Muslim Historiography* (Leyden, 1952).

Ruiz Martín, F., 'Los planes frustrados para crear una red de erarios y montes de piedad (1576–1626)', in *Cuadernos Hispano-americanos*, nos 238–40 (October–December 1969), pp. 613 *et seq.*

Saavedra Fajardo, Diego, *Empresas politicas o idea de un principe politico cristiano* (Münster, 1640).

Sachau, E., *Muhammedanisches Recht* (Stuttgart, 1897).

Sachau, E., *Syrische Rechstbücher*, 2 vols (Berlin, 1914).

Salas, Juan de, *Commentarii in secundam secundae D. Thomas* (Lyons, 1617).

Salón, Miguel, *De Justitia in 2.2. S. Thomae* (Valencia, 1581).

Sanchez-Albornoz, C., *La España musulmana según los autores islamitas y cristianas medievales* (Buenos Aires, 1946).

Sanchez-Albornoz, C., *España, un enigma histórico* (Buenos Aires, 1956).

Saravia de la Calle Veroñense, Luis, *Instrucción de mercaderes muy provechosa* (Medina del Campo, 1544).

Sayous, A. E., 'Observations d'écrivains du XVIe siècle sur les changes', in *Revue économique internationale*, vol. 4 (November 1928).

Schacht, J., *An Introduction to Islamic Law* (Oxford, 1949).

Schumpeter, J. A., *History of Economic Analysis* (New York, 1954).

Schreiber, E., *Die volkswirtschaftlichen Anschauungen der Scholastik seit Thomas von Aquin* (Jena, 1913).

Scott, J. Brown, *The Spanish Origin of International Law and of Sanctions* (Washington, D.C., 1934).

Sempere y Guarinos, J., *Biblioteca española económico-política*, 4 vols (Madrid, 1801–21).

Sierra Bravo, R., *Doctrina social y económica de los Padres de la Iglesia* (Madrid, 1967).

Sierra Bravo, R., *El pensamiento social y económico de la escolástica*, 2 vols (Madrid, 1975).

Sierra Corella, A., 'Los forjadores de la grandeza de Madrid. El Doctor Cristóbal Pérez de Herrera', in *Revista de la Biblioteca y Museo del Ayuntamiento de Madrid*, nos. 59–60, (January–December 1950), pp. 231–49.

Smith, Adam, *Wealth of Nations* (1776)

Sombart, W., *Die Juden und das Wirtschaftsleben* (Leipzig, 1911).

Solís, Feliciano de, *De Censibus* (Alcalá, 1594).

Soto, Domingo de, *Deliberación en la causa de los pobres* (Salamanca, 1545); reprinted by Instituto de Estudios Políticos (Madrid, 1964).

Soto, Domingo de, *Libri decem de justitia et jure* (Salamanca, 1553).

Struzzi, Alberto, *Diálogo sobre el comercio de estos reinos de Castilla* (1624).

Suarez, Francisco, *Opera omnia*, 25 vols (Paris, 1856–78).

Sureda Carrión, J. L., 'Las doctrines fiscales de Jacinto Alcazar y Francisco Centani', *Anales de Economía*, vol. 6, no. 24 (1945), pp. 7 et seq.

Sureda Carrión, J. L., *La Hacienda castellana y los economistas del siglo XVII* (Madrid, 1949).

Sylvester of Prierio, *Summa summarum quae Silvestrina dicitur* (Bologna, 1514).

Tawney, R. H., *Religion and the Rise of Capitalism. A Historical Study* (London, 1926).

Tawney, R. H. and Power, Eileen, *Tudor Economic Documents*, 3 vols (London, 1924).

Thomas Aquinas, St, *Opera omnia* (Paris, 1871–80).

Thomas Aquinas, St, *In X libros ethicorum*, Vol. 25, edn cit.

Thomas Aquinas, St, *Summa theologica*, Vol. 3, edn cit.

Turgot, A. R. J., *Oeuvres* (Paris, 1807–11).

Turgot, A. R. J., *Valeurs et monnaies*, Vol. 3, edn cit.

Ullastres Calvo, A., 'La teoría de la mutación monetaria del P. Juan de Mariana', in *Anales de Economía*, nos. 4 (1944) and 5 (1945).

Ulloa, Bernardo de, *Restablecimiento de las fábricas y comercio español*, 2 vols (Madrid, 1740).

Usher, A. P., *The Early History of Deposit Banking in Mediterranean Europe* (Cambridge, Mass., 1943).

Utzáriz, Geronimo de, *Theorica y práctica de comercio y de marina* (Madrid, 1724; 2nd edn, Madrid, 1742; repr., with Introduction by Gabriel Franco, Madrid, 1968; Eng. tr. by John Kippax, *The Theory and Practice of Commerce and Maritime Affairs*, London, 1751).

Valencia, Pedro de, 'Discurso sobre el precio del trigo' (1605) in *Pedro de Valencia, Escritos Sociales*, ed. C. Viñas Mey (Madrid, 1945), pp. 85–144.

Valencia, Pedro de, 'Discurso sobre el acrecentamiento de la labor de la tierra' (1605), edn cit., pp. 49–83.

Valencia, Pedro de, 'Discurso contra la ociosidad' (1618), edn cit., pp. 29–47.

Valle de la Cerda, Luis, *Desempeño del Patrimonio Real . . . por medio de los erarios públicos* (Madrid, 1618).

Vaux, Baron Carra de, *Les Penseurs de l'Islam*, 5 vols (Paris, 1923).

Venusti, A. M., *Compendio utilissimo di quelle cose, le quali a nobili e christiani mercanti appartengono* (Milan, 1561).

Vicens Vives, J., *Manuel de historia económica de España* 4th edn (Barcelona, 1965). English translation, *Economic History of Spain* (Princeton, NJ, 1969).

Vilar, P., 'Les primitifs espagnoles de la pensée économique, quantitavisme et bullionisme', in *Mélanges Marcel Bataillon*, special number of *Bulletin Hispanique* (1962), pp. 261–84.

Vilar, P., 'Le Temps du Quichotte', in *Europa* (January 1956).

Vilar, P., *Crecimiento y Desarrollo* (Barcelona, 1964) includes both the above-mentioned articles.

Vilar, P., *Oro y Moneda en la Historia, 1450–1920* (Barcelona, 1969). English translation, *A History of Gold and Money, 1450–1920* (London, 1976).

Vilar Berrogain, J., *Literatura y economía. La figura satírica del arbitrista en el siglo de oro* (Madrid, 1973).

Villalón, Cristóbal de, *Provechoso tratado de cambios y contrataciones de mercaderes y reprobación de usura* (Seville, 1542).

Viñas y Mey, C., *El problema de la tierra en la España de los siglos XVI y XVII* (Madrid, 1941).

Viñas y Mey, C., *Doctrinas de los tratadistas españoles de los siglos XVI y XVII sobre el comunismo* (Madrid, 1945).

Viñas y Mey, C., *Pedro de Valencia, Escritos sociales* (Madrid, 1945).

Vitoria, Francisco de, *Commentarios a la Secunda secundae de Santo Tomás*, in Biblioteca de Teólogos españoles, ed. V. Beltran de Heredia, Vols 4–6 (Salamanca, 1934).

Vives, Juan Luís, *De subventione pauperum* (Paris, 1530). Spanish translation, *Tratado de socorro de los pobres*, in Nueva biblioteca filosófica, no. 49 (Madrid, 1931).

Walzer, R. R., *The Arabic Transmission of Greek Thought to Medieval Europe* (Manchester, 1945).

Weber, W., *Wirtschaftethik am Vorabend des Liberalismus* (Münster, 1959).

Weber, W., *Geld und Zins in der spanischen Spätscholastik* (Münster, 1962).

Weber, W. and Wingate, S. D., *The Medieval Latin Versions of the Aristotelian Scientific Corpus* (London, 1951).

Wirminghaus, A., *Zwei spanische Merkantilisten* (Jena, 1886).

Zavala y Auñon, Miguel de *Representación al Rey Nuestro Señor D. Felipe V, dirigida al más seguro aumento del Real Erario* (Madrid, 1732).

Index

For Product Safety Concerns and Information please contact our EU representative GPSR@taylorandfrancis.com Taylor & Francis Verlag GmbH, Kaufingerstraße 24, 80331 München, Germany

Printed and bound by CPI Group (UK) Ltd, Croydon, CR0 4YY

01/05/2025

01858414-0001